Council for Standards in Human Service Education (CSHSE) St

The Council for Standards in Human Service Education (CSHSE) developed 10
departments and help students understand the knowledge, values, and skills as d
guidelines reflect the interdisciplinary nature of human services.

STANDARD	CHAPTER
Professional History	
Understanding and Mastery ...	
Historical roots of human services	Intro, 1
Creation of human services profession	Intro
Historical and current legislation affecting services delivery	Intro, 1, 4, 7, 9
How public and private attitudes influence legislation and the interpretation of policies related to human services	Intro, 4, 9
Differences between systems of governance and economics	4
Exposure to a spectrum of political ideologies	Intro, 4, 8, 9
Skills to analyze and interpret historical data application in advocacy and social changes	7, 8, 9
Human Systems	
Understanding and Mastery ...	
Theories of human development	
How small groups are utilized, theories of group dynamics, and group facilitation skills	2, 8, 9
Changing family structures and roles	
Organizational structures of communities	4, 8
An understanding of capacities, limitations, and resiliency of human systems	1, 7, 8, 9
Emphasis on context and the role of diversity in determining and meeting human needs	1, 2
Processes to effect social change through advocacy (e.g., community development, community and grassroots organizing, local and global activism)	7, 8, 9
Processes to analyze, interpret, and effect policies and laws at local, state, and national levels	2, 7, 8, 9
Human Services Delivery Systems	
Understanding and Mastery ...	
Range and characteristics of human services delivery systems and organizations	1, 4, 9
Range of populations served and needs addressed by human services	1, 2, 3, 4
Major models used to conceptualize and integrate prevention, maintenance, intervention, rehabilitation, and healthy functioning	1, 2, 3, 5
Economic and social class systems including systemic causes of poverty	
Political and ideological aspects of human services	Intro, 1, 8, 9
International and global influences on services delivery	4, 8
Skills to effect and influence social policy	2, 7, 8, 9

Adapted from the October 2010 Revised CSHSE National Standards

Council for Standards in Human Service Education (CSHSE) Standards Covered in This Text

STANDARD	CHAPTER
Information Management	
Understanding and Mastery ...	
Obtain information through interviewing, active listening, consultation with others, library or other research, and the observation of clients and systems	3, 6
Recording, organizing, and assessing the relevance, adequacy, accuracy, and validity of information provided by others	3
Compiling, synthesizing, and categorizing information	3, 6, 9
Disseminating routine and critical information to clients, colleagues, or other members of the related services system that is provided in written or oral form and in a timely manner	2, 3
Maintaining client confidentiality and appropriate use of client data	3
Using technology for word processing, sending email, and locating and evaluating information	3, 6, 9
Performing elementary community-needs assessment	8, 9
Conducting basic program evaluation	8
Utilizing research findings and other information for community education and public relations and using technology to create and manage spreadsheets and databases	7, 8, 9
Planning & Evaluating	
Understanding and Mastery ...	
Analysis and assessment of the needs of clients or client groups	3, 5, 6, 7, 8, 9
Skills to develop goals, and design and implement a plan of action	3, 6, 7, 8, 9
Skills to evaluate the outcomes of the plan and the impact on the client or client group	3
Program design, implementation, and evaluation	8, 9
Interventions & Direct Services	
Understanding and Mastery ...	
Theory and knowledge bases of prevention, intervention, and maintenance strategies to achieve maximum autonomy and functioning	1, 3
Skills to facilitate appropriate direct services and interventions related to specific client or client group goals	1, 2, 3
Knowledge and skill development in: case management, intake interviewing, individual counseling, group facilitation and counseling, location and use of appropriate resources and referrals, use of consultation	1, 2, 3
Interpersonal Communication	
Understanding and Mastery ...	
Clarifying expectations	1, 2, 5, 7
Dealing effectively with conflict	7, 9
Establishing rapport with clients	2, 3, 8
Developing and sustaining behaviors that are congruent with the values and ethics of the profession	2, 3, 5, 7, 8, 9

Council for Standards in Human Service Education (CSHSE) Standards Covered in This Text

STANDARD	CHAPTER
Administration	
Understanding and Mastery ...	
Managing organizations through leadership and strategic planning	5, 8, 9
Supervision and human resource management	5, 8, 9
Planning and evaluating programs, services, and operational functions	5, 7, 8, 9
Developing budgets and monitoring expenditures	6
Grant and contract negotiation	6
Legal/regulatory issues and risk management	5, 6
Managing professional development of staff	5, 7, 9
Recruiting and managing volunteers	5, 6, 8, 9
Constituency building and other advocacy techniques such as lobbying, grassroots movements, and community development and organizing	7, 8, 9
Client-Related Values & Attitudes	
Understanding and Mastery ...	
The least intrusive intervention in the least restrictive environment	1, 2
Client self-determination	1, 2, 3, 8
Confidentiality of information	3
The worth and uniqueness of individuals including ethnicity, culture, gender, sexual orientation, and other expressions of diversity	2, 3
Belief that individuals, services systems, and society change	1, 7, 8, 9
Interdisciplinary team approaches to problem solving	1, 8, 9
Appropriate professional boundaries	2, 3, 8
Integration of the ethical standards outlined by the National Organization for Human Services and Council for Standards in human service education	1-9
Self-Development	
Understanding and Mastery ...	
Conscious use of self	3, 7, 8
Clarification of personal and professional values	3, 7, 8
Awareness of diversity	1, 2, 3, 5
Strategies for self-care	3
Reflection on professional self (e.g., journaling, development of a portfolio, project demonstrating competency)	3, 7, 8, 9

Designed to help students advance their knowledge, values, and skills, the Standards for Excellence Series assists students in associating the Council for Standards in Human Services Education (CSHSE) National Standards to all levels of human services practice.

FEATURES INCLUDE

- **Standards for Excellence grid**—highlighting chapters where various standards are addressed.
- **Standards for Excellence critical thinking questions**—challenges students to think critically about the standards in relation to chapter content.
- **Multimedia links**—correlates content to multimedia assets throughout the text, including video, additional readings, and more.
- **Self-study quizzes**—found throughout the text, self-study quizzes test student knowledge and comprehension of key chapter topics.
- **Chapter review**—links to a scenario-based chapter review, including short-answer discussion questions.

Foundations in
Human Services Practice

A Generalist Perspective on Individual,
Agency, and Community

Judith T. Herzberg

Boston Columbus Indianapolis New York San Francisco Upper Saddle River
Amsterdam Cape Town Dubai London Madrid Milan Munich Paris Montréal Toronto
Delhi Mexico City São Paulo Sydney Hong Kong Seoul Singapore Taipei Tokyo

Editor in Chief: Ashley Dodge
Editorial Assistant: Amandria Guadalupe
Managing Editor: Denise Forlow
Program Manager: Carly Czech
Project Manager: Doug Bell,
  PreMediaGlobal
Executive Marketing Manager:
  Kelly May
Marketing Coordinator: Jessica Warren
Procurement Manager: Mary Fisher
Procurement Specialist: Eileen Collaro
Art Director: Jayne Conte

Cover Designer: Karen Salzbach
Interior Designer: Joyce Weston Design
Cover Art: Fotolia/© yellowj
Digital Media Director: Brian Hyland
Digital Media Project Manager: Tina
  Gagliostro
Full-Service Project Management:
  PreMediaGlobal/Sudip Sinha
Composition: PreMediaGlobal
Printer/Binder: LSC Communications
Cover Printer: LSC Communications

Credits and acknowledgments borrowed from other sources and reproduced, with permission, in this textbook appear on appropriate page within text.

Many of the designations by manufacturers and seller to distinguish their products are claimed as trademarks. Where those designations appear in this book, and the publisher was aware of a trademark claim, the designations have been printed in initial caps or all caps.

Library of Congress Cataloging-in-Publication Data
Herzberg, Judith T.
  Foundations in human services practice: a generalist perspective on individual, agency, and community/Judith Herzberg. —First Edition.
    pages cm
  Includes bibliographical references and index.
  ISBN-13: 978-0-205-85825-5
  ISBN-10: 0-205-85825-2
  1. Human services—Management. I. Title.
  HV41.H473 2014
  361.0068—dc23
                                                    2013035554

21 18

ISBN-10: 0-205-85825-2
ISBN-13: 978-0-205-85825-5

Contents

. . . .

8. Becoming a Community Organizer   149

9. Lobbying in the Political Arena   168

Preface

· ·

Foundations in Human Services Practice explores theories, models, and practices by human services practitioners. This text will provide you with a base of information that can be built upon to assist you with practice essentials for working with clients, agencies, and communities.

As a distinct academic field of study, human services focuses on social technologies (such as models and methods of practice) as well as service technologies (such as programs and delivery systems) that are designed to provide human benefits. As an introduction, a history about human services is included. The history of human services will set the stage by providing a concrete explanation of how the human services profession differs from other helping fields, providing students with a better sense of professional identity and appreciation of the progressive history behind human services.

When developing this text, I endeavored to write it in such a way that captures the human services ideology of helping the whole person by providing content that focuses on theories and practices with clients, agencies, and communities that are important to human services practice. I designed this text to help students realize that helping the whole person entails work in many different spheres:

- **Direct Service**—case management theory, case management process, and interviewing
- **Organizational Structure**—management, supervision, and fundraising
- **Community**—organizing, advocating, and lobbying

Features

Many features have been included in this text to enhance your experience; however, they are only as useful as you make them. By engaging with this text and its resources, you'll gain an understanding and mastery of:

- **Human Service History**—covers the history of social welfare from the colonial period to the modern day so that students understand the sources of current practices and institutions.
- **A Multidisciplinary View of Human Services Practice**—examines practices in the context of social, economic, and political factors at all levels of society focused on alleviating human problems.
- **Micro, Mezzo, and Macro Approaches to Practice**—covers the theories and models of case management, interviewing, nonprofit structure and operations, fundraising, grassroots organizing, and more.

Learning Outcomes

Students will be able to achieve a variety of learning outcomes by using this text and its resources, including:

- **Critical Thinking Skills**—students can develop their critical thinking skills by reviewing the standards boxes (indicated by the National Standards series band) and engaging with the multimedia resources highlighted in boxes throughout the chapter.
- **Oral Communication Skills**—students can develop their oral communication skills by engaging with others in and out of class to discuss their comprehension of the chapter based on the chapter's learning objectives.
- **Assessment and Writing Skills**—students can develop their assessment and writing skills in preparation for future certification exams by completing topic-based and chapter review assessments for each chapter.
- **CSHSE National Standards**—students can develop their understanding and mastery of CSHSE's national standards by discussing the standards box critical thinking questions.

Acknowledgments

This edition of *Foundations in Human Services Practice* has been a collaborative effort among many people. I want to first mention those at Pearson Allyn & Bacon who understood my vision for the human services field. Many thanks to Ashley Dodge, Executive Editor, and Carly Czech, Human Services Program Manager, for believing in this project.

In addition, I have had the benefit of careful reviews of this edition. I wish to thank Uma R. Kukathas, University of Washington, who has been vital to this project as its primary developmental editor. I would like to thank Doug Bell, the senior project manager, for his expert oversight of this project. He assured me there was light at the end of the tunnel and indeed there was light. To Rebecca Burlew, my former human services student, I offer many thanks for her close reading of the manuscript and suggestions that improved the text.

I want to thank my husband, Bruce Herzberg, Bentley University, for his love and support throughout the project. Besides playing the role of husband, he also served as my in-house development editor. His expertise in rhetoric served me well, especially as we worked to create a manuscript that would be clear and spoke to its intended audience—human services students.

Finally, I dedicate this book to all the human services students I have taught and met over the past two decades because they were my inspiration for creating this textbook.

This text is available in a variety of formats—digital and print.
To learn more about our programs, pricing options, and customization,
visit **http://www.pearsonhighered.com.**

Introduction

The human services academic discipline is relatively new when compared with other disciplines. To help clarify what the human services discipline is, a short history is offered in this introduction. Writing a history about the human services discipline is challenging because the historical material comes from several related disciplines. In this introduction, you will be offered some insight as to when and why human services began as a distinct discipline. What is the importance of knowing the history of human services? This history will help clarify how graduates from human services academic programs are different from graduates of other academic programs. Understanding the history of your profession will help to solidify your professional identity.

The History of the Human Services Profession

Perhaps, surprisingly, the academic discipline of human services appears to have been started as an educational movement. This movement was initiated by higher education professionals during the countercultural period of progressive social action that occurred in the 1960s. Individuals, groups, and communities were engaged in activism against social, economic, and political inequalities in the United States. Many professors and students on college campuses throughout the country were actively involved in the counterculture. Events like "teach-ins" and open public debates were used to educate people about public affairs. Many people also engaged in mass demonstrations to show their disapproval of the establishment (Roszak, 1995). So it might not be a surprise that several new human services movements sprang to life in this period.

THE NEW HUMAN SERVICES MOVEMENT   In the late 1960s, the **new human services movement** began as the brainchild of independent social work and psychology educators who wanted to reform the "elitist practices of the helping professions" (Chenault & Burnford, 1978). These educational reformers believed that the academic disciplines of education, nursing, medicine, social work, public administration, criminal justice, and psychology were focused on specialized knowledge and skill sets, which were designed to distinguish them from those of other professions and raise their own academic and professional stature. This culture of competition among professional disciplines led them to protect their professional turf from encroachment, which stifled cooperation. Worse, within this culture of careerism, the state of clients and human services systems seemed to have become a secondary concern.

Educators in the human services movement wanted professional students to learn about sharing power and resources with clients, creating humane and responsive delivery services, and serving as change agents to promote greater social equity and justice (Chenault & Burnford, 1978). It was proposed that professional programs be refocused and incorporate the following five central concepts into their curriculum:

1. Systemic integration of human services systems.
2. Comprehensiveness and accessibility of services.
3. Client troubles defined as problems in living.
4. Generic characteristics of helping activities.
5. Accountability of service providers to clients.

One could imagine that in the context of the counterculture and new progressive educational movements the five central educational concepts from the human services movement might have appealed to educators. Chenault and Burnford (Chenault and Burnford 1978) reported that educators in professional programs such as education, social work, nursing, medicine, and psychology initially had some interest in the new concepts. In fact, some educators attempted to change their students' attitudes about careerism. Others attempted to incorporate the human services educational concepts into their professional curriculum. However, in most cases, "human services" was simply a title tagged onto traditional professional courses or programs (e.g., Education and Human Services). In the long run, no significant changes were made to the curricula of professional programs.

Once it became clear that educators in professional programs were not changing their curricula, a group of educators took matters into their own hands. They went on to create a new and distinct profession that reflected the educational concept of the human services movement (Chenault & Burnford, 1978). By the mid-1960s, human services began to emerge as a new academic discipline, though without the benefit of national standards. In consequence, new human services programs had different missions and goals that reflected the influences of social, political, and economic factors in which they developed.

HOW ASSOCIATE HUMAN SERVICES PROGRAMS STARTED   Under President Lyndon Baines Johnson's Great Society, there were numerous efforts to educate and train people so that they could become productive citizens. Johnson believed there was nothing to be gained by maintaining a nonproductive class in society. Under the Great Society initiative, federal funds were made available through legislation like the Economic Opportunity Act of 1966. Thirty-three million dollars was allocated to Scheuer's New Careers Program (Nixon, 1969). This program was also supported under antipoverty legislations, such as the Manpower Development and Training Act of

1962, the Community Mental Health Centers Act of 1963 (Woodside & McClam, 2006), the Health Manpower Act of 1968, Title I Health Professions Training, and the Allied Health Professions Health Training (Kadish, 1969). The New Careers Program was based on the belief that the poor were not responsible for their condition in society. Therefore, the poor should be given an opportunity to be educated and trained for employment that offered a living wage. According to Pearl and Riessman (1965), the New Careers Program goals were to

1. provide a sufficient number of jobs to the unemployed,
2. have jobs defined and distributed to unskilled and uneducated workers,
3. create permanent jobs and provide opportunity for life-long careers to the poor,
4. create opportunities for the poor to have equal chances for upward mobility, and
5. have jobs that contribute to the good of society.

Promoters of the New Careers Program maintained that poverty could be eradicated. However, several specific conditions were needed for poor recipients: (a) gainful employment, (b) secure employment, and (c) on-the-job training, so they had an opportunity for career advancement. Under these conditions, the poor would have more resources, skills, and flexibility to escape poverty. Officials from the New Careers Program anticipated that job creation would occur in education, health, and social services. For example, human services technical and associate degree programs were created, and community colleges would play a large role in the education of human services workers.

In 1965, the National Institute of Mental Health (NIMH) also played a major role in the creation of new human services programs when they funded the Southern Regional Education Board (SREB). NIMH awarded a five-year grant to SREB for the development of an experimental pilot Mental Health Worker Program that would be used by community colleges in 14 southern states (McPheeters & King, 1971).

Dr. Harold L. McPheeters, a psychiatrist, headed the SREB project (Box 1: Harold McPheeters, the "Father of Human Services"). McPheeters led a taskforce comprising 55 higher education and mental health professionals from across the United States. The taskforce worked to determine the need for human service workers and how to educate them.

In an analysis of the manpower studies, done by SREB, it was determined that there was a need to train paraprofessionals who could be generalist workers. The generalist would fill the growing personnel shortage in the mental health systems. In addition, the generalist was to take over tasks performed by mental health professionals, like social workers and psychologists. It was believed that some professionals' tasks could

---

Box 1	**Harold McPheeters, the "Father of Human Services" (1923–)**

In 1963, the Kennedy administration successfully signed into law the Community Mental Health Center Act that mandated the deinstitutionalization of individuals with chronic mental illness. This legislation created an immediate need for outpatient care and a host of direct service workers to assist the thousands of mentally ill released from state hospitals. Dr. Harold Lawrence McPheeters, a practicing psychiatrist, was instrumental in leading a taskforce that developed guidelines for mental health and human services programs at the associate and bachelor's degree levels. Currently, Dr. McPheeters is considered the "father of human services" education. During his career, he authored nine books and dozens of journal articles about mental health education, service integration, medical education, and funding health professions.

be performed by paraprofessionals. This would free professionals to engage in more complex tasks (Ginsberg, Shiffman, & Rogers, 1969).

SREB outlined the scope of practice of the generalist: (a) work with a limited number of clients or families in conjunction with mental health professionals to provide an array of services, (b) be able to work in a variety of agencies that provided mental health services, (c) be able to work cooperatively with all of the existing professions in the field rather than affiliating directly with any one of the existing professions, (d) become familiar with a number of therapeutic services and techniques rather than specializing in one or two areas, (e) be a beginning professional who is expected to continue to learn and grow (McPheeters & King, 1971). SREB successfully created an associate-level human services curriculum that was used at community colleges throughout the South.

SREB was not alone in its efforts in the development of associate-level human services curricula and programs. In the same time period, Audrey Cohen (Box 2: Audrey Cohen, "The Mother of Human Services") was in the midst of establishing the College of Human Services (CHS) in New York City (Grant & Riesman, 1978). In 1966, CHS received a federal grant from the Office of Economic Opportunity for educating and training poor students for paraprofessional jobs in the human services field.

In 1970, the college was accredited by the New York Regents and was permitted to grant associate in arts degrees. However, after running the program for several years, Cohen realized that the pathway to becoming a professional was much harder than expected for the poor, minorities, and women. She started to believe that it would take a radical approach to advance poor CHS graduates up the career ladder.

Under the influence of the **Telic Reforms Movement,** Cohen altered the college's curriculum. *Telic* by definition means "goal directed" and is derived from the Greek word *telikos*. Telic reformers sought to change traditional undergraduate education. They felt that undergraduate education should focus on student autonomy, personal growth, and have innovative teaching methods and curricula (Grant & Riesman, 1978). Telic reformers also believed that undergraduate education should focus on notions of the ideal community and be responsive to marginalized groups. Cohen adopted one of the Telic Reforms models called the **Activist-Radical Impulse Model.** Under this model, educators in CHS were encouraged to oppose the traditional university model that led to disaffection with traditional educational models, mainstream politics, and other social institutions that perpetuated the status quo (Grant & Riesman, 1978).

| Box 2 | Audrey Cohen, the "Mother of Human Services" (1932–1996) |

Audrey Cohen was born in Pittsburgh, Pennsylvania, and brought up in a middle-class Jewish family. She attended the University of Pittsburgh and studied political science. After graduation in 1953, she taught in a Washington, DC, high school, became involved in the Civil Rights Movement, and later founded a research business. In 1964, this innovative educator, who was also a wife and mother, founded the Women's Talent Corps to educate female welfare recipients for paraprofessional jobs. The Corps successfully created employment opportunities for many women. The Women's Talent Corps later became the College of Human Services—now called the Metropolitan College of New York. Cohen's vision was to reform helping professions and higher education so that anyone who desired an education in the growing field of human services could acquire it. The college became co-ed, and remained committed to admitting and assisting nontraditional students. All CHS students received a transdisciplinary education that employed progressive teaching methods to ensure that students could achieve their professional aspirations. Audrey Cohen should be called the "mother of human services" education.

The CHS curriculum focused on integration of services, opening service systems to minorities, and changing human services systems to be more responsive to human needs (Grant & Riesman, 1978). Furthermore, the CHS curriculum became competency based. For example, the competencies were divided into four categories: (a) learning competency, (b) relationship competency, (c) group competency, and (d) teaching competency. In this restructured program, students were asked to act with purpose and contemplative awareness. In addition, they were expected to engage in planning and researching that would improve human services delivery.

The growing need for generalists in the job market resulted in the proliferation of associate-level human services programs throughout the United States. By the early 1970s, there were approximately 174 colleges in 44 states that offered an associate degree with a human services focus. In total, associate-level programs graduated an estimated 11,000 students by 1974 (True & Young, 1974). Sadly, only 50% of these human services graduates were gainfully employed. The majority worked in state hospitals or mental health settings; a smaller percentage became employed in special education or treatment programs. Graduates of associate-level human services programs were viewed as beginning-level professionals or paraprofessionals who had upward mobility potential in the job market.

However, an in-depth study of CHS associate-level graduates' employment revealed that the jobs offered were often dead-end jobs that could have been attained with a high school diploma. Employers reported that associate-level graduates had little to no upward mobility because they lacked the education and skills needed to advance. This realization motivated Cohen and other educators to create bachelor-level and graduate-level human services programs so that their students could attain higher level jobs that allowed for upward mobility in their organizations.

BACCALAUREATE AND GRADUATE HUMAN SERVICES PROGRAMS In the mid- to late 1960s, bachelor-level human services programs were being established. The bachelor-level programs were often designed to create workers who would serve as professional change agents. These programs often embraced the Activist-Radical Impulse Model, and so teaching approaches were progressive and egalitarian as compared to traditional college programs. Curricula were focused on social change as a means to improve human services delivery and the condition of the client.

One notable example of a four-year human services program was at Franconia College in New Hampshire. The educators in Franconia's School of Human Services were committed to community and participatory democracy as opposed to traditional higher education that perpetuated mainstream views and privileges (Osher & Goldenberg, 1987). Franconia's educational policies were designed to exclude biases based on class, race, and gender in curriculum, teaching methods, and the learning environment. Educators believed that the college culture should reflect a world that functioned under the forces of freedom, justice, and beauty rather than greed, bigotry, and oppression. The school's administration supported the human services faculty as they translated their beliefs into the program. The program's curriculum was designed so that students could become skilled change agents in a variety of human services organizations and communities.

The human services faculty also challenged and redressed the exclusion of disenfranchised groups from higher education. Efforts were made to have full participation of the poor, minorities, women, and community lay workers who as a collective group had been victims of the dominant culture's policies and practices. Admission and financial aid policies were altered at the college to ensure that nontraditional and marginalized students could be admitted into the human services program.

The Franconia School of Human Services was growing and generating revenue for the college, but it was not enough to forestall the closing of the institution. Luckily, because of the high profile and revenue-generating potential of Franconia's School of Human Services, the faculty brokered a deal and moved the entire program to New Hampshire College. In 1978, once the new program was up and running, the student enrollment reached 700 full-time students. To support the expanding program, the faculty sought grants to further their educational initiatives and social change activities. Grants came from the Ford Foundation, U.S. Department of Labor, and a variety of other public and private donors, which enabled the program to support work in hunger, work with the elderly, and economic development among the poor. Graduates of the program were prepared to take on significant roles in different human services systems.

SREB also formed the Undergraduate Social Welfare Manpower Project, which helped colleges develop baccalaureate human services programs in six states: West Virginia, Virginia, Texas, Tennessee, Maryland, and Kentucky (McPheeters & King, 1971).

This Manpower Project had several objectives that included increasing the number of human services programs, increasing the number of bachelor-level workers, and enhancing the training and employability of these graduates. The Manpower Project helped colleges establish relevant curriculum objectives such as a generalist curriculum with an eclectic knowledge base. Students were educated and trained to help service users cope with, prevent, and alleviate social stresses. However curricula did not focus on altering infrastructures of service delivery systems or the social conditions that contributed to clients' current status. SREB's general concern was to ensure the employability of graduates and to alleviate a personnel shortage in the human services sector. Baccalaureate graduates would be considered middle-level workers trained to engage in a broad range of duties to an individual, family, or a community, and they would serve as advocates and community organizers (McPheeters & King, 1971).

In terms of graduate education, some educators felt that undergraduate programs could not prepare the type of professional originally envisioned by the new human services movement. Chenault and Burnford (1978) argued that human services programs should educate and train students only at the graduate or postgraduate levels to ensure that the profession would be considered a professional discipline. Currently, graduate programs in human services focus on administration, community organization, leadership, and social policy analysis. Terminal degrees are offered at several institutions.

Professional History

Understanding and Mastery: Historical roots of human services.

Critical Thinking Question: The history of human services is challenging to fully understand because its historical roots are in several related disciplines. However, the CSHSE standards say that understanding the history of your profession will help to solidify your professional identity. Why do you think this is so? What have you learned from this chapter that gives you a better sense of your professional identity?

● ●

The Creation of an Academic Discipline

What defines a professional discipline? One definition for a **professional discipline** is that it must have a new pattern of knowledge, theory, and skills that will make it different from other disciplines (Thompson, 2003). A professional discipline develops a distinctive theoretical base, which supports its identity as a profession and separates it from more dominant and established professions. Furthermore, graduates of a professional program have specialized knowledge, keen analytical abilities, specific skills for practice, preparation for passing licensing exams, and professional values and identity (Wheeler & Gibbons, 1992).

What is the human services discipline? According to Susan Kincaid (2009), a human services researcher and educator at Western Washington University, there hasn't been a clear and concise definition for the study of human services. Is it important to have a concrete definition for a discipline? Yes! Kincaid believes that students should be able to receive a succinct definition for the study of human services, similar to definitions for sociology, psychology, and anthropology. Here is the definition for the study of human services that underlies this book:

> **Human services** is the study of social technologies (practice methods, models, and theories) and service technologies (programs, organizations, and systems) that benefit a service user.

Here are definitions for the mission and academic discipline of human services:

> The **human services mission** is to promote a practice that involves simultaneously working at all levels of society in the process of promoting the autonomy of individuals or groups, making informal or formal human services systems more efficient and effective, and advocating for positive social change within society.

> The **human services academic discipline** has an interdisciplinary educational approach to ensure that students can critically analyze complex social problems of individuals, communities, and society from multiple vantage points.

Assess your comprehension of the **Three Related Definitions** that pertain to the human services profession by completing this quiz.

The struggle to be recognized as a distinct field of study is not unique to human services. For instance, the nursing discipline fought to distinguish itself from the medical field, psychology struggled to be considered a distinct field of study from philosophy, and social work fought to be considered a profession unto itself.

In the human services field, there are dedicated human services educators, scholars, students, and practitioners who are working to get greater recognition for the field. Each year new human services programs are being created, conferences are held, and innovative research is done. In addition, more terminal degrees (doctorates) are being awarded, which means there will be more human services educators, researchers, and scholars working for greater recognition and position in the academy.

EDUCATIONAL STANDARDS FOR HUMAN SERVICES PROGRAMS There is also an ongoing effort to standardize curricula, which is being advanced by the **Council of Standards for Human Services Education (CSHSE)**. CSHSE—generally referred to simply as the Council—is a nonprofit organization established in 1976. The mission of the Council is to establish national standards as a way to promote excellence in human services education, provide quality assurance, and guarantee standards of performance and practice among human services graduates. Presently, program accreditation is voluntary, but the Council is working to bring more human services programs on board.

Are curriculum standards necessary for a discipline? The purpose of having curriculum standards is to ensure that students in different schools are receiving a comparable education that prepares them for human services practice. The absence of national curriculum standards can make it difficult for students to understand and explain what they are being educated and trained to do. In addition, other professionals and prospective employers will have no standards for determining what human services graduates are capable of doing if each human services program is different. Social work and nursing are two disciplines that have successfully standardized their curricula across the country. The CSHSE has developed curriculum guidelines for all degree levels and delineates the scope of practice for human services students graduating from different degree programs (Table 1).

Table 1	CSHSE National Curricula Standards for Human Services Degrees	
Standards for Associate Curriculum	**Standards for Bachelor's Curriculum**	**Standards for Master's Curriculum**
Standard 11: The curriculum shall include the historical development of human services.	Standard 11: The curriculum shall include the historical development of human services.	Standard 9: The curriculum shall include the historical development of human services.
Standard 12: The curriculum shall include knowledge and theory of the interaction of human systems including individual, interpersonal, group, family, organizational, community, & societal.	Standard 12: The curriculum shall include knowledge and theory of the interaction of human systems including individual, interpersonal, group, family, organizational, community, & societal.	Standard 10: The curriculum shall include knowledge and theory of the interaction of human systems including individual, interpersonal, group, family, organizational, community, & societal.
Standard 13: The curriculum shall address the scope of conditions that promote or inhibit human functioning.	Standard 13: The curriculum shall address the scope of conditions that promote or inhibit human functioning.	Standard 11: The curriculum shall address the scope of conditions that promote or inhibit human functioning.
Standard 14: The curriculum shall provide knowledge and skills in information management.	Standard 14: The curriculum shall provide knowledge and skills in information management.	Standard 12: The curriculum shall provide knowledge and skills in information management.
Standard 15: The curriculum shall provide knowledge and skill development in systematic analysis of service needs; planning appropriate strategies, services, and implementation; and evaluation of outcomes.	Standard 15: The curriculum shall provide knowledge and skill development in systematic analysis of service needs; planning appropriate strategies, services, and implementation; and evaluation of outcomes.	Standard 13: The curriculum shall provide knowledge, theory, and skills in systematic analysis of service needs; selection of appropriate strategies, services, or interventions; and evaluation of outcomes.
Standard 16: The curriculum shall provide knowledge and skills in direct service delivery and appropriate interventions.	Standard 16: The curriculum shall provide knowledge and skills in direct service delivery and appropriate interventions.	Standard 14: The curriculum shall provide knowledge and skills in direct service delivery and appropriate interventions.

Standards for Associate Curriculum	Standards for Bachelor's Curriculum	Standards for Master's Curriculum
Standard 17: Learning experiences shall be provided for the student to develop his or her interpersonal skills.	Standard 17: Learning experiences shall be provided for the student to develop his or her interpersonal skills.	Standard 15: Learning experiences shall be provided for the student to develop his or her interpersonal skills.
Standard 18: The curriculum shall incorporate human services values and attitudes and promote understanding of human services ethics and their application in practice.	Standard 18: The curriculum shall provide knowledge, theory, and skills in the administrative aspects of the services delivery system.	Standard 16: The curriculum shall provide knowledge, theory, and skills in the administrative aspects of the services delivery system.
Standard 19: The program shall provide experiences and support to enable students to develop awareness of their own values, personalities, reaction patterns, interpersonal styles, and limitations.	Standard 19: The program shall incorporate human services values and attitudes and promote understanding of human services ethics and their application in practice.	Standard 17: The program shall incorporate human services values and attitudes and promote understanding of human services ethics and their application in practice.
Standard 20: The program shall provide field experience that is integrated with the curriculum.	Standard 20: The program shall provide experiences and support to enable students to develop awareness of their own values, personalities, reaction patterns, interpersonal styles, and limitations.	Standard 18: The program shall provide experiences and support to enable students to develop awareness of their own values, personalities, reaction patterns, interpersonal styles, and limitations
	Standard 21: The program shall provide field experience that is integrated with the curriculum.	Standard 19: The program shall provide field experience that is integrated with the curriculum and demonstrates conceptual mastery of the field of professional practice.
		Standard 20: The program shall provide a capstone experience that demonstrates conceptual mastery of the field of professional practice; for example, a portfolio, project, or thesis.

Reprinted by permission of Council of Standards for Human Services Education (CSHSE)

Council aims to standardize human services curricula without limiting program flexibility. In other words, depending on the needs of a community, a human services program may have additional courses designed to address the needs of a specific service population. Therefore, creative and relevant programs are not sacrificed to rigid standards.

In Table 1, you will see that each higher degree level requires both additional content and a greater depth of knowledge, theory, and skills. What is the difference among the human services degree levels? An associate-level degree has a vocational or technical emphasis. Graduates from these programs are often considered paraprofessionals and are engaged in direct service in a variety of human services settings. The next level is the bachelor's degree, which is awarded in four-year colleges. Graduates from bachelor-level programs are often considered beginning professionals who engage in direct service and administration of human services systems. According to CSHSE, the master's-level degree provides students the opportunity for conceptual mastery of the field through subject matter, theory, practice, and research. Students learn to interpret, analyze, synthesize, communicate knowledge, and develop skills to effectively practice and advance the profession. Master-level graduates should be able to enter mid- and upper management in a variety of human services settings. A summary of the knowledge and skill objectives that are identified by CSHSE for the associate and bachelor levels is provided in Table 2.

Professional History

Understanding and Mastery: Creation of human services profession.

Critical Thinking Question: Educational reformers believed that many helping disciplines were focused on specialized knowledge and skill sets, which were designed to distinguish them from other professions and raise their own academic and professional stature. In the creation of the human services profession, what knowledge and skill sets are supposed to distinguish it from other academic helping professions?

A CAREER PATH IN HUMAN SERVICES: Some have argued that if human services graduates were licensed or had certification they would be more employable. In response to this request from human services students, educators, and practitioners, the National Organization of Human Services (NOHS) and the CSHSE worked in collaboration with the Center for Credentialing and Education and created a national certification. The credential is named the **Human Services Board Certified Practitioner (HS-BCP).** Its purpose is to

1. demonstrate professional identity,
2. demonstrate a commitment to quality services,
3. demonstrate competency to provide human services to clients,
4. assert a commitment to high standards with human services, and
5. assert adherence to the human services ethical and behavioral codes.

Since the inception of the human services profession, there have been debates about licensing and certification. Historically, credentialing in the human services profession was avoided because some believed that traditional professions had used credentialing as an oppressive tool against poor people, minorities, and women. These groups were often denied professional legitimacy, which would have led to lucrative employment opportunities. Moreover, the concept of credentialing went against the spirit of the Telic Reforms Movement, which had inspired many human services educators and programs throughout the country. The debate about the value of a credential is ongoing within the human services field.

Despite human services being a valid field of study and profession, it sometimes is inaccurately represented. For example, in the *Occupational Outlook Handbook 2010*, 11th edition, produced by the U.S. Department of Labor, the only job title that is related to the human services profession is Social and Human Service Assistant. This job title appears to be a generic term used to describe a broad range of paraprofessional job titles (workers who assist helping professionals like social workers, teachers, and psychologists). The minimum educational requirement for the Social and Human Service Assistant is a high school diploma, and their job duties focus on direct services.

| Table 2 | Human Services Knowledge and Skills by Degree Level | 11 |

Associate-Level Knowledge	Associate-Level Skills
1. Knowledge of the history of human services systems and the profession.	1. Skills to compile, synthesize, and categorize data.
2. Knowledge of historical and current legislation affecting human services.	2. Skill to do case management.
3. Knowledge of theories in human development, small groups, family structures, and organizational systems.	3. Skill to do intake interviewing
4. Knowledge of major models of prevention, maintenance, intervention, rehabilitation, and health functioning for a broad range of service populations.	4. Skill to do individual counseling.
5. Knowledge of assessment and outcomes for determining individual or group needs.	5. Skill to do group facilitation.
6. Knowledge about the characteristics of human services delivery systems.	6. Skills to make referrals and do consultations.

Bachelor-Level Knowledge	Bachelor-Level Skills
1. Knowledge of a spectrum of political ideologies.	1. Skills to analyze and interpret data for application in advocacy and social change.
2. Knowledge to analyze and interpret how policy and law affects service delivery systems.	2. Skills to affect social change through advocacy work at all levels of society.
3. Knowledge of socioeconomics that explains the systemic causes of poverty.	3. Skills to effect and influence social policy.
4. Knowledge of the political economy of human services programs.	4. Skills to do community needs assessment.
5. Knowledge of international and global influences on service delivery.	5. Skills to conduct program evaluations.
6. Knowledge to use research findings and other data for education and public relations.	6. Skill to manage organizations through leadership and strategic planning.
7. Knowledge of program design, implementation, and evaluation.	7. Skill to manage human resources.
8. Knowledge of legal and regulatory issues and risk management.	8. Skill to plan and evaluate programs, services, and operational functions.
	9. Skill to develop budgets and monitor finances.
	10. Skill for grant writing and contract negotiations.

Reprinted by permission of the Council of Standards for Human Services Education (CSHSE)

The *Occupational Handbook* does state that employers prefer workers with an associate, bachelor's, or master's degree, but there is no mention of human services degrees. The good news is that the U.S. Department of Labor has projected that human services–related job opportunities are growing faster than all other job categories. The bad news is that human services students, graduates, and practitioners are still battling with the lack of recognition from other professionals and employers. Therefore, it is important to join and be actively involved in professional organizations (Table 3).

Joining one or more of the many professional human services organizations gives you the opportunity to network with individuals in your field. Networking gives you the opportunity to learn and share with other professionals. You will

Table 3	Professional Human Services Organizations

Organization Name	Website
American Educational Research Association (AERA) Subsection: Education in Social Context	www.aera.net
American Public Human Services Association (APHSA)	www.aphsa.org
American Society for Public Administration (ASPA) Subsection: Health and Human Services Administration	www.aspaonline.org/shhsa
National Organization for Human Services (NOHS)	www.nationalhumanservices.org

Regional Human Services Organizations	Email Address
Western Region of Human Service Professionals	west@nationalhumanservices.org
Southern Organization for Human Services	sohs@nationalhumanservices.org
Northwest Human Services Association	nwest@nationalhumanservices.org
New England Organization for Human Services	neohs@nationalhumanservices.org
Mid-West Organization for Human Services	mwohs@nationalhumanservices.org
Mid-Atlantic Consortium for Human Services	machs@nationalhumanservices.org

Explore the Center for Credentialing and Education to learn about the Human Services Board Certified Practitioner (HS-BCP) certification. Consider why a human services practitioner with a license or HS-BCP certification will be more employable.

have access to conferences and journals geared to your professional interests. As a member you will also be in the informational loop that keeps you abreast of social, political, and economic factors affecting the field. Moreover, when you join a professional organization, it enhances your professional identity. As the field continues to grow, the stature of the human services professional will change because there is power in numbers.

Assess your analysis and evaluation of this chapter's content by completing the Chapter Review.

Section One

···

Direct Service

Human services practice—at the individual level—is geared to assist clients with finding options or solutions to their problems in living. To perform this role, you will engage in direct service activities such as conducting interviews, doing intakes, and creating individual treatment plans. The three chapters of Section 1 focus on these direct services practices. In Chapter 1 there is an examination of human services models and theories so that you gain some exposure to evidence-based practices. This theoretical material is followed by an examination of systems theories and how they are used in human services practice. In Chapter 2 there is a discussion about the essential elements of the case management process that covers assessment, planning, and monitoring outcomes of the client. The final discussion in this chapter focuses on the complexities of assuming the role of legal guardianship while being a case manager. The focus of Chapter 3 is the interviewing process. Interviewing is a singular practice that can be used in multiple ways, and you will explore different interview types, formats, and skills. Legal issues related to interviewing clients and managing clients' legal records will also be covered.

The chapters in Section 1 of this text are intended to provide a foundation in direct service approaches that can be applied to work in a wide variety of public agencies and nonprofit human services settings. Mastering these approaches is essential to human services practice, but it should be remembered that direct service is not the only practice of a human services generalist. Human services practice is also about creating efficient and effective delivery systems and promoting community change, and these topics will be covered in Sections 1 and 2 of the book.

Case Management Models and Theories

· ·

As a human services generalist, your work will encompass doing direct service, which means you need to develop a case management knowledge base and acquire interviewing skills to work with clients one on one. When working one on one with a client, you will typically engage in case management, which is a process that involves assessing the needs of clients so that services can be arranged, coordinated, evaluated, and monitored. In addition, the process involves advocating for services and resources to meet specific client needs.

At no time in the history of case management has any one profession laid claim to it. At present, case management is used by professionals in human services, nursing, criminal justice, social work, and psychology. Professionals who use case management (whatever the approach) are working with their clients rather than telling them what to do, which is typical under the medical model.

In this chapter you will learn about case management history and models, system theories, case management process, and the art of interviewing. All of this material is presented to give you a theoretical foundation in human services practice.

A Historical Perspective of Case Management

The use of **case management** by health and human service workers can be traced back to the early 1800s (Murphy, Tobias, Rajabium, & Abuchar, 2003). It was at this time that case management was first conceptualized as a way to coordinate a complex network of services for vulnerable populations in need of social and medical care because clients were unfamiliar with the myriad services available to them and the associated bureaucracy. Therefore, each client would be assigned a case worker to help him or her to navigate complex delivery systems. For example, in the late 1800s, during the American public health movement, case management was used by nurses who were working to track the spread of communicable diseases in communities. Case management was also used by settlement workers—like Jane Addams of Hull House—to track clients and coordinate complex services for the poor in Chicago (Knight, 2005).

After World War II, the federal government began using case management to coordinate complex services for people receiving veterans' benefits, Medicare, and Medicaid (Finkelman, 2011). The use of case management would increase in both the public and private sectors over the next several decades. For instance, in 1964 the Johnson administration initiated the War on Poverty; this was an initiative that led to the creation of a new series of community programs throughout the United States (Milkis, 2005). As these federally funded anti-poverty programs increased in number, so did the use of case management as an approach to assist clients better utilize new service programs in their communities.

Some believed that the use of case management would ensure better coordination and continuity of federal services (Holt, 2000). Federal policymakers then began to mandate that the delivery of health and human services be done in a coordinated manner for veterans, families, children, elderly, and the disabled. Legislation like the Older Americans Act of 1965, for example, also had mandates for coordinated services. This mandate specified that a case manager would be assigned to individuals enrolled in specific federal welfare programs. The case manager would oversee each client to ensure that he or she was receiving services in an efficient and coordinated manner.

However, not all human services legislation was so explicit about mandating coordinated services. For example, in the 1970s, a new federal policy mandated the deinstitutionalization of patients with chronic mental health problems. This new policy caused massive systemic changes among human service delivery systems in the United States. Costly long-term mental health facilities were closed and replaced with community mental health centers (Burns & Perkins, 2000). Newly released mentally ill clients were placed into residential community settings to ensure that they had the least restrictive environment, which was to improve their mental health. Yet the concept of the least restrictive environment, in reality, resulted in the mentally ill having little to no care or support with their activities of daily living. The use of mental health case managers to oversee the newly deinstitutionalized mentally ill would be an afterthought.

By the 1980s, some believed that case management could be the most efficient way of handling mental health clients (Rothman & Sager, 1998). Case management became the default intervention to assist deinstitutionalized clients in a community setting. Workers who used case management during the deinstitutionalization period were called "systems agents." Systems agents used a brokerage case management approach to handle their clients (Burns & Perkins, 2000), which meant that they only coordinated services to ensure the continuity of care for their mentally ill clients. Systems agents did not provide direct care (Intagliata, 1982). Direct care involved engaging in a therapeutic relationship with mental health clients, which was left to licensed professionals such as psychiatrists, psychologists, and clinical social workers.

The Meaning of Case Management

In the last few decades, there has been a renewed interest in formalizing the use of case management in many helping fields (Roberts-DeGennaro, 1993). This renewed interest in case management has resulted in several debates. One debate is whether case management should be considered its own profession or come under the control of some other profession. Another debate concerns whether case management is a method or intervention. What is apparent from the literature is that there is no standard methodology for case management.

Case management means different things to different people and to different professions, but there are some core components that most would agree upon. In this book, we will consider case management as a process with several overlapping steps: (a) assessment, (b) planning, (c) service coordination, (d) observation, (e) evaluation, and (f) advocating for services. Case management can be used as a short-term intervention to prevent or help manage a crisis in a client's life. On the other hand, case management can be used for an extended period of time; for example, a practitioner can assist clients with complex or unremitting problems in living. Overall, the goals of case management are to assist clients to their highest level of functioning and/or help clients manage their personal life challenges so that they can regain and maintain their personal autonomy.

Because case management is used for various purposes among professions, the definitions are different. Review the definitions of case management from two other professional groups:

Interventions & Direct Services

Understanding and Mastery: Skills to facilitate appropriate direct services and interventions related to specific client or client group goals.

Critical Thinking Questions: Different professions have different case management definitions. If human services generalists were to facilitate appropriate direct services to specific clients, would it be possible to create a standardized case management model? If so, what would be the essential features of your case management approach and how would you know it was appropriate for the client?

Social work case management is a method of providing services whereby a professional social worker assesses the needs of the client and the client's family, when appropriate, and arranges, coordinates, monitors, evaluates, and advocates for a package of multiple services to meet the specific client's complex needs. [Social work] case management is both micro and macro in nature: intervention occurs at both the client and system levels. It requires the social worker to develop and maintain a therapeutic relationship with the client, which may include linking the client with systems that provide him or her with needed services, resources, and opportunities. (Retrieved from National Association of Social Workers website).

Case Management Society of America defines case management as a collaborative process that has assessment, planning, facilitation and advocacy for options and services to meet an individual's health needs through communication and available resources to promote quality cost-effective outcomes (Finkelman, 2011).

When you review the different definitions of case management in this chapter, you will note similarities and differences among the definitions. However, there is much more to case management than any single definition.

How Case Management Is Used in Human Services

Case management practice often depends on the practitioner's education and training. It is also affected by the organization's financial resources and structure (Greene & Kropf, 1995). Human services practitioners in both private organizations and public agencies use case management to assist different types of clients who are in need of varying degrees of assistance, services, and resources. In general, a human services generalist as case manager performs a variety of roles to assist the client through complex human service systems. Both the client and case manager collaborate about coordinating formal services, informal resources, and care.

Your role as a case manager will vary according to the agency or organization by which you are employed. In other words, the organizational structure in which you work will determine how you function as a case manager (Woodside & McClam, 2003). Therefore, it is important that you understand the type of organization you are working in. According to Edgar Schein (1997), an expert in organizational cultures, the reason you should understand an organization's culture is because it helps you see how the organization goes about doing its work. And in terms of a human services organization, understanding its culture will also help you understand what you can and cannot do for your clients.

Consider the following example. Government policy makers have determined that case management is an effective means for public service providers to help clients navigate complex human service systems, and that case management is also a cost-effective method for helping vulnerable populations (Murphy, Tobias, Rajabium, & Abuchar, 2003). In addition, the Government Performance and Results Act of 1993 mandates that federal agencies reduce waste and inefficiency. Therefore, public agencies are accountable for achieving planned results, program outcomes, service quality, and consumer satisfaction. If you are a case manager in a government agency, you will be directly impacted by these policies. You will have to adopt a federally approved case management model while also holding down costs, reducing waste, achieving planned results, keeping up service quality, and ensuring that your clients are satisfied with services. Does this all seem a little overwhelming? I give you this example to impress upon you that where you work will determine how you engage in case management. Your practice is not simply determined by your education and training. Be open to the fact that your employer will have a say in how you work with the agency's clients.

Case Management Models and Theories

It is time to talk about case management models as an evidence-based practice. **"Evidence-based practice"** is a term that refers to the use of practices that have been researched and proven to be effective. Research involves the process of collecting data that are statistically measured. Statistical measurements are reported as significant or insignificant. In terms of case management, the statistical measurement tells whether the practice under study is effective or not with clients. All the models that are examined in this section of the chapter have been researched and have been statistically measured and found to have varying degrees of effectiveness. The following six case management models are examined:

1. Assertive Community Treatment
2. Intensive Case Management
3. Comprehensive Enhancement Practice Model
4. Kinship Care Case Management
5. Strength-Based Case Management
6. Brokerage Case Management

As you examine the six different models, it is important to think critically about the research that pertains to each model before making a determination about its worth. An evidence-based practice should be your goal because this will ensure that your clients are receiving care that has been scientifically proven to be effective. By no stretch of the imagination does this book review all the case management models that are available to you. The models that are offered are promising for use in human services practice.

Assertive Community Treatment

Assertive Community Treatment (ACT) was developed in the 1970s out of a program called Training in Community Living (TCL), an intensive community-based program for the severely mentally ill (it is now used with other vulnerable populations like battered women and AIDS clients). ACT is a team case management approach where the caseload is shared among a team who collectively create comprehensive individualized service plans for clients and do intense outreach. Yet clients are managed by a primary case manager who is a member of the team. It is believed that helping professionals who work as a team will experience less burnout on the job and in turn clients have greater continuity in care.

Before a full explanation is given about how this approach works, here is a brief outline of how it was first conceptualized. First, Stein and Test (1980) developed ACT through extensive research of community-based programs. ACTs critical practice features initially included the following:

1. maintaining low client or staff caseloads,
2. having 24-hour crisis support by the treatment team,
3. using a whole-team approach with a multidisciplinary team,
4. providing direct services such as monitoring client medication,
5. creating individualized care plans,
6. working with clients in the community,
7. holding regular staff meetings to collaborate on caseload, and
8. maintaining a no discharge policy of clients.

After two landmark studies about ACT, it was hailed as an innovative case management approach for the care of the severely mentally ill (Burns, 2010). During the 1980s, ACT became a routine clinical delivery approach that was widely used in the mental health field around the world. After more extensive research, changes and additions were made to ACT to make it more effective with different types of clients. Currently, ACT has the following core features:

1. multidisciplinary staffing,
2. integration of services,
3. team approach,
4. small caseloads (staff–client ratio 1:10 or 1:12),
5. locus of contact in the community,
6. management of medications,
7. focus on activities of daily living,
8. rapid access,
9. assertive outreach,
10. individualized services, and
11. time-unlimited services.

HOW THE ACT MODEL WORKS   In general, if your agency is using the ACT approach you would be assigned to a multidisciplinary team. Typically, a multidisciplinary team of professionals comprises a variety of practitioners like a human services generalist, nurse, crisis mobile team member, social worker, occupational therapist, vocational rehabilitation counselor, and physician. Each team member possesses different specialized skills and knowledge to address a client's problems; having practitioners from different disciplines allows team members to use different approaches as they coordinate care for the client. A human services generalist, for example, who has a rehabilitative or substance abuse background would have a different approach of looking at a client's problems versus a physician who would primarily be focused on a client's medical problems.

Each team member is assigned a part of the team caseload, usually between 10 and 12 clients. ACT teams maintain low staff–client ratio (e.g., 10 team members are responsible for approximately 100 clients), which allows the team to give comprehensive and individualized care, offer clients rapid access to services, and increase service continuity for the client. Having low caseloads also allows the team to engage in assertive outreach to clients who are reluctant or resistant to accepting care. Assertive outreach is based on the premise that once a case is open, the client and team have a lifelong relationship. Ideally no case is ever closed; therefore clients always have a group of professionals who are prepared to help when needed. However, the ACT approach necessitates that the team must have frequent case meetings to discuss their shared caseloads.

As the case manager you will be the primary coordinator for a specific group of clients, which means you would regularly interface with the client, monitor client outcomes, and oversee the client's records. You would also help create an individual service plan with each client (if the client is able). This plan focuses on activities such as how the client would manage handling personal hygiene, taking medication, paying rent, working, and other activities of daily living.

Typically, the case manager is the first person on the team whom the client would reach out to when he or she needed something. However, even though you might be the primary case manager, your work is never done in isolation because you are part of a multidisciplinary team. ACT is a team approach, which means that you are equally invested in the welfare of your assigned clients and the clients of other team members. For example, a client's service plan is further developed with the help and expertise of other team members. The overall goal of the individual service plan is focused on strategizing how to help the client independently function in a community setting, and this might involve several team members and the primary case manager.

ACT team members have frequent contacts with clients in settings outside the agency. Ideally, 80% of client contact occurs in their homes or a natural setting, for example, their jobsite. Contacts outside the therapeutic setting are called "in vivo" contacts. During in vivo contacts, team members have the opportunity to meet with the client's family or caretaker. The benefit of this is it gives the team the opportunity to communicate and gather client information from the family or caretaker. Moreover, the in vivo visit gives multiple team members an opportunity to work with and teach clients new skills. For instance, the nurse team member could assess and determine the best way for the client to take his or her medication. The vocational rehabilitation counselor team member could do supervised job training with the client on the job site. The human services generalist who is also the primary case manager could work with the client on activities of daily living such as riding public transportation, managing money, paying bills, finding housing, shopping, and cooking in either a home or a natural setting.

During in vivo contacts, team members engage in direct observations of clients, which allows for a more accurate client assessment rather than solely relying on client self-reports, and team members can better determine whether clients are accomplishing their activities of daily living (e.g., taking medication or maintaining personal hygiene) and making adequate adjustment to living in the community.

Moreover, the ACT team uses an integrated service approach that allows them to tailor in-house services for the client. Client services are integrated at the practitioner level rather than coordinated at the administrative level. (Schaedle, McGrew, Bond, & Epstein, 2002). In other words, the team directly offers services to the client, such as direct counseling, skill building, and family advising. Every effort is made by the team to offer clients direct integrated services rather than referring them out for services; in turn, this creates greater continuity of care for clients. Overall, each team member acts as a case manager for one set of clients, but the team works together to ensure that the group's clients all receive the best care in the most efficient and effective manner.

POPULATIONS BEST SERVED BY ACT   ACT has been extensively researched, compared with other case management approaches. This approach has also been found to be a relatively effective approach that can be used to address problems of a variety of client populations and can be used as a whole-person approach because it allows the case manager to address client-in-context problems.

Overall, it has been suggested that ACT is an effective case management approach with different client populations. ACT has also been successfully adapted to accommodate different ethnic minority groups and can be used in different settings (Ackerson & Karoll, 2005). For example, when an ACT team is working with ethnic minorities who have chronic mental illness, efforts are made to include team members who are culturally similar to the clients. These team members must have an in-depth understanding of the clients' cultures, which will help with implementing the case management process (Law, 2007).

ACT has also been adapted for use in the criminal justice field and is called the Forensic Assertive Community Treatment (FACT). In this instance, FACT is designed as a reentry case management approach to help mentally ill prisoners. Case managers are focused on helping newly released prisoners—known as parolees—adjust to the demands of living in a community. It was reported that parolees receiving FACT case management were less likely to be re-incarcerated, less likely to need outpatient care, and less likely to be admitted to a psychiatric unit.

RESEARCH FINDINGS ABOUT ACT   Many practitioners find ACT to be an effective case management approach. It was reported that ACT reduces the length and frequency of inpatient psychiatric stays of different service users that include the homeless mentally ill (Coldwell & Bender, 2007), ethnic minorities with severe chronic mental illness (Law, 2007), the mentally ill with schizophrenia, psychosis (Bond et al., 2001), depression, bipolar disorder, and the dual diagnosed (Ackerson & Karoll, 2005).

In studies about ACT, the positive outcomes reported were as follows: (a) clients had greater success in independent living, (b) improved quality of life, and (c) improved social functioning when they received more services (Bigelow & Young, 1991). Other positive outcomes reported about ACT were that clients had reduced psychiatric hospital stays, increased housing stability, and controlled mental health symptoms (Schaedle et al., 2002). Plus clients reported that the best parts about ACT were the staff availability, home visits, and help with activities of daily living (McGrew & Wilson, 1996).

From the team perspective, the most important client service of ACT was the frequent home visits (Prince, Demidenko, & Gerber, 2000). The research indicated that when staff worked as a team, it decreased practitioner burnout. In turn, when there was a lower rate of burnout, there was lower rate of turnover among staff, which resulted in better continuity of care of clients. However, in the process of implementing ACT it was unclear which specific practices reduced psychiatric readmissions (Udechuku et al., 2005). Similarly, it was not clear what elements of the case management approach worked or could be eliminated if implementation costs were a concern to practitioners (Burns & Perkins, 2000). There were also concerns about the capability of team members to effectively engage in a team approach because the concept was not clearly defined (Burns, 2010). It was inferred that practitioners didn't have the background in building teams and managing work groups.

Because of ACT's general success, many countries around the world use ACT in place of institutional care (Mowbray, Plum, & Materson, 1997). However, it has been reported that ACT has not effectively reduced hospital admissions of the mentally ill in the United Kingdom (Marshall & Francis, 2000) and in the Netherlands (Sytema et al., 2007). All case management approaches have problems that should be considered before using them with clients.

Intensive Case Management

Intensive Case Management (ICM) is a team approach where practitioners support each other as they independently work to link and coordinate services for clients. Some believe that ICM is not represented by one well-defined model but seems to be based on different case management models (Schaedle, 1999). In general, the ICM approach is more extreme or intense than those used in general case management (Vanderplasschen, Wolf, Rapp, & Broekaert, 2007). Although there is no consensus for one definition for ICM, some critical features include the following:

1. The practitioner individually manages small caseloads.
2. The primary function of the practitioner is to link and coordinate client services.
3. The practitioner encourages client empowerment.
4. Client outreach occurs only when it is necessary.
5. Cases are closed when clients refuse services or when they are institutionalized.
6. Team management is considered less important.

Originally, ICM was focused on maintaining continuity of client services, reducing costs for services, and increasing the mentally ill client's quality of life and function. You might be thinking that ACT and ICM approaches have a similar focus on the mentally ill. You are correct: Both approaches were designed to help chronically mentally ill clients integrate into their communities. The common features between the two models are as follows: (a) both serve clients in need of intensive care, (b) both are used in a community setting, and (c) both address practical client problems (Schaedle et al., 2002). So what makes ICM different from ACT? You will see the differences between the models when you examine how ICM works.

HOW ICM WORKS Implementing ICM involves assembling a team of professionals. The team serves as a support for its members instead of the arena in which client problems are collectively handled. Therefore, team management is less important in the ICM approach because each team member is expected to work independently with his or her clients.

The primary function of ICM is to link and coordinate client services and encourage client empowerment. Case managers handle multiple client problems because they have small caseloads. They also view clients as autonomous beings who make individual choices and take responsibility for their own lives. Therefore, a case manger makes little effort to do outreach to clients. Finally, under the IMC approach when clients refuse services or are institutionalized, the case manager will close the case.

POPULATIONS BEST SERVED BY ICM   The clients that seem to be best served by ICM include a full range of vulnerable populations. The literature contains data that reveal that the following groups have benefited from ICM: the severely mentally ill with and without a history of violence (Dvoskin & Steadman, 1994), frail older adults in need of health services (Young, 2003), homeless mothers with severe mental illness seeking reunification with their minor children (Hoffman & Rosenheck, 2001), adults with schizophrenia (Preston, 2000), women who have been stalked by former intimate partners (Spence-Diehl, 2004), and people with HIV/AIDS.

RESEARCH FINDINGS ABOUT ICM   Research study outcomes have shown that ICM varies in its effectiveness. However, there is research that indicates that ICM is effective with clients with mental illness (Dvoskin & Steadman, 1994). It was reported that mentally ill clients receiving ICM were more likely to live independently and less likely to be hospitalized. Overall, a broad array of clients reported satisfaction with their care, having access to tangible services and greater support (Hoffman & Rosenheck, 2001; Preston, 2000; Young, 2003).

Comprehensive Enhancement Practice Model

Comprehensive Enhancement Practice Model (CEPM) is an empirically based case management model with 15 overlapping functions performed in a time-phased sequence that begins with client referral for service and proceeds through therapeutic interventions and advocacy for additional services to meet the client's needs. This case management approach is a time-phased sequence of functions used with vulnerable populations that have long-term complex problems in living (Rothman & Sager, 1998). Overall, CEPM has the case manager focusing on the individual client. One limitation of CEPM is that it does not focus on social action or community development on behalf of different client populations, which would be useful for engaging in a whole-person approach.

CEPM was developed by a group of researchers at the University of California Los Angeles Center for the Child and Family Policy Studies and the Los Angeles Department of Mental Health. This group of researchers sought to create a standard practice for case management based on effective practices in the field and case management literature. After an in-depth study, CEPM was conceptualized (Rothman, 1991). The model has 15 sequential functions that the case manager uses to help clients with complex problems (Rothman & Sager, 1998). The 15 sequential case management functions are as follows:

1. referral,
2. intake,
3. assessment,
4. goal setting,

5. intervention planning,
6. resource identification and indexing,
7. formal linkage to external sources,
8. informal linkage to family and social networks,
9. monitoring,
10. reassessment,
11. outcome evaluation for termination,
12. interagency coordination,
13. counseling,
14. therapy, and
15. advocacy.

HOW CEPM WORKS   The 15 sequential functions are used by the case manager during the case management process. Each function is performed in a time-phased sequence, but some functions overlap and other functions become alternative options or recur at different times (Rothman, 1991).

REFERRAL TO THE AGENCY   The first function is getting a referral, which is how prospective clients come to the organization for service. Typically, clients come to the organization via referrals from social networks and/or professional networks. In addition, administrators in the organization work to develop reciprocal referral systems with other organizations and have staff engage in community outreach. Once a referral is received, it is incumbent upon staff to make every effort to be responsive to the referred client by quickly accommodating him or her with an appointment. Overall, the access function is to ensure that there is a continual flow of viable clients into the organization.

INTAKE FUNCTION   Once a prospective client comes into the agency, a formal intake interview is done. The intake function is the time when client information that is required to complete organizational forms is gathered. This information will help the organization determine whether the client is eligible for services and can pay for services. After completion of the intake, the prospective client receives information about the agency services, requirements, and limitations.

ASSESSMENT FUNCTION   If the client qualifies for services with the agency, then the next function is the assessment. During the assessment, the case manager begins to gather information to determine what type of problem the client is experiencing. Client problems are determined by doing a case history. If necessary, psychosocial assessment or psychological tests are needed, and they are typically done by licensed professionals like psychologists or clinical social workers. Moreover, an assessment will not be complete until client records are requested from outside agencies. This will ensure that the most comprehensive client assessment is being done.

GOAL-SETTING FUNCTION   Goal setting is built on the assessment. Goal setting is a part of developing a client's individual service plan. Short- and long-term goal setting should occur with client input. In the process of setting goals, there should be a realistic outlook regarding the limitations of vulnerable clients. These limitations should be calculated into all forms of future planning made by the case manager. The case manager will also determine whether immediate services to handle a crisis are needed for the client during this planning phase.

INTERVENTION FUNCTION Intervention planning is the fifth function, which is when the practitioner will make a choice about the type of treatment (e.g., counseling or therapy) the client will need in the long term. This choice involves linking the client to external services and occurs in conjunction with the development of the individual service plan. The major objective of intervention planning is to help clients move through their short- and long-term goals.

The next three functions are resource identification and indexing, formal linkage to agencies and programs, and informal linkages to families and social networks. These three functions don't follow a logical progression because client resources and service delivery systems are constantly changing.

RESOURCE IDENTIFICATION AND INDEXING FUNCTION When case managers work to discover what barriers exist at the client and system levels, this is the first part of resource identification and indexing. Once those barriers are identified, the case manager can systematically determine what relevant informal and formal resource linkages are accessible to the client. Then the case manager would create a database of resources in the community and service area that might be of importance or use to the client. Once a database of informal and formal resource linkages is created, the next two functions deal with formal and informal linkages that can be made on behalf of the client.

FORMAL LINKAGE FUNCTION An important case management function involves formally linking clients, which means (a) making sure the correct service is provided, (b) making initial contact with an agency on behalf of the client, (c) orienting clients about agency processes, (d) preparing documentation, and (e) visiting external agencies to ensure appropriate referrals are made in the future. Linking clients to external services means that the case manager must remain vigilant about updating and developing resource information about formal resources because they change or become defunct.

INFORMAL LINKAGE FUNCTION To make informal linkages, the case manager must learn about a client's immediate and extended family members and who might be of assistance to the client. The other resource would be determining who the client believes might be available to help among his or her social network like friends, clergy members, and employers. Linking clients to family or social networks means that the case manager must again remain vigilant about updating and developing resource information about informal resources because they change. The next two functions are monitoring and reassessment, and they are overlapping functions.

MONITORING FUNCTION The purpose of the monitoring function in case management is to appraise whether the different interventions are working for the client. The case manager needs a substantial amount of time to engage in monitoring, which includes telephoning external agency staff, doing a crisis intervention, visiting with the client, or communicating with the client via telephone or email.

REASSESSMENT FUNCTION Reassessment means the case manager is readjusting the client's service plan or revising goals with the client if things are not working as planned. The case manager will make both informal and formal reassessments of goals with the client on a regular basis. The reassessment function is when the case manager should probe for additional client information and determine if new obstacles or problems have occurred. If the case manager is working with a client for a long-term period, he or she will repeatedly engage in monitoring and reassessment over the duration of the case management process. In turn, the practitioner will be working with the client to set new goals and will repeatedly be doing intervention planning, monitoring, and reassessing as needed.

OUTCOME EVALUATION FOR TERMINATION The next function is intermittently used in the case management sequence. This function is outcome evaluation, which is when the case manager is focusing on termination or discharge of the client because the client no longer needs ongoing professional services. Termination of case management rarely occurs with vulnerable populations like the chronically mentally disabled or physically disabled clients.

INTERAGENCY COORDINATION FUNCTION This function is not usually done by the case manager. Interagency coordination is usually done by the administration. Typically, only administrators have the power to create policy agreements with other organizations. Because administrators are knowledgeable about service patterns, type and number of clients, legal issues, and fiscal obligations, they are in a better position to do interagency coordination.

COUNSELING AND THERAPY FUNCTIONS Counseling function is short term and is a form of advice or information giving to help the client with day-to-day problems. And the case manager can offer this type of counseling to clients. In CEPM, counseling is a function that is different from therapy, which is usually done by licensed practitioners. Therapy is used for personality restructuring and is based on decreasing psychological dysfunctions. In addition, therapy helps clients manage their immediate social realities.

ADVOCACY FUNCTION The final function of CEPM is advocacy. The case manager will intermittently advocate on behalf of the client to get services or resources that are being unjustly withheld from them. The case manager may guide clients through a bureaucratic process and teach them to advocate on their own behalf to obtain benefits that are due them. However, to be an effective advocate, the case manager needs to be knowledgeable about the advocacy process and lobbying in the political arena.

CLIENTS BEST SERVED BY CEPM The model is designed to be used with vulnerable populations that include the elderly, children, and disabled. Researchers have determined from data that vulnerable populations commonly needed long-term services to live in the community (Rothman & Sager, 1998). CEPM is a comprehensive case management approach that could easily be used to scaffold clients throughout their life.

RESEARCH FINDINGS ABOUT CEPM The CEPM is an empirically grounded model that guides the practice of case managers, which is not considered rigid practice. It is assumed that before using the model a case manager has basic knowledge and skills about interpersonal processes. This model was designed as a working tool to help professionals manage their caseloads with flexible and overlapping functions. It is based on data obtained from a large group of case managers working in the field. Most of the follow-up research about CEPM was done by Jack Rothman who also created the model. Overall, it is a promising case management approach.

Kinship Care Case Management

In 1992, the Michigan Kinship Project worked to identify best practice approaches for kinship care of children at risk (Rothman, 1991). After extensive field testing, the **Kinship Care Case Management** Model was developed. The model is designed to help family members who are willing to be kinship caregivers of a minor child who is at risk of being put into foster care. Both the child and kinship caregiver have overlapping concerns that are taken into consideration as the individual service plan is created. The objective of the case management approach is to support the family that is caring for the child and avoid placing the child into foster care. The featured components of the Kinship Care Case Management Model are as follows:

1. attention to cultural diversity,
2. family participation and decision making,
3. systematic assessment, and
4. individualized and comprehensive services.

HOW KINSHIP CARE WORKS   The first step in this case management process is an assessment of the minor child—who is the client. This assessment is also done in conjunction with a family conference. During the assessment process, the client (if he or she is capable) is asked to provide personal information and is encouraged to be an active partner in creating a treatment plan. In addition, information is collected from the foster parent (a designated family member) about the client's needs, formal supports, finances, resources, strengths, goals, and tasks related to placement decisions. Because the client is cared for by a family member, it is essential to get information about the child's family system and social network.

When using the Kinship Care Model, the assessment data are collected in three steps. The first step involves getting a picture of the client's family system. The two

FIGURE 1.1

Ecomap

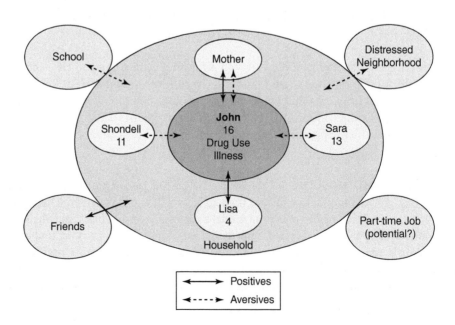

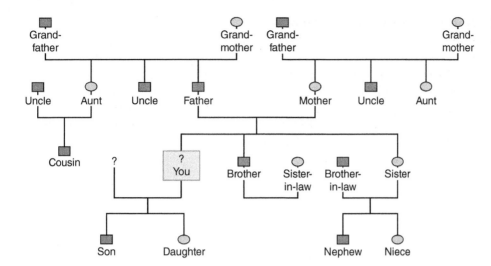

FIGURE 1.2
Family Genogram

diagrams typically used to depict a family system are an **ecomap** and a **genogram**. Why use diagrams? These diagrams are visual aids that summarize information about your client, which allows you or another team member to get a sense of the client's family dynamic in one glance. The diagrams also efficiently relay complex information without having to rummage through pages of a client's case report. Both the ecomap and genogram are tools that help the case manager organize complex client information and reduce the need for writing lengthy reports.

The ecomap depicts the client's relationship with his or her family and social networks (see Figure 1.1). The ecomap is also a visual representation of the positive and aversive relationships among family members and the client's social network.

The genogram is used to depict data about the client's multigenerational family system (see Figure 1.2). With one glance, you can visualize the client's family roles and relationships with the genogram.

The second step of data collection involves asking critical questions of the kinship caregiver to determine what formal services and support will be necessary to maintain the child in his or her household. Focus the questions on family finances, stressors, and whether the current housing situation is adequate.

The third step of data collection involves asking the child (if he or she is able to communicate) questions about his or her life and needs. In addition, the child's academic records and health records should also be obtained.

After data are collected for the assessment, there will be a family conference. During the family conference, the case manager reviews the collected data with the kinship caregiver. The caregiver is encouraged to be actively involved in the preparation of the client's service plan. In the service plan, there are action steps and measurable objectives to be completed within a 90-day period. The service plan should be signed by the kinship caregiver. Then a weekly meeting is scheduled with the child and the caregiver to ensure there is progression toward the client's goals. During these weekly meetings, the client or caregiver can address any concerns during the process.

Watch the video **Constructing a Genogram** to learn how this tool is used to map the client's family tree and personal events that occur in the client's family system.

To effectively use the Kinship Care Case Management approach, practitioners must work at being culturally aware. They must become knowledgeable about multicultural interactions in the context of their work. Becoming a competent multicultural practitioner takes time and great effort. Please be advised that when you work with minor children, it is essential that you know and understand the dos and don'ts. Do not assume that you understand all the policies and laws for working with children. To be safe, double-check with your agency about their policies and get clarification of state laws before beginning work with minor children and their families.

CLIENTS BEST SERVED BY THE KINSHIP MODEL   The kinship case management approach uses the natural strength found in the family network to help support children at risk (Mills & Usher, 1996). The research indicates that kinship case management is effective with children involved in foster care and adoption services. With minor modifications, this model may be appropriate for prevention and protective services for children.

RESEARCH FINDINGS ABOUT THE KINSHIP MODEL   It was reported that there are instances where the kinship system will fail because the adult family member is overwhelmed with the level of care or the child begins to act out. As a result, a formal agency will have to intervene. In some cases, the minor child—who is the client—is removed from the designated caregiver and put into the regular foster care system (Mills & Usher, 1996).

There is a body of literature about the effectiveness of kinship foster care, but there is little literature about the kinship case management model. Yet the lack of research about the kinship case management model doesn't diminish its importance. Providing support and protection to children should be a major concern of all the helping professions.

Strength-Based Case Management

The **Strength-Based Case Management (SCM)** approach is designed to activate the client's abilities and inner resources so that he or she can cope with personal challenges. The approach emphasizes the client's strengths and does not dwell on his or her deficits. The features of SCM are as follows:

1. help clients discover their strengths,
2. focus on client strengths and self-direction,
3. promote use of informal helping networks,
4. offer assertive community involvement,
5. develop a strong positive relationship with the client.

Starting in the 1980s, SCM was used in community mental health centers and hospitals to help clients effectively function in the community. SCM is based on four major assumptions about people. First, all people possess the inner strength and abilities to deal with the world they live in. It is also assumed that people possess the knowledge to explain all aspects of the life and have the potential to find solutions to their own problems. Third, it is assumed that individuals will ultimately survive and thrive despite their misfortunes experienced in life. The final assumption is that some people will need assistance to find their strengths and abilities to change their life.

HOW THE SCM MODEL WORKS   When a practitioner uses SCM, the first step is to do an assessment. During the assessment, the client is asked to identify his or her personal capabilities and assets. To get to this information, the client is encouraged to share personal stories of life challenges. The client is helped with exploring his or her perceptions and rediscovering personal abilities.

Next the treatment plan—also known as the service plan—is developed. This plan is based on the strengths, needs, and goals identified by the client. The practitioner plans activities that are flexible and tailored to the client's needs and internal strengths. Then the planned activities are used to move the client toward his or her goals.

During all interactions, the practitioner focuses on the client's strengths, explores the client's strength perceptions, and learns about the oppression the client endures. The client is encouraged to offer insights about personal capabilities, which are used as a foundation to be built on in the future. And clients are encouraged to use informal help networks rather than formal community resources (e.g., social service agencies) to help them develop their own abilities to deal with personal challenges.

To avoid an oppressive interaction, the practitioner repeatedly asks the client to make a critical analysis of the case management process. The practitioner works to develop a close professional relationship with his or her clients but maintains professional boundaries at all times.

CLIENTS BEST SERVED BY SCM   The SCM approach has been successfully used with a variety of client populations. The groups that benefit from this case management approach are the elderly, mentally ill, and individuals with substance abuse problems.

RESEARCH FINDINGS ABOUT SCM   There is a growing body of empirical evidence that reports positive outcomes of SCM. Clients who received SCM had higher levels of satisfaction with services than clients that received standard care (Bjorkman, Hansson, & Sandlund, 2002). In addition, mentally ill clients who received SCM spent significantly fewer days in the psychiatric unit.

Clients receiving SCM reported that it was useful to reflect on their problems and appreciated the close relationship developed with their case managers (Brun, Rapp, 2001). Yet this close relationship was sometimes a strain on clients and thwarted their progress.

It has also been reported that SCM does not have any significant impact on psychological symptoms, quality of life, and social and vocational functioning (Bjorkman, Hansson, & Sandlund, 2002). It is suggested that SCM is a naïve approach because it merely encourages clients to engage in positive thinking. Therefore, it doesn't help the client to reframe the objective reality that is behind the problems being experienced. Moreover, some consider SCM to be a questionable intervention or think it should not be used at all.

Brokerage Case Management

Brokerage Case Management (BCM) is considered a brief case management approach, which means the contact between the client and case manager is limited to one or two sessions. The case manager acts as a broker working on behalf of the client to secure information about client services, locate external linkages to agencies, and find financial support for clients (Moseley, 2004). The goals of BCM are to prevent inpatient hospital stays, improve the client's quality of life, and elevate the client's personal functioning (Bond et al., 2001).

HOW THE BCM MODEL WORKS In the BCM process, a client assessment is done by the case manager. This assessment helps prioritizes client needs and deficits. The case manager uses the assessment information to locate, coordinate, and refer clients to services. The goal of BCM is to reduce the institutional care of clients in favor of community-based care.

Brokerage case managers typically have relatively heavy caseloads, and this leaves them no time to create formal external linkages to other organizations. If BCM is to work, case managers must have the support of their administrations to develop informal or formal collaborative agreements with external agencies. These collaborative agreements are designed to promote professional communication among staff from different organizations. As a result, collaborating agencies are supposed to accept appropriate referrals from each other. This collaboration creates a seamless network among formal community resources, which allows the practitioner to better serve and support clients.

CLIENTS BEST SERVED BY BCM It has been reported that mentally ill clients are best served by BCM (Bond et al., 2001). However, it was not clear why. Little research was found about the BCM model. Nevertheless, from my own practical experiences in the field, I have seen BCM used in some shape or form in organizations for HIV/AIDS, domestic violence, and mental health. Case managers using BCM were often put in the position of trying to create collaborative agreements with external agencies. In the real world, this meant that collaborative agreements were not made because frontline workers didn't have the time or the clout to create interorganizational contracts.

Assess your comprehension of the differences between the six case management models by completing this quiz.

RESEARCH FINDINGS ABOUT BCM In the few studies done on BCM, the results indicated that the client group that received BCM were given only a referral to external services, and clients failed to use the services provided. For example, referring elderly clients (65 years or older) to services in the community resulted in low rates of access and usage of mental health and substance abuse services (Bond et al., 2001). In addition, it was reported that BCM did not reduce these clients' use of the hospital to manage mental health and substance abuse problems.

Systems Theories

In the 1930s, Ludwig von Bertalanffy, a biologist, developed **general systems theory,** which describes the relationship among individual internal organic systems in their interactions with their external environment. Followers of Bertalanffy proposed that many phenomena could be viewed as a web of relationships or interactions among systems, and, moreover, that all systems have common patterns or behaviors. The knowledge of systemic patterns or behaviors and their interactions could be used to increase the understanding of complex phenomena. Bertalanffy's work went beyond biology and was used in different fields of study, including engineering and psychology. By the mid-1900s, social scientists began to adapt the concepts of general systems theory to metaphorically explain how human beings interacted with human systems that started at the level of family, workplace, and neighborhood and extended to religious and educational affiliations, which were all encompassed by political and government systems, the economic system, and systems of transit, commerce and industry, mass media, and finally social norms derived from dominant belief and value systems.

Bioecological Theory

Urie Bronfenbrenner (2005), a social scientist, worked on a **bioecological theory** that would influence the fields of human services and social work. Bronfenbrenner proposes that human development, throughout one's lifetime, is influenced by the events that occur in the social environment in which a person lives (e.g., a family or community). In addition, events that occur outside the person's personal sphere, like social policies and practices, regulate one's behavior in society. However, these external events also indirectly influence human development. For instance, you live in a society that has laws prohibiting the murder of people and this law in turn regulates your behavior. Are there people who break the public laws, norms, or social conventions? Yes! Nevertheless, human behavior is influenced by external forces that are not under the control of that individual. Bronfenbrenner struggled to test the synergistic interaction between the biopsychological makeup of humans and their environment. He wanted know how the human physical body and mind all interacted with the physical environment and how it affected human development.

HOW THE BIOECOLOGICAL THEORY WORKS   Bronfenbrenner (1979) theorized that some critical elements that drive human development are the objective and subjective experiences that humans have with their environment. The objective experience refers to concrete things that people come into contact with in the environment, and the subjective experience refers to the full range of feelings (both positive and negative) about self, others, and events experienced throughout life. He characterized feelings as both stable and changeable plus they are emotionally and motivationally loaded. Through the human life cycle, human development is based on progressively more complex shared interactions with people, objects, and symbols in the external environment, which Bronfenbrenner called the "proximal processes." For instance, if a child is to effectively develop intellectually, emotionally, socially, and morally, shared interactions (proximal processes) must occur on a regular basis for extended periods of time.

Some examples of proximal processes are learning, playing, reading, and learning a new skill. These and other shared interactions are considered the primary engines of human development. Bronfenbrenner believed that these shared interactions develop strong emotional attachment between a child and a committed caregiver. Over time the child internalizes the caregiver's feelings and activities, which results in motivating a child to explore, manipulate, and engage in his or her environment. Support of the caregiver by a third party (another adult or parent) serves to increase the quality of the interaction and leads to more positive development. However, human development during the proximal process systematically varies because there are differences in people's genetic inheritance, immediate and remote environments, and environmental permanencies and changes over an extended period of time.

Some say that the bioecological theory has a gap between the social development of individuals and their social networks; plus there is also a problem understanding changes over time (Cairns & Cairns, 2005). Yet social scientists started using system theory terminology such as open/closed systems, positive/negative feedback, steady state, and equilibrium to help explain micro-level through macro-level workings of people, groups, and organizations independently and interactively. In practical terms, translating Bronfenbrenner's bioecological theory into practice has not been as successful as some might have hoped. However, there have been attempts to make the theory relevant to human services practice.

Human Services Organic Model: A Whole-Person Approach

Joann Chenault, a pioneer in human services education, created the **Human Services Organic Model** to conceptualize the different levels of society, which factor into human problems and influence human development. The Human Services Organic Model has two fundamental principles, which are the principle of interconnection and the principle of constant change that govern the overall functioning of the systems and environments of human interaction (Chenault, 1975).

HOW THE HUMAN SERVICES ORGANIC MODEL WORKS   The principle of interconnection refers to the connection of human systems that form larger organic (i.e., living) networks. Human systems include individuals, groups, communities, organizations, and different societies. Chenault (1975) theorizes that all human systems are interconnected and compose complex networks. The complexity of an individual's interconnection with other systems is infinite. Yet, the reality of the interconnections within a human system is that each connection has some type of influence upon the individual that you must be aware of, so you can work to change it, when necessary. Furthermore, the principle of interconnection means that you must consider your client's problems from a multidimensional perspective (i.e., whole-person perspective).

The second concept of the Human Services Organic Model is that there is constant change within human systems, which means that human systems are always fluid, self-correcting, and renewing. Therefore, individuals, families, communities, social institutions, organizations, and societies are all continually changing, self-correcting, and renewing themselves. Clients don't live in a vacuum; whether they like it or not, they are caught in the flow of constant change, which can create a series of problems for the client. Change is also caused by the individual, and some is caused by external forces. If not all change comes from the individual, then you must be cognizant of what external forces are causing change.

Chenault created her model to challenge human services practitioners' rigid and absolute beliefs. The model requires practitioners to be cognizant of multiple possibilities for choices, rather than automatically defaulting to simple either-or choices. She felt that simple either-or choices were based on people's assumptions and result in the suppression of their creative choices. Creative choices increase alternatives to new concepts and innovative ways of dealing with issues and problems. Chenault maintained that comfort with one's positions or answers should be a signal that other viable options might have been overlooked, especially when attempting to solve client problems.

Overall, the Human Services Organic Model was an attempt to illustrate the complexities of determining the influences upon an individual. It illustrates why practitioners might have difficultly choosing innovative ways of solving a client's problems. There is little research about this model; therefore, it cannot be put into the category of evidence-based practice. However, the importance of the whole-person approach continues to be an overarching practice in human services. Using a whole-person approach poses challenges to your practice. Nevertheless, striving to better serve our clients in their environmental context remains a major concern despite the limitations of models or theories.

In the case management process, you will do an assessment of the client's problems from a whole-person perspective, which means looking at a client's problems in the context of the person, his or her social environment, and the society he or she is a part of. When you are working with clients you should be asking yourself: (a) How does the client contribute to his or her problems? (b) How does the client's personal environment contribute to his or her problems? and (c) How does society contribute to the client's problems? If you are going to address the root cause of a client's problems, you have to ask all of these three questions, which means you are using a whole-person approach.

Summary

Since the early 1900s, government agencies and nonprofit organizations have used case management for coordinating human services. Yet, there is no single definition for case management, and case management practice is not controlled by any one profession. How a practitioner engages in case management practice will depend on where the individual works. Generally, case management has several overlapping steps: (a) assessment, (b) planning, (c) service coordination, (d) observation, (e) evaluation, and (f) advocating for client services. Some case management models are designed for specific service populations. ACT and ICM, for example, are two case management approaches that focus on reintegrating chronically mentally ill clients back into communities. The Comprehensive Enhancement Practice Model is used with vulnerable populations like the disabled, elderly, and children, while the Kinship Care Model is used only with children. SCM focuses on empowerment of the client, and BCM focuses on coordinating services for the client. In choosing a case management approach, it is important to consider client problems in context by using systems theory. Systems theories have been designed to help practitioners conceptualize client's problems as a result of the interconnection between the client and external environments that are not under the control of the client. However, the adoption of general systems theory into human services practice has not been as successful as some might have hoped.

Human Services Delivery Systems

Understanding and Mastery: Major models used to conceptualize and integrate prevention, maintenance, intervention, rehabilitation, and healthy functioning

Critical Thinking Question: The human services organic model requires the generalist to contextualize a client's problems across different human systems. If the generalist uses this model to conceptualize and integrate services for the client, what questions would have to be asked to get a realistic understanding about how other systems are affecting the client's overall functioning?

Assess your analysis and evaluation of this chapter's content by completing the **Chapter Review**.

Case Management

A Human Services Practice

There is no agreed-upon method of case management among the different helping professions. Yet, there are some practices that can be found in almost every case management approach. These practices involve getting information from clients and strategizing a client plan. This chapter will cover these two essential practices and, in addition, introduce the important principles surrounding legal guardianship—an essential element of human services practice that may be appropriate in a number of different situations.

This chapter is designed to give you a general sense of the case management process, but there is no focus on any specific case management approach. First, you will examine what is involved in doing a client assessment. Client assessment means gathering information, analyzing it, and then drawing conclusions about what problems in life the client is having. Next you will examine what it takes to develop an individual service plan to address a client's problems in living. Finally, there is a discussion about what is involved if you must act as a legal guardian or case manager for a client. Overall, you will be given a foundation on some essential case management components and a related legal issue that can be built upon regardless of the case management approach you adopt.

Case Management Assessment

Case management is used in an array of settings that include social service agencies, drug programs, community mental health facilities, schools, and hospitals. Yet across different agencies the process of learning about and how to do case management is neither systematic nor comprehensive. Different types of practitioners will emerge with different knowledge about how to do case management, because agency-based learning depends on whatever in-house learning opportunities and expertise are available to practitioners at the time (Schneider & Amerman, 1997). Similarly, case management is taught in different academic disciplines, and there is no standardized case management approach used by all disciplines and their practitioners. However, almost all case management approaches have assessment and planning components.

When you are assigned to be the case manager for a client, one of the first things you will do is an assessment. There is no agreed-upon method on how to do an assessment among different professions. Nonetheless, the purpose of an assessment is to gather information from a client and other sources so that you can calculate what problems you will be helping the client address, understand the factors causing the problem, find resources for creating change, anticipate unintended problems, and measure the amount of change in the client's life (Fischer, 1978). To help you understand the complexity of the assessment process, it is broken down into the following three steps: (a) gathering information, (b) analyzing the information, and (c) drawing conclusions.

Gathering Information

The first step of doing an **assessment** involves gathering information directly from the client, from the client's family, from peer and support networks of the client, and from professionals who have worked with the client in other institutions. In other words, you should be using a whole-person approach for gathering client information, which necessitates getting information from the individual and the individual's social network, plus gathering information about the sociocultural environments and society that impact the client.

During an assessment interview, the questions asked of clients are designed to assess their level of functioning, current problems, and needs in terms of resources that will sustain them. In an ideal world, an assessment interview would last as long as necessary to get all the relevant information. However, in the real world you will typically have a very short period of time to complete an entire assessment. If the client is in crisis, for example, is the victim of abuse, domestic violence, or elder neglect, your agency might push you to complete the assessment and take action all in the same day.

You will now examine the type of information that is typically gathered from an assessment interview. Consider an assessment as an ongoing event in which information is gathered in snapshots that will be assembled over time and will give you a detailed view of the client's life. In many agencies, the assessment interview is structured so that each client is asked the same set of questions. This process is considered a standardized assessment.

Why have standardized assessments? It allows agencies to determine the types and quantities of services offered to clients (Rothman, 1991). The limitations of a structured assessment are that it may not highlight the root causes of the client's problems because not enough interrelated information is gathered about the client and the context he or she lives in (Schneider & Amerman, 1997). Therefore, the case manager must determine which standardized answers signal the need to probe for additional information related to a client's problem. However, if you lack extensive knowledge about the problems of the service population that you intend to work with, your standardized assessment may be incomplete, because you might not know what questions to ask or might not comprehend what critical information you are lacking.

In other instances, you might be required to construct questions for specific information categories that are based on the type of service population you are working with. In this instance, you will conduct what is considered a semistructured assessment interview. Regardless of the interviewing format—structured or unstructured—using well-designed questions is an efficient way to gather information from clients and external informants (e.g., family members, friends, or professionals).

Questions used in an assessment interview focus on information from different sources. The first source is your client. Assessment questions should be designed to elicit information that will give you the necessary information to assist the client. Depending on the agency and available community resources, questions during the assessment interview might focus on one or more of the following topics: housing, employment, health, education, finances, social interaction, legal issues, recreation, independent living, personal relationships, transportation, and social barriers.

Furthermore, assessment questions should be designed to get clients to explain how the overall social, political, and economic circumstances they are in affect their lives. Questions should also be asked so that it can be determined whether human service programs that are servicing the client are effective and efficient. These social-service questions are asked because quality of life is directly affected by the quality of services produced by social welfare, education, medical and mental health-care programs. There should be a set of questions that will help you determine whether clients understand social welfare policies (e.g., Social Security, Medicare, and Medicaid) that may impact their life. There should also be a set of questions to determine what clients perceive as social barriers to achieving their goals. If assessment questions are properly designed, you will get a comprehensive understanding of the many different social factors that have shaped the client's views and life.

Another source of information for the client's assessment can come from secondary sources such as school records, bank records, health records, legal documents, service records from other agencies, and standardized tests (Box 2.1). Some of the records collected and standardized tests assessed are done by licensed professionals and can be beyond your comprehension. Don't be afraid to ask for help if you are unable

---

Box 2.1   **Examples of Standardized Assessment Tools**

Intelligence Tests
- Stanford-Binet IQ Test
- Wechsler Adult Intelligence Scale
- Wechsler Intelligence Scale for Children (WISC)
- Wechsler Preschool and Primary Scale of Intelligence

Cognitive Development Tests
- Cambridge Neuropsychological Test Automated Battery
- Draw-a-Person Test

Personality Tests
- Minnesota Multiphasic Personality Inventory (MMPI)
- Thematic Apperception Test (TAT)
- Rorschach Test
- Myers-Briggs Type Indicator (MBTI)

to interpret certain records or test results. It's more important that you understand the information—so ask for help from team members in your agency.

To get client records from a secondary source, you will need the proper releases, or what is called a signed informed consent document from the client. You must do this before you can make a request for records (e.g., school transcripts) or speak with professionals (e.g., drug rehab counselors) from another agency. Getting information from external informants who know your client will involve interviewing people like family members, friends, or professionals. I will stress this point once again—the appropriate releases must first be obtained from the client before you speak with any external informant.

Analyzing Information

The second step of doing an assessment involves analyzing a client's records, which is done solely by the practitioner. An analysis of intake summaries, case notes, and secondary sources can offer an in-depth view of a client from many different perspectives that are represented in the formal notes written by other professionals. Even if the client is new to your agency, I guarantee they will have a paper or digital record trail, which means you need to be prepared to obtain them so you can do a thorough analysis.

Is a comprehensive review of records labor intensive? Yes! It takes a lot of time and practice to review client records. So you must learn how to assemble client records in a manner that will help you better understand your client. The discussion now focuses on what it means to analyze information contained in client records.

First, you need to be open to the information in the client records. In other words, try not to look for information that will confirm your preconceived ideas about the client, because if you search for information to confirm your beliefs about the client's problems and needs you may not be open to other information in the records. When you first get a set of records, do a quick review of them to get a general idea of what they contain. Are there several intakes from different agencies? Do the case notes have any relevant information? Are you missing important information about the client? Was there any indication that referrals had been made for the client?

Next, get pen and paper and begin taking notes during your second review of the client records. At this time you will begin a critical analysis of the records. To make the analysis easier, use the sample document titled "Client Information Analysis Outline" (Exhibit 2.1), which will help you organize the information in the client record that you are analyzing. I use this document to do a record analysis, but you can develop your own. The major objective is to look for similarities and differences across the records.

Where do you start? Start looking for similarities across the data for problems described by the client. For instance, during a data analysis, does the client describe his or her problem consistently and in the same manner across all the internal and external case notes under review? If so, you can look in the records for similarities in plans, actions, and outcomes.

You must also look for differences across the data. For example, are the client's presenting problems described the same way across all records? If not, why not? As you assess the case, can you determine why the client's descriptions of his or her presenting problems have been inconsistent? Did the client express his or her needs differently to different practitioners? Were different plans and actions taken? If there are differences across the records, you will need to find out why this is the case.

EXHIBIT 2.1
Sample Client
Information Analysis
Outline

I. SIMILARITIES AMONG CLIENT RECORDS:

II. DIFFERENCES AMONG CLIENT RECORDS:

III. MAJOR MACRO-THEMES: SOCIETAL CAUSES AND BARRIERS RELATED TO THE PROBLEMS:

IV. MAJOR MEZZO-THEMES: COMMUNITY AND FAMILY CAUSES AND BARRIERS RELATED TO THE PROBLEMS

V. MAJOR MICRO-THEMES: CLIENT'S DESCRIPTIONS OF PROBLEMS, STRENGTHS, AND NEEDS:

- -

A critical analysis also involves looking for major themes throughout the records. For example, you note that the client has a crisis and begins to drink and drug to self-medicate, which is reported in case notes from several different agencies. Another theme that is reported throughout the client's records is that the client takes a job and then does something to get fired from the job, which creates another crisis. When you discover repeating themes in the client's record, make short summaries of themes and keep track of where you found the information.

If you aren't sure what a major theme is, examine the client's records with these questions in mind: (a) What problems does the client identify as a challenge? (b) What are the client's needs? (c) What client strengths and weaknesses have been identified? (d) What have other agencies done for the client, and was it effective? (e) What external factors or barriers might have caused the client's problems? If you systematically analyze the client's records and then organize the information around meaningful themes, you should be able to see definite themes and patterns. You can then draw more accurate conclusions.

Drawing Conclusions

The third step in doing an assessment involves the following: (a) drawing conclusions about the client's problems, (b) determining the causes of the client's problems, (c) assessing the client's ability to deal with his or her problems, and (d) deciding the best methods to deal with the client's problems. Conclusions are based on your analysis of the client's records and not on experiences you have had in the past with other clients.

Factually based conclusions guide the planning phase of the case management process, in which the individual service plan is created. You and the client may conclude, for example, that a certain set of problems should be addressed in the individual service plan because the problems have repeatedly been addressed and not adequately solved, which is supported by the client's records. Conclusions can also be made with respect to the duration of the problems, the severity of the problems, and whether the client is motivated to address the problems. In addition, conclusions can be drawn about the different external pressures that might be contributing to the client's problem followed by determining possible plans of actions that can be taken.

We have examined the most basic components of assessment. What I want you to take away from this discussion is some general understanding of how to do a systematic assessment that includes gathering information, analyzing information, and drawing conclusions based on the information. As you create an individual service plan with your client, you should do so based on facts rather than on arbitrary beliefs of what is best for the client.

As you become more knowledgeable about working with clients, you will begin to understand the difficulties of implementing change at different social levels (individual, group, and societal).Why is change so hard to implement? According to Saul Alinsky (1971), "the fear of change is one of [peoples'] deepest fears, and a new idea must be at the least couched in the language of past ideas; often, it must be, at first, diluted with vestiges of the past" (p. 108). Remember Alinsky's words as you begin your work with clients—it might help you understand the complexity of change for all people, especially your clients.

Case Management Planning

Another essential component of most case management approaches is planning, which typically deals with creating an individual service plan. The overall goal of creating the individual service plan is to connect clients to both formal and informal services, so that they can achieve their desired life goals.

Person-Centered Planning

Planning should be person centered, which means putting the client at the center of the planning process. In addition, **person-centered planning** involves respecting the client's personal preferences, culture, and values. Person-centered planning was originally an approach used to plan services for disabled adults (Houston, 2003), but now it is an accepted practice with all service populations. Planning focused on the client's view of his or her circumstances, support networks, and ambitions for the future is planning that humanizes the rigid bureaucracies within human service systems that are more focused on expediently getting the job done despite the fact that it is impersonal.

Person-centered planning can be difficult because the practitioner's and client's approach to setting goals may be different because of influencing factors such as economic status, cultural norms, religious beliefs, and individual characteristics. When there is no agreement, you will need to be open to the client's world views and be prepared to compromise to keep an open exchange between you and the client. Current research suggests that clients who define their needs and participate in forming solutions to their problems are more likely to remain involved in the service planning process (Anthony & Crawford, 2000).

PLANNING WITH CHILDREN   When you are working with children, the approach to get them involved in service planning might not be as straightforward as outlined previously. Thomson and Walker (2010) suggest that to involve children in service planning you first need to read the child's file and speak with other professionals who have worked with the child so that you have something to work with. If possible, meet the child at his or her home. This is an opportunity to gather information to make an assessment about the home situation, and it's an opportunity to build a relationship with the child outside of the office.

Be prepared to ask questions that will encourage a dialogue and will get you additional information about the client (Thomson & Walker, 2010). Asking questions that have already been asked and answered is a turnoff. Furthermore, children are sometimes more willing to speak in an environment that is nonthreatening and where they don't have to have eye contact with the practitioner. If possible, find a neutral venue like a game room in your center or a public park to develop a relationship with the client before the actual work begins. You will need to be mindful of confidentiality issues in the different venues to which you take your client.

Finally, as you engage a child in a conversation, follow the rapport-building techniques outlined in Chapter 3 because they apply in this situation too. When you answer a child, be prepared to repeat your answer several times. The number of times you might have to repeat information will be dependent on the child's age. Therefore, be prepared to have the same conversation when working with children because it takes time for them to digest what is being said.

Planning Goals With the Client

Creating goals for the service plan is a collaborative (two-way) process between the practitioner and client. This process is also a democratic dialogue in which the client and practitioner mutually agree on the best goals to be included in the service plan. Goals in the service plan should also be derived from the client assessment. Moreover, goals should be realistic and attainable within a limited timeframe. The goals for the service plan are designed to

1. have clients strive for positive changes in thoughts and behaviors,
2. have clients strive for the greatest self-determination possible,
3. have clients better utilize their support network for positive growth, and
4. have clients effectively utilize community service agencies and resources.

Here is a sample document for an individual service plan (see Exhibit 2.2). This is a collaborative and flexible plan between the client and case manager and can be changed by both parties when mutually agreed upon. Note that the sample service plan has five categories to be filled in: (a) responsible person, (b) short-term goals, (c) plan/strategy and begin date, (d) outcome and target date, and (e) outcome completion date.

The first thing to be entered into the service plan is the name of the person responsible for carrying out the plan to meet a specific goal. Having an identified responsible party ensures that the person assigned understands what is expected of him or her. The next column is where the goal is written. The service plan can have both short-term and long-term goals. *Short-term goals* typically address a crisis that the client is having or some immediate need of the client. *Long-term goals* address changes that the

Client Name: _____ **Client ID#** _____

Summary of Problems: _____

EXHIBIT 2.2
Sample Individual
Service Plan

SHORT-TERM GOALS

	Responsible Person, Title & Agency or Relationship to Client	Short-term Goals	Plan/ Strategy and Begin Date	Outcome and Target Date	Outcome Completed Date
1					
2					
3					
4					
5					

LONG-TERM GOALS

	Responsible Person, Title & Agency or Relationship to Client	Long-term Goals	Plan/ Strategy and Begin Date	Outcome and Target Date	Outcome Completed Date
1					
2					
3					
4					
5					

Case Manager Signature: _____ **Date:** _____

Supervisor Signature: _____ **Date:** _____

. . . .

client wants to make, with the understanding that it takes a relatively longer amount of time to initiate change. All goals should be unambiguous, which means they should be clear-cut. Examples of short-term and long-term service plan goals are listed below (see Exhibit 2.3).

Strategy Planning

A plan is a tentative course of action that—in terms of case management—is written down by the client and case manager before the delivery of services. The plan describes the activities that different parties will engage in to reach a planned objective related to the client's needs (e.g. services, shelter, or other resources). When you look at the sample document of the individual service plan, please note that it has a space for the person that is responsible for a specific strategy and the date the strategy began. How do you write a good strategy? The strategy should be based on the goal

Client Name: _____ **Client ID#** _____

EXHIBIT 2.3

Example Individual
Service Plan With
Goals

Summary of Problems: _____

SHORT-TERM GOALS FOR THE SERVICE PLAN

	Responsible Person, Title & Agency or Relationship to Client	Short-Term Goals
1	Client	Obtain room at women's shelter.
2	Client	Move to shelter when you feel safe.
3	Client's Sister	Serve as a support when client transitions into women's shelter
4	Client and Attorney	Obtain a temporary restraining order against partner
5		

LONG-TERM GOALS FOR SERVICE PLAN

	Responsible Person, Title & Agency or Relationship to Client	Long-term Goals
1	Client and Money Manager	Work to improve money management.
2	Client	Secure new housing near job.
3	Client	Have better relationship with family.
4		
5		

that was determined from the analysis of the client's records. The ultimate goal is to ensure that the client will achieve a desired outcome. Planning strategies is a creative process that you and the client will be involved in together. There are no books or checklists that will help you develop the perfect plan. What you have at your disposal is the information from the client file that you have systematically synthesized, information about the success (or otherwise) of strategies that have been used in the past, strategies not taken, strategies that were considered but there was no follow through. You may also have a client who will express a preference for a particular strategy that is appropriate for his or her lifestyle. Don't lose sight of the fact that this planning is supposed to be a teachable moment in which clients are learning to take control of their lives.

Will you make the perfect plan? It's best to remember that a plan is not set in stone. Be ready to revise your plan if need be as circumstances change, as steps in the plan work or falter, or as opportunities arise. A plan should not constantly change—it is supposed to provide some stability, attainable milestones, and sought-after improvements. However, the plan is not life, and life is full of surprises. Be flexible.

What should the plan do if it's helpful? A useful plan is a guide for both client and case manager, a statement of concrete actions to be undertaken in succession, with identifiable and measurable milestones toward accomplishment of larger goals. Celebrate the accomplishments and strategize about reaching the next milestone.

For example, one long-term goal on the client's list in Exhibit 2.3 was to secure new housing near near her job. The sample document in Exhibit 2.4 outlines a three-step strategy that moves the client from thinking about where she might move to concrete steps to make the move followed by actual places to rent his or her new apartment. Once you have a plan, make sure the client signs it, which indicates that he or she agreed with you about the plan.

Monitoring the Outcomes

Completed outcomes and the outcome targets are both components in the plan, which can be used to monitor and evaluate the effectiveness of planned strategies. Outcomes can be used to inform clients of their individual progress. Outcomes can be used to report to the team members, supervisors, external delivery services, administrators, stakeholders, and funding sources. Reports can detail what worked, how it worked, and time and resources needed to make things work.

What if the plan fails? Plans will fail, but you and the client must learn to be open to learning from failures. Confronting failure is an issue studied and discussed in organizational psychology, but it is applicable to human services. According to Cannon and Edmondson (2001), identifying failure is essential to learning from it, followed by a discussion and analysis of the relevant lesson learned, and finally learning to cope during a discussion of failures and identified causes. In the context of monitoring outcomes, if there are failures, you and the client should be prepared to learn from the failures, which means that you and the client are willing to identify a failure, discuss, and analyze it, and productively deal with the fallout. I want you to be prepared and have the attitude that you and the client can learn from mistakes or failures.

THE IMPORTANCE OF WORKING WELL WITH OTHERS While working in a human service organization, you will have to deal with both internal organizational and external organizational processes with respect to their service delivery networks (Austin, 2002). The coordination and integration of services improves outcomes for clients that have multiple, complex, and long-term service needs (Gans & Horton, 1975). The effectiveness of community service delivery is dependent on the effectiveness of the working relationships of agency practitioners delivering services plus the quality of services they provide (Sauber, 1983).

A place where internal and external organizational processes come together is in the case conference. The case conference is a formal meeting in which the case manager meets face to face with team members (internal and external) working with the same client. Using a team approach can build trust and cohesion that leads to achieving

Client Name:_____ **Client ID#** _____

Summary of Problems:_____

LONG-TERM GOALS

	Responsible Person, Title & Agency or Relationship to Client	Long-Term Goals	Plan/Strategy and Begin Date	Target Outcome and Date	Outcome Completed Date
1	Client	Secure new housing near job	Step 1. Identify neighborhoods that have housing that fits client's budget. 9/1	1. Client will have information to review with case manager in two weeks. 9/15	
			Step 2. Review things that will be needed to move into new housing: security deposits for apartment and utilities. 9/3	2. Client will outline all possible expenses to make the move. 9/7	
			Step 3. Identify at least 3 possible housing options. Have addresses, monthly rental rate, and landlord name and phone number. 10/15	3. Client will choose which apartment he or she desires most. 10/30	
2					
3					
4					
5					

common goals for the client in a coordinated fashion. However, teams can also be dysfunctional because of factors like turf wars, personal conflicts, mismatched goals, poor communication, and the lack of coordinated leadership (Rothman & Sager, 1998). While such conflicts are unfortunate, your best approach in this situation is to remain focused on your client's need.

Before your presentation, do your homework and be prepared to present the case in a logical and succinct manner. (see Exhibit 2.5, which is a sample of a case conference form; you could use a form such as this to organize your case presentation). Typically you would explain the reason for the meeting, which should be important because team members don't want you wasting their time. Quickly summarize the client's current problems and needs—this is followed by making a brief outline of planned actions. Check with team members about what has or has not been done, ask that answers be brief and to the point. The discussion that follows the presentation is when team members share additional information and updates, which all can be used to make adjustments to the client's individual care plan.

Client Name:_____ **Client ID#** _____

Case Conference Date: _____ **Client File No:** _____

EXHIBIT 2.5
Sample Case
Conference Form

Participant's Name & Position	Agency Name & Direct-Dial Phone & Email	Phone, Skype, or In-person

Did the client attend the case conference? Yes _____ **No** _____

Is there a written and signed informed consent from the client for every participating agency listed above? Yes _____ **No** _____

Reason for Case Conference:

_____

_____

Assessment of Client's Current Problems and Needs:

_____

Planned Actions	Individual & Agency	Agrees to:	Date to be Completed

Case Manager Signature: _____ **Date:** _____

· ·

Legal Guardianship and Case Management

You have examined some essential components of case management in this chapter, but what happens if you are appointed a **legal guardian** of your client? How does that change your role if you are the case manager? For instance, your agency might be appointed to be the legal guardian for a client who is defined as legally incompetent, which is a complex legal concept. According to Donald Dickson (1995), individuals are presumed to be incompetent if they are mentally ill and civilly committed, mentally disabled, drug addicted, or alcohol dependent. In addition, a child under the age of 18 is a minor and is considered to be incompetent and in some circumstances to be a ward of the court (Jenson & Fraser, 2006). The concept of competency varies according to different state laws and the criteria for being a legal guardian also varies, and so check your state laws.

If you are acting as the agency's representative who assumes the role of legal guardian, you are technically the client's case manager. The twist is, as legal guardian you can have either partial or total control of the decision-making process for the incompetent client (Dickson, 1995), which is not in line with client-centered case management. To have complete or partial control of a client or his or her property can be a daunting task because of the unequal power dynamic introduced into the case management process.

What's the difference between total and partial control? To have total control means you have guardianship of both the client and his or her property. If you are given only control of either the client or the client's property, then you have partial control. Guardianship of the client means you have the power to make personal decisions for the client, such as health care, living arrangements, or travel. As the guardian of the client's property, you can make decisions about paying bills, selling, buying, or investing assets for the client. However, as a legal guardian you might be responsible to the court—depending on the laws of the state—to make periodic or annual reports about actions taken on behalf of the client. If you are handling the client's finances, the court might require your agency to post a cash bond to ensure the safety of the client's funds plus require an accounting of financial transactions made on behalf of the client. If you are wondering why all these measures are taken to safeguard the client, I would have you look no further than the local and national stories of human service professionals mishandling funds and donations of their organizations. Being a legal guardian is a huge responsibility, because you have the power to make life-altering decisions for an adult or child.

Primary Role of the Legal Guardian

Human Systems

Understanding and Mastery: Processes to analyze, interpret, and effect policies and laws at local, state, and national levels.

Critical Thinking Question: A human services practitioner is obligated to analyze laws at all levels of government that affect human service delivery systems. Find and carefully read the laws in your state that guide the activities of a legal guardian. Make a list of the things a legal guardian can and cannot do. Take note of the things you don't understand about these laws and seek clarification from your instructor or a legal professional. Is there a separation between the roles of the legal guardian and the case manager in your state? If so, how do their roles differ? Finally, explain who can get a legal guardian and what makes a person legally incompetent.

The primary role of the legal guardian is to make decisions for the incompetent client. Courts have devised standards for making decisions on behalf of the client, which are the substitute judgment standard and the best interests standard. According to the legal scholar Dickson (1995), the substitute judgment standard requires that the legal guardian attempt to replicate the decision that the incapacitated person would make if he or she were able to make a choice. In addition, prior to being incompetent, an individual might have expressed a preference that you should take under consideration despite the fact that it might not be the best decision. As we discussed earlier in the chapter, your personal values and goals might be different from the client's; keep in mind that as a human services practitioner you are working on behalf of the client even if you're the legal guardian. Another approach to decision making for an incompetent client is a best interests standard, which means the legal guardian has to determine what is best for the incompetent client. From an objective perspective, your decisions are guided by what is best for the client, even if it's in conflict with the client's or your preference.

I have only touched upon the legal complexities of being a guardian for a client. If you assume this role, as a representative of your organization, make sure that you understand the legal implications for taking that role. Talk with a supervisor and have a clear understanding of what is expected of you and if you believe this is beyond your professional scope, inform your superiors.

Summary

Currently there is no standardized case management approach. However, case management models do have similar components such as assessment, planning, and monitoring outcomes. Assessment deals with gathering and analyzing client information that helps the practitioner determine the cause of the client's problems. After the assessment comes planning, when the practitioner and the client create an individual service plan for the client. To ensure a plan is working, the practitioner continually monitors the client's outcomes. The case management process is fluid. The practitioner must be prepared to make needed adjustments to a client's individual service plan to reflect the changes in the client's life. Moreover, a practitioner should make regular use of case conferences to work with team members and clients to find the most effective approach to address the client's problems in living. Legal guardianship is an option in some states for the case management of an incompetent client, but much care must be taken to understand and observe the state's laws and practices.

Assess your analysis and evaluation of this chapter's content by completing the **Chapter Review**.

Interviewing

A Human Services Practice

Interviewing is a very important human services practice that you will engage in. But what exactly is an interview? It is more than a casual conversation with a client. It might be more appropriate to think of an interview as a purposeful exchange of information between a human services practitioner and client. The key term here is "purposeful." This purposeful exchange is a conversation in which the practitioner asks questions of the client to obtain information and also to learn more about the client through personal stories.

In a human services setting, the interview usually occurs between parties who don't know each other, yet both parties have a stake in the outcome. During an interview, the practitioner typically prompts the verbal exchange by asking the client questions. Interview questions are formulated by the practitioner to elicit different types of information from a client such as (a) demographics, (b) personal needs, (c) eligibility status for services, and (d) personal information.

The interview is structured so that the practitioner talks less and reveals relatively little personal information to the client. The client typically talks more and shares personal or sensitive information with the practitioner. This type of interviewing should not be confused with psychological therapy, which is provided by licensed professionals.

The practitioner's education, simply by virtue of his or her expertise, training, and position, has more power and control than the client during the interview. This creates an unequal power dynamic between the practitioner and client. As a result, the practitioner should maintain appropriate professional boundaries to ensure the client's comfort and emotional well-being throughout the interviewing process.

To become a good interviewer, you must genuinely like people, and you need to know the mechanics of interviewing and develop good interviewing skills. If you understand interviewing mechanics and learn the necessary skills, you will begin to master an essential human services practice.

Different Interview Types and Formats

The process of doing an **interview** is basically the same across all types of settings and fields, whether it is for human services, business, or research. Before looking in detail at an interview in a human services setting, it might be helpful for you to understand how interviews are used in business and research. Why? You should know about business interviews because you might be put in charge of hiring or promoting workers and volunteers in your organization. You should know about research interviews because you might need to interview clients or workers to evaluate whether a program is working.

In the context of the business world, interviews are designed to elicit information that is desired by employers. The information obtained from the interviewee will enable the interviewer to make an appropriate decision about making a new hire or recommending someone for a promotion. Box 3.1—Types of Business Interviews—outlines six different types of interviews that are primarily used for hiring and promotion.

Interviews are also used in research. Why should you know about different types of interviews for research? You might be called on, for instance, to do research to help justify why potential donors should fund your community agency or new program. Information from potential donors can be obtained by using a qualitative research strategy such as a case study.

Imagine that you have chosen to do a case study, which means you will gather information by doing interviews with specific groups, in a specific agency, and at a specific time. The interviews for the case study are collected from clients in your agency

---

Box 3.1 ▸ **Types of Business Interviews**

- **Case Interview.** The purpose of the case interview is to gauge what type of problem-solving skills a prospective employee possesses. The interviewer presents a case study with an assortment of problems for which the interviewee must formulate solutions. The case interview is typically done face to face between the interviewer and interviewee.
- **Face-to-face Interview.** The purpose of the face-to-face interview is a traditional conversation with an employer to determine the fit between the prospective employee and the employer.
- **Group Interview.** The purpose of the group interview is to determine leadership potential among a group of employees. The interviewer starts an informal group discussion by asking specific open-ended questions. The goal is to see which employee will take the lead in the discussion, how they interact with others, and whether they possess skills to persuade others.
- **Dinner Interview.** The dinner interview is an informal discussion to determine whether the prospective employee can develop common ground with the interviewer. This interview is done in a casual setting such as a restaurant or at a dinner party.
- **Panel Interview.** The panel interview is done with more than one interviewer but fewer than 10. This group asks the prospective employee a series of questions related to the position he or she has applied for. The goal of the interview is to determine whether the interviewee has good presentation skills, can build rapport with his or her audience, and can think on his or her feet.
- **Stress Interview.** In a stress interview, the prospective employee is deliberately put under pressure to determine how he or she handles stress. This type of interview is typically done for jobs that are considered high pressure and require individuals who cannot be unnerved.

Box 3.2   **Qualitative Research Designs**

- **Ethnography.** The goal of ethnographic interviewing is to learn about the interviewee's culture, language, values, and behaviors solely through the client's descriptions. The modality to collect information is done by engaging in nonthreatening conversations with the client who is considered the expert cultural guide teaching the professional (Leigh, 1998). In some instances, the goal is to assist the client in the development of culturally sensitive interventions, which promote the client's right to self-determination.
- **Phenomenology.** Phenomenology is a research strategy in which the researcher focuses on the detailed description of the interviewee's experience of a lived situation. This strategy requires that a researcher be self-aware because personal beliefs can create biases in what is heard. The researcher stays attentive and has a naïve openness to the phenomena described by the participant. In other words, the researcher will not use personal knowledge and experiences to interpret the data.
- **Grounded theory.** Grounded theory is a research strategy used for the development of general theories that are based on data collected through interviews and verified with other data.
- **Case Study.** A case study approach is one in which a researcher studies a specific instance or person, which is bounded by time, case, or person. It is a process of gathering information from multiple sources via interviews and other resources, as a means of recording findings about the complexity of social environments that are unattainable from quantitative research.

who have been receiving services for at least a year. From each interviewee—the clients chosen for the study—you get an in-depth narrative, which is his or her personal story about receiving services from your agency. Once the narratives are all collected, you then analyze them for specific data to determine what the interviewees think (both positive and negative) about your agency. Overall, the data help generate understanding of social actors in complex social contexts. In Box 3.2, you will find a list of different types of research designs in which interviews are used to collect data.

Interviewing is not under the control of any one profession and does not require an advanced degree. Interviewing itself is not regulated under the law; however, some legal restrictions apply to the information obtained in an interview (discussed later in this chapter). Moreover, interviewing is one of the core skills on which human services practice is built (Mandell & Schram, 2011). A human services generalist might conduct: (a) an intake interview or (b) a case management interview. Each interview is done for different reasons. The purpose of an intake interview is to determine whether a prospective client is eligible for services with a specific agency. A case management interview is conducted to help a client develop a plan to address personal problems. The other types of interviews that you might conduct as a human services practitioner are listed in Box 3.3.

Box 3.3   **Human Service Interview Types**

- **Intake Interview.** The purpose of an intake interview is to determine whether an applicant fits an agency's criteria for services.
- **Case Management Interview.** The interview in the case management process is done to make an assessment of the client's situation and needs (see Chapter 2).
- **Agency Interview.** An agency interview is done with an agency that accepts client referrals. During this interview, information is gathered about services offered and what is needed to make a successful referral to that agency.
- **Community or Group Interviews.** The purpose of this type of interview is to gather information about a common concern that is affecting a community or group. Interviewing in this context may occur when a needs assessment is being done with respect to community development.
- **Political Interview.** Interviews are done with local, state, and federal politicians as an advocacy strategy.

For the most part, the different interview types are self-explanatory, but then there is also the issue of how interviews are formatted. In other words, there are three basic interview formats: structured, unstructured, and semi-structured. The interview format determines how the interview is conducted. All three formats can be used with any type of interview. Despite the interview format, they may be conducted via telephone or done face to face with a client.

Structured Interview Format

Structured interviews are conducted in a standardized manner with preset questions that come in the form of surveys or questionnaires. A survey and questionnaire are instruments designed to get specific information from a respondent. The preset questions can be open-ended (which produces phrases and short narratives) or closed-ended (which produces a short specific response). The role of the interviewer during a structured interview is to ask a client preset questions in an established order. Prior to the start of the interview, the client is told to answer the questions without asking for clarification from the practitioner conducting the interview. Furthermore, during the interview the practitioner will not ask probing questions or deviate from the preset questions to clarify or instruct the client. In addition, the practitioner will maintain a neutral poise with respect to body language and emotional affect while conducting the interview so as not to influence the client being interviewed. When asked a question, the interviewee directly answers the set of questions asked by the interviewer.

Under what circumstances would you conduct a structured interview? Imagine that your agency has been running a new program for over a year that is not performing well. The executive administrator now wants some specific answers about why clients are not using a provided service. To get specific answers to specific questions, the agency might have a practitioner or a team of practitioners administer a survey or questionnaire. Both instruments have preset, standardized, or closed-ended questions that you would ask of each client. You would ask each client the same set of questions in the same manner and under the same conditions. Data collected from these instruments can be compiled and quantified to determine the answer to a specific question or a set of questions.

Unstructured Interview Format

The **unstructured interview** is conducted under a more relaxed interview protocol. In other words, questions need not be standardized and questioning need not follow in a specific order or with a script. The interviewer uses open-ended questions to elicit client information that is of interest to him or her. Probing questions are used to get in-depth information from the client and to keep the discussion focused on the areas of interest. The interviewer acknowledges that the client is an expert about his or her stories, perspectives, culture, and interpretations of experiences.

Under what circumstances would an unstructured interview be done? Imagine you are the case manager and a new client has been assigned to you. During the case management interview, the objective is to find out what the client wants to work on. Each client is different, and so there is no one way to do an unstructured interview. As a result, the interview will be relatively fluid as you work to complete the client's individual plan of services. You use open-ended questions to get the client to talk about his or her life, goals, and strategies. Open-questions are designed to get information from the client by allowing it to unfold in the least mechanical fashion. Remember, no one unstructured interview is like another. In terms of case management, you are trying to help the client find his or her way in life.

Semi-structured Interview Format

The **semi-structured interview** is a blend of the structured and unstructured interviews. The semi-structured interview is conducted under a set of less-stringent research rules. An interviewer uses a standard set of questions in the order of his or her own choosing to gain an in-depth understanding about a specific topic of interest. Probing questions are also used to get clients to further expand their stories or for them to offer greater clarification during the course of the interview.

The interviewer asks questions, which have varying degrees of standardization, which allows for great flexibility. It is assumed that the flexibility in questioning is needed to get in-depth information from the client during the interview. Therefore, the interview is composed of open-ended questions embedded with closed-ended questions to ensure that specific client information is obtained.

When would you most likely conduct a semi-structured interview? The intake interview for an agency is an example of a semi-structured interview. You will need to ask a standard set of questions for each applicant seeking services from your agency. In the event a client is upset or distracted, you might reorder the standard set of questions because you feel the client isn't ready to answer difficult questions. Therefore, you would move on to another question until the client seems ready to answer more difficult questions. In the semi-structured interview, you can also ask probing questions to get an applicant to give accurate and complete information. It is important to obtain the right client information if the agency has to make a determination about whether an applicant qualifies for services.

Interviewing Process

To become a good interviewer you need to be interested in others, be capable of centering your attention on others, and have the ability to communicate that you value the stories of others (Seidman, 2006). However, there are a lot of things you must know about the interviewing process. We will therefore examine what you must do before the interview, during the interview, and after the interview.

The Process Before the Interview

The purpose of the interview will determine how much advance work may be needed for research or developing questions. It is important to know what type of interview you will be conducting (e.g., an unstructured or semi-structured interview) before you begin creating interview questions. The process of creating questions is addressed later in this chapter under the section Interviewing Skills. It is important to review your questions and remind yourself of the purpose of the interview before you meet the interviewee.

You need to ready yourself so you can meet with the client without interruption. First make sure that you are physically comfortable. There is nothing more distracting than having an urgent call to use the restroom during an interview. It can also be difficult for you to concentrate if you're seated on an uncomfortable chair or in a room that is too hot. Therefore, it is important for you to be physically comfortable so that you can attend to the client during the interview. As a helping practitioner, you need to learn to take care of yourself so that you are in a good place to assist others.

Step 1: Building Rapport	Step 2: Asking Basic Questions	Step 3: Asking Difficult Questions	Step 4: Sensitive Closing
• Creating calm and building rapport for the client.	• Start questioning with the least challenging questions to encourage dialogue.	• Asking the most challenging questions.	• Concluding the interview in a sensitive and humane manner for the safety of the client.

FIGURE 3.1
Interviewing Process Steps

Next, unplug. Looking at your computer or checking your phone is highly disruptive and is an impediment to active listening. Take care of your business and turn off your technology before the start of the interview, to ensure there are no interruptions while you are interviewing a client. In short, put aside personal distractions so that the client will have your full attention (Murphy & Dillon, 1998).

The Process During the Interview

All interviews have structure. This includes the unstructured interview. Remember an interview is a purposeful exchange of information between a practitioner and client. During the interview you should make your client comfortable. A comfortable client is more likely to be open and willing to share personal information. Figure 3.1 outlines a simple four-step structure that should be easy to keep in mind during any interview.

STEP 1—BUILDING RAPPORT   Step one is marked by the arrival of the client. Make sure the client is comfortable and prepared to start the interview. During this initial period, it is appropriate to engage in informal discussion with the client to create a calm atmosphere, which builds **rapport**. Treating a client with dignity and respect also helps to build rapport and should be present throughout the interviewing process. Remember, according to the *Ethical Standards of Human Service Professionals* you are obligated to respect the cultures and beliefs of individuals and groups.

If you are going to take notes during the interview, explain to the client why it is necessary. It can be distressing to some clients if you are writing while they are talking. Assure the client that your note-taking is necessary but minimize the amount of writing you do during the interview and remember to make frequent eye contact with your client. Every gesture demonstrates your concern for the client as positive body language and active listening, which help build rapport with your client.

During the interview, watching the clock is a necessary evil; agencies are dependent on practitioners being efficient and effective workers. Before the actual interview begins, let the client know how much time you have for the interview and apologize, if necessary, for watching the clock. See the Interviewing Skills section for more suggestions about managing your time in an interview.

STEP 2—ASKING THE BASIC QUESTIONS   As you begin asking a client questions, it is best to ask the least complicated and nonthreatening questions first. Asking the right questions at the right time promotes conversation competence in the client. In other words, the client develops a sense that the information being shared is unfolding in manner that respects his or her privacy. If the client has control of how personal information is revealed it empowers the client during the interview.

After you have asked the client a question, it is important you demonstrate that you are listening carefully to the client's stories and personal information. To demonstrate you are listening to the client, you can repeat and rephrase what the client has said; this ensures the accuracy of what you have heard from the client. Demonstrating understanding promotes an easy conversational flow and a sense of openness in which in-depth information can be shared. At all times, during the interview you should be observing the nonverbal communication of the client. Nonverbal communication might cue you to what a client is feeling during the interview process. Again, see the section on Interviewing Skills for further discussion of ways to manage this step in the process.

STEP 3—ASKING THE DIFFICULT QUESTIONS   The most difficult questions are those that may cause the client embarrassment or discomfort. You must determine the most opportune time to ask the difficult questions, but be prepared to abandon the effort in the face of client resistance. You will need to wait until there is a better time to ask the difficult questions. What you can do in the meantime is reinforce the client's sense of privacy about all the information he or she has shared. In time the client will share sensitive information. Once sensitive information is revealed, a client often feels exposed. Therefore, you must ensure that the client is in a safe psychological place before you end the interview.

STEP 4—CLOSING THE INTERVIEW   The final step during the interview process is to terminate the interview, which should be done with great sensitivity. As the interview comes to a close, you should be thinking about how to slowly return the client to a safe psychological place. First, the client should be cued about five minutes before the end of the interview that things are going to be wrapped up. Having a five-minute period to close gives the client a sense that he or she won't be abruptly shut down. Toward the end of the interview is not the time to have the client to begin talking about emotion-laden topics or new material. Instead, you should be preparing the client to leave on a good note.

In the process of closing the interview you should quickly summarize what occurred during the interview. Major themes should be quickly outlined along with summary of the general discussion. During the closing, the client should have an opportunity to clarify what has been said in the session. Moreover, as you summarize what has transpired in the session this again lets the client know that you were listening. If there is to be a follow-up interview with the client, explain its purpose and check for the best way to get in touch. Thank the client for sharing information and repeat your assurances that his or her personal information will remain confidential. End as you began, with a cordial and respectful exchange.

The Process After the Interview

If there is supposed to be a follow-up visit, you should ask the client the best phone number or address to use to reach him or her. Follow-up is not done enough by human services agencies because it is labor intensive, and there aren't enough hours in a day for practitioners to keep track of everyone who comes through the door. Yet doing follow-ups can offer agencies vital client data that could assist in making their service systems more humane, effective, and efficient.

After the interview is completed and the client is gone, you must complete your documentation. When you do interviews with clients, it is your responsibility to keep a written record of what has occurred during a client–practitioner contact. Furthermore, your record of events also keeps other professionals in your organization informed about what has been done with your clients.

When a client is referred to another agency, a copy of his or her records will most likely be transferred too. It is important that a client file contains accurate information about what has been done with the client in the agency. Remember, if an event has not been recorded it is assumed that it has not been done. So accuracy in documentation keeps the next agency in the know about what has and has not been done for the client.

General Interviewing Skills

To become a good interviewer, you must practice skills such as preparing questions, asking questions, active listening, attending to meaningful interview content, and engaging in direct observations. In this section of the chapter, we examine what it takes for you to conduct a good interview.

Preparing Interview Questions

An interview is not an interview without questions. To have a good interview, the questions must be thoughtfully prepared. To prepare thoughtful interview questions, the interviewer needs to understand how these questions are constructed. We will examine two basic types of question: standardized and open-ended.

PREPARING STANDARDIZED QUESTIONS: First, many **standardized questions** are closed-ended questions that are designed to elicit specific information from the client. For instance, a person who applies for social service benefits would be asked the following closed-ended questions:

1. Did you have a job title?
2. How many children do you have?
3. Have you ever been unemployed?
4. Are you without a permanent home?

A good closed-ended question doesn't have complicated words and asks for one bit of information per question. Creating complex questions may cause the client to become confused and unable to give an accurate response. When writing closed-ended questions, first consider what information you need to have. Then ask the question in the simplest and most straightforward way. And ask one thing at a time. What might seem clear to you might not be clear to others, so test your questions with colleagues and with individuals similar to the group you intend to ask the questions. It is important to test your questions to ensure they are consistently getting to the information that is desired.

PREPARING OPEN-ENDED QUESTIONS If you need a client to give details about his or her problems, it is best to ask the client a series of open-ended questions. **Open-ended questions** are not standardized, not judgmental, and have no right answers (Rubin & Rubin, 2005). Open-ended questions are designed to promote natural responses from the client. Here are examples of open-ended questions:

1. What was your work life like?
2. How are your relationships with your children?
3. What did you do when you became unemployed?
4. What is your housing situation like?

Open-ended questions invite clients to give unstructured answers. The problem with unstructured answers is that a client might end up talking about everything not related to his or her problems. The practitioner must know how to redirect the client to give information that highlights personal problems and needs. Remember, open-ended questions are not asked so that you can begin a general conversation with the client.

Consider the purpose of the interview: What information will you or your agency need later to do your work and help the client? Questions may be divided into simple categories for your convenience: (a) main questions, (b) follow-up questions, and (c) probing questions. In addition, each question format can be either closed-ended or open-ended. All three question formats should be used to get the client's in-depth information (Ulin, Robinson, & Tolley, 2005). Each question format gets to different layers of the client's story, experience, or problem. Use of the three types of questions demonstrates to the client how detailed you need them to be to clarify different aspects of the conversation in the interview. Well-designed questions should encourage clients to interpret each question as it relates to their life (Seidman, 2006). Questions can also be designed to focus the client or to allow the client to control the direction of the interview. Overall, a question should be simply designed to ask the client about one thing at a time, as this will reduce the client's misunderstanding of what is being asked.

Main questions should be derived from the problem the client is experiencing. These questions should allow clients to share their stories in a fashion that suits them. Here are examples of main questions:

1. What brings you to the agency?
2. How would you describe your problem?
3. Have you attempted to resolve the problem?

Follow-up questions are designed to help clients move further and elaborate upon the main question and to get to a deeper level of personal content. Some examples of follow-up questions are listed:

1. You said that you need services, but how quickly?
2. You said that you haven't been handling the problems we have discussed; can you explain the problems that you have been handling?
3. Tell me what would be the first thing you want to address?

Finally, probing questions are designed to get clients onto an even deeper level of content that is not necessarily related to the main problem. Examples of probing questions are as follows:

1. What factors contributed to the problem?
2. Can you explain your feelings about unfinished business?
3. How would you pick what problem should be solved first?

PHRASING QUESTIONS   You now have a sense of the different types of questions that can be asked of clients. However, you need to understand how to effectively and delicately phrase these questions. First, when phrasing questions avoid starting questions with "why" because that could make you sound judgmental. Second, carefully weigh whether a question will get the information you want without harming or humiliating the client. Constructed questions should reflect sensitivity toward a person's culture, race, ethnicity, gender, and sexual orientation, to name a few things. It is important that you don't construct questions from only a mainstream perspective. The *Ethical Standards of Human Service Professionals* says:

> **Statement 17:** Human service professionals provide services without discrimination or preferences based on age, ethnicity, culture, race, disability, gender, religion, sexual orientation, or socioeconomic status. (Reprinted by permission of the National Organization for Human Services.)

The Art of Asking, Listening, and Observing

Interviewing is a complex process that takes time to master. If you are committed to learning how to do a good interview, you will become a good interviewer in time. Practice is the name of the game and don't be afraid to make a mistake. Mistakes are learning opportunities; take note of them and remember what not to do in the future.

ASKING INTERVIEW QUESTIONS   The interview should be reserved for the client's voice. Your voice is introduced in the interview as a guiding force to gently direct clients to specific information and to move them through the interview. Asking questions is an effective and reliable method for collecting data and getting a conversation going between two parties, but it is one of the hardest skills to master (Murphy & Dillon, 1998). Asking the right question at the right time takes practice. Developing good timing can be enhanced if you understand the different question formats and know how to order questions during an interview.

Question ordering (if you are not doing a structured interview) involves anticipating the logical flow of the conversation and understanding when to intentionally ask the right type of question at the right time. An interview should start with easy and non-threatening questions and carefully progress toward difficult questions that the client could perceive as threatening. You must be flexible and back off if the client is not ready to answer difficult questions. Therefore, you might have to find some other way to ask difficult questions. Clients often won't answer difficult questions until they feel safe in the interviewing process. It is your job to create a warm and inviting environment so that the client feels respected and safe. The manner in which you ask questions will demonstrate whether you are empathic and have respect for the client. Moreover, questioning in the context of the interview is done with the intention of learning and understanding the client. Questioning that is done to satisfy your curiosity is disrespectful to the client and should be avoided. According to the *Ethical Standards of Human Service Professionals*:

> **Statement 2:** Human service professionals respect the integrity and welfare of the client at all times. Each client is treated with respect, acceptance, and dignity. (Reprinted by permission of the National Organization for Human Services.)

ACTIVE LISTENING SKILLS   The skill of **active listening** means you are attentive to the client as he or she shares personal information and life stories with you. Active listening is represented without words. For example, during the interview your physical posture communicates to the client whether you are listening or not. When your body posture is relaxed and open, you are nonverbally communicating to the client you are prepared to fully listen. As the interview progresses you can position yourself so that you are slightly leaning toward the client; this signals you are engaged in the interview.

If you aren't sure about the effects of your body posture, imagine being seated next to someone you don't want to talk to. In this scenario, many people become tense and position their body away from the person they have no interest in talking with. However, if you are interviewing someone, the goal is to do just the opposite, to turn toward the person and relax your body posture.

I can't tell you exactly how to sit, but it is your responsibility as the practitioner to remain aware that your body position can communicate to the client whether or not you are attentive and open during the interviewing process. However, I can tell you this: Look directly at your client during the interview. Eye contact is another nonverbal communication that demonstrates that you are or aren't being attentive to the client. Give an occasional nod of the head, as this also demonstrates acknowledgement of what the client is saying during the interview.

As for direct verbal communication directed toward the client during the interview, there are several things that can be done. As the client progresses through his or her story, you will offer verbal encouragement that demonstrates you are actively listening. Occasionally, you should also paraphrase what the client has told you. Paraphrasing means restating what the client said but in your own words without changing the content. An example of paraphrasing follows:

Client	I hate my boss because he dogs me for no reason and I can't focus on my work and then there are times I just feel like what's the point? And I just want to end the whole thing and walk out. The thought of going into work gives me a stomach ache and I don't know how much longer I can handle it.
Practitioner	I hear you saying that going to work is physically and mentally distressing because your boss is micro-managing your work without reason. And this is making you think about quitting your job. Is that what you're saying?

Another form of active listening occurs when you need to ask for clarification of the facts offered by the client. In an interview, the conversations ebb and flow, which means there are natural pauses in the stream of the conversation. One of the best times to ask for clarification is during a natural pause in the conversation. You want to avoid cutting a client off in mid-sentence because the client may construe it as being rude. Furthermore, when a client uses words or phrases that you don't understand, you should get clarification. Words and jargon should not be barriers to understanding what is being said during the interview. If a word or jargon is not understood make sure you get clarification from the client for greater accuracy. An example of seeking clarification is given here:

Client	I want to jack my boss! But. . . I don't know what to say.
Practitioner	What do you mean by jack?
Client	Oh! It means you want to hurt someone.
Practitioner	Do you want to hurt your boss?
Client	Not for real, I mean I think about it. . .but I'm not gonna act on it.
Practitioner	So you're saying you're not going to hurt your boss?
Client	Yeah! I wouldn't hurt a fly or my boss.

The last active listening skill that we will examine is called reflecting. This is a little tricky to use because you are offering your impressions about what the client is feeling.

Client	But I hate my boss because he dogs me for no reason and I can't focus on my work then there are times I just feel like what's the point? I just want to end the whole thing and walk out. The thought of going in to work gives me a stomach ache and I don't know how much longer I can handle it.
Practitioner	I sense you feel dread about your job combined with hopelessness about changing the conditions you are working under. And you're frightened about not having a job.
Client	Yeah, you hit the nail on the head. That's exactly how I feel!

To ensure that you are hearing what the client is saying, don't forget to use active listening strategies like paraphrasing, clarification, and reflecting. Because it is hard to recall a client's exact words from an interview with great accuracy, these three strategies will help you more accurately recall the content of your interviews with clients.

How you listen during an interview is shaped by the type of information that you need from the client. For instance, if you were working in a temporary shelter for battered men, you might be listening more for the client's feelings about living away from his spouse as opposed to his thoughts about events occurring at his job. You also will be listening to what the client says and does not say. Strategies to listen in this manner necessitate that you pay close attention to how the client's narrative unfolds. For instance, when listening to the narrative you would (a) focus on emerging themes, (b) note the story order, and (c) pay attention to speech patterns.

To help organize the client's narrative that you are hearing in the interview, listen for and list emerging themes, which are sets of beliefs or ideas. Examples of some conversational themes are as follows:

Client	I feel I have accomplished little in my lifetime.
Client	I believe men should take a role with raising kids.
Client	There is no getting around racism. I can't get ahead of it.

Typically, the client's narrative will have several dominant themes that will emerge during the interview. Recurring themes in the client's conversation might indicate that the topic should be further explored, if you have the opportunity. Overall, try to make a note about when themes emerge and determine how often the themes occur over the lifecycle of the interview. For instance, you might write the following note in the client's file:

> NOTE ABOUT CLIENT'S INTERVIEW:
>
> The client opened the interview with a story that represented she felt like a failure. In three successive discussions of her life's work she repeatedly made reference to her personal failures.

Story sequence is another thing that you will listen for; this is the order in which the story unfolds. Does the story have a beginning, middle, and end? A client's storytelling and explanations should be relatively clear and orderly. Nevertheless, if a story becomes convoluted and confusing you should question the accuracy and reliability of the client's information. He or she might have left out critical information for reasons unknown to you. On the other hand, you might have an incomplete story because the client has organic problems (i.e., mental or medical problems) that interfere with his or her ability to construct a story in a logical sequence.

As a human services practitioner you won't be responsible for the psychological reparative work with clients, yet you still need to be aware of the psychology of the person sitting before you. Therefore, in an interview you should listen to how the client expresses his or her feelings. Consideration should be given to whether the feelings are consistent with the client's behaviors. For example, if the client was crying throughout the interview and says he or she is not upset, that would be something to note and should be followed up. You should also be able to determine whether the client is psychologically open and prepared to work on his or her problems in a productive manner or if the client is inflexible in his or her approach to problem solving because of an overwhelming emotional state.

You should also be listening and observing the client's speech patterns. What are speech patterns? Speech patterns can be described as the way a client speaks and uses tone, pitch, volume, and rate while talking. Clients who are nervous sometimes have pressured speech, which means they speak rapidly and seem like they are trying to get everything out at once. Or a client might appear to you to be shouting but be unaware of the increased volume of his or her voice.

During an interview one of the hardest things to do is listen to silence. Yes, silence! There will be a lot of reasons why clients might fall silent in an interview. At the time the silence occurs, you must be prepared not to fill it with your nervous chatter. Leave the silence open and wait for the client to fill it. There are many ways to interpret silence. When it occurs, watch the client carefully and remember what he or she does. Sitting in silence with a client will be uncomfortable! But you must be prepared to hear the richness in the silence.

Finally, listening without bias can be defined as being aware of one's own cultural and social assumptions because they can affect how one listens during the interviewing process. As the interviewer it is your job to collect the most accurate data from the client. But that means you must effectively hear the client and be open to the fact that information will come in forms that are foreign to your world experience. Being nonjudgmental and accepting of a client sounds easy, but it is harder than you might anticipate. The *Ethical Standards of Human Service Professionals* says:

> **Statement 36:** Human service professionals foster self-awareness and personal growth in themselves. They recognize that when professionals are aware of their own values, attitudes, cultural background, and personal needs the process of helping others is less likely to be negatively impacted by those factors. (Reprinted by permission of the National Organization for Human Services.)

When you can listen without bias, it can make clients feel they are being heard without being judged for their unique perspectives. Moreover, clients will feel free to interpret and make sense of their world experiences, emotions, thoughts, and behaviors in context. "In context" means that client information is shaped by social, economic, and political systems in which the client lives. In other words, clients interpret their world in their own context, which often is different from your own. As a result, you must remain open to hearing things that might not fit your world concept. Review the section in Chapter 2 on working with diverse service populations.

MAKING DIRECT OBSERVATIONS   During an interview, there is much to learn about clients through **direct observation**. This interviewing skill involves observing the client's body language. How much can you observe? There is a treasure trove of nonverbal communication that comes through facial expressions, physical appearances, and gross body movements (e.g., head nodding, facial expressions, eye movement, and posture).

In our everyday activities, we engage in direct observation of people at the mall, at the school, or in the streets. Without hearing a word from people whom you observe, you can tell a lot about what is going on. Have you ever seen a couple in the mall who appear to be mad at each other? Have you ever seen a student who appears uninterested in the classroom activities? Have you sat across the table from your date and without speaking a word know the date is doomed? There are thousands of instances that a person's body language effectively conveys what they are feeling and thinking. Now it's time to take that people-watching skill up a notch, so that you can use it to enhance your understanding of clients during the interviewing process.

When you are interviewing a client, observe his or her facial expressions. The complex production of human facial expressions involves movements of eyes and facial muscles that control the eyebrows, cheeks, nose, and mouth. Once you have identified the client's facial expression (e.g., sad, anxious, or happy), you will compare the expression in the context of what the client is talking about. Much has been written about human facial expressions. Classic studies about human expressions claim there are six facial expressions that are universally recognized: happiness, sadness, fear, disgust, surprise, and anger. However, it has been argued that facial expressions and emotion labeling are probably influenced by the cultural context (Russell, 1994). That is, facial expressions in Western cultures might not be labeled the same way in other cultures. Yet, new research suggests that greater generalizations might be possible. Researchers used a video sequence to track a range of expressions from neutral to fully expressive and then analyzed them using a computerized algorithm. The researchers have discovered they might be able to make a generalization about human facial expressions among different racial groups if the method is applied to a large-enough sample (Krinidis & Pitas, 2010). The research above demonstrates that you should be cognizant of how you interpret human facial expressions; there is no one right way.

It is important to observe a client's eye contact during the interview. As discussed earlier, a practitioner's direct eye contact with the client helps establish rapport, but it also allows the practitioner to directly observe the client. The literature is filled with discussions of direct and indirect eye contact and what it means within the context of the interview. It has been found that eye contact is a complex nonverbal behavior, and it's hard to determine what is too much and what is too little. In addition, there are cultural considerations to be aware of when practitioners attempt to interpret eye contact of clients who are not members of the mainstream culture. For instance, a young woman comes to your agency and you might be thinking she belongs to a cultural group that avoids direct eye contact. After speaking with her, you find that she actually grew up in a neighborhood close to yours. In fact, both of you have a similar cultural background despite the fact that both of you belong to two distinct racial and cultural groups. To make sure that you don't function from your stereotypical assumptions, first let the client's story unfold and then make an informed assessment of your direct observations with respect to eye contact.

In the interview that is done face to face with a client, the practitioner has the opportunity to observe a client's body movements. Body movements would include actions like walking, sitting, hand motions, and leg movements. How would you report about body movements? Body movements can be described in the following ways: tense, spastic, nervous, relaxed, unbalanced, or lethargic. Imagine you just started an interview and the client reaches for her cell phone and then begins to repeatedly open and close the cell phone through the entire interview. You might report your direct observation in the following manner: "The client opened and closed her phone for the duration of the interview. Her hands were tense and she sat on the edge of the chair. When she stood to leave the office she described having pins and needles sensation in both legs. She presented as nervous and apprehensive." This short description is an example of an initial impression of a client.

Another group of observable body movements are those classified as autonomic responses such as flushing, blinking, tearing, swallowing, sweating, and breathing. These physical responses are relatively automatic but can radically change when the client is under stress. For instance, at the start of the interview the client finds it hard to talk because her mouth feels dry; this is a stress response that occurs due to anxiety. Don't forget that clients are people who we are trying to help. The simple gesture of offering a client some water or opening a window to get a cool breeze shows your client that you care and helps build rapport.

As the interview progresses, it is important to observe if the client is mentally alert. The client's mental alertness is often described as oriented times three—also known as *oriented x 3*—which means the client is aware of (a) self, (b) time, and (c) place. If you have a client in your office who is not oriented to self, time, or place it might be a good time to suspend the interview and consult with your supervisor. Because when a client presents as disoriented, he or she might have an undiagnosed medical or mental health problem and that needs to be attended to first.

Another thing you should be observing is the client's physical make-up like body type, clothes, and hygiene. All of these things can tell you some things about the client. You will be engaged in direct observation and will make mental notes about your clients, but don't forget to demonstrate concern about their well-being. If you have a client who is elderly, overweight, or physically disabled and having a hard time sitting for an extended period of time, make sure he or she is comfortable by arranging for different seating. If you see the client for several different sessions, try to anticipate some of his or her future needs. When a client's overall hygiene is lacking, you need to determine if this is due to cultural differences, life style choice, or related to mental health problems. Typically, when I had a client in my office who appeared disheveled and unkempt, there often was an underlying mental health problem. This brings us to the issue of keeping yourself safe.

Cultivating your direct observation skills should make a difference in the way you go about working with your clients. It might also alert you to the fact that your client might be a danger to themselves, you, and others. As you observe the behavior of a client, always remain aware of your own safety. If that little voice in the back of your head is screaming "DANGER! DANGER!" it should not be ignored. If you feel unsafe, remove yourself from the situation and contact your supervisor and security to report your concerns. In some agencies, offices are equipped with a panic button so the practitioner can alert security that there is a pending threat. In my own practice, I didn't hesitate to push the panic button when one of my clients seemed threatening. Security guards knocked on my door to ensure that I was safe and remained outside of the door until the client was gone. If you feel unsafe, call for help; it's better to be safe than sorry.

> Assess your comprehension of <u>things you need to be aware of while doing an interview</u> by completing this quiz.

Legal Concerns in Human Services Practice

Because we live in a litigious world, it is important to have a basic understanding of several legal concepts related to human services practices such as interviewing. Never assume that you know the laws that govern your practice without consulting the legal office in your agency. It is your responsibility to know the laws at the local, state, and federal levels before you begin to practice.

Legal Concepts Related to Interviewing

There are some important concepts that all human services practitioners should know, such as (a) duty to warn, (b) confidentiality, (c) privacy, (d) informed consent, and (e) privileged communications. We are reviewing these concepts because they have special meaning to human services practice but are often not understood. Consider the following scenario. You are in the process of doing a case management interview with a client you have been working with for nearly a year. She unexpectedly states she intends to harm a third party and also reveals she has killed someone in the past. Question number one: Does a human services generalist have the legal duty to warn a third party if his or her client may cause harm to that third party? Question number two: Does a human services generalist have to keep the client's bad acts confidential and does the client have the right to assume the right of privacy? Question three: Is a human services generalist covered under privileged communication laws? Before you answer any of these questions let's review the aforementioned legal concepts.

THE LEGAL CONCEPT OF DUTY TO WARN The **duty to warn** is based on the landmark case decision made in *Tarasoff v. Regents of the University of California*, in which the court determined that a psychotherapist has the legal duty to protect a third party from foreseeable harm that his or her client may inflict upon that party. This case came about because in October 1969, a graduate student at University of California, Berkeley, named Prosenjit Poddar, murdered a student named Tatianna Tarasoff because she refused his romantic advances. Prior to this murder, Poddar had confided in his psychotherapist about his intention to kill Tarasoff. Poddar's psychotherapist notified the campus police about his intentions, which resulted in Poddar being taken into custody. But Poddar would later be released by the campus police. However, neither Poddar's therapist nor the campus police warned Tarasoff about the threat against her life. This lack of warning ultimately resulted in Tatianna Tarasoff's murder.

Tarasoff's parents brought suit against Poddar's psychotherapist for failure to warn their daughter about the impending threat against her life. In 1976, the Supreme Court of California found that if a psychotherapist's client poses a serious threat of violence to another, then that professional has a duty to warn a third party. In other words, the psychotherapist is obligated to breach confidentiality to protect a third party against harm when there is foreseeable evidence of danger to the client or other persons (Glosoff & Pate, 2002).

Precisely who is legally compelled to warn a third party against harm from their client? On one hand, the Tarasoff statute legally compels psychotherapists to warn a third party. On the other hand, it does not compel human services generalists to warn a third party about an imminent danger from his or her client. What are human services practitioners supposed to do if they have a client who might harm an individual or others? The *Ethical Standards of Human Service Professionals* explains what to do if a third party is in imminent danger from a client:

> **Statement 4:** If it is suspected that danger or harm may occur to the client or to others as a result of a client's behavior, the human service professional acts in an appropriate and professional manner to protect the safety of those individuals. This may involve seeking consultation, supervision, and/or breaking the confidentiality of the relationship. (Reprinted by permission of the National Organization for Human Services.)

Information Management

Understanding and Mastery: Maintaining client confidentiality and appropriate use of client data.

Critical Thinking Question: Maintaining client confidentiality is critical to promoting trust between the client and practitioner. Yet, if it is suspected that danger or harm may occur to the client or to others as a result of a client's behavior, the human services practitioner acts in an appropriate and professional manner to protect the safety of those individuals. This may involve seeking consultation, supervision, and/or breaking the confidentiality of the relationship. What would make you suspect that your client might cause harm to others?

However, a profession's ethical standards are not legally binding; therefore, the standards impose only a moral obligation upon professionals to work for the good of the client. It is ultimately up to the professional whether he or she will choose to adhere to a set of ethical standards. Again I ask, what would you do if a client revealed that he or she might do harm to a third party? To be safe, immediately speak with your supervisor to get clear instructions about what to do and whom to contact in and outside of your agency if you feel a client might harm others. However, you should also be aware that your professional ethical standards may be in conflict with local, state, or federal laws. Without exception, a legal statute supersedes the ethical standards of a profession. This means you must obey the laws in your state and country even when they are in conflict with the ethical standards of your profession. Once again, request clarification from the legal office at your agency.

CLIENT CONFIDENTIALITY   Confidentiality means protecting a client's personal information and privacy from public disclosure. The concept of **confidentiality** can be based on statutes, court decisions, or professional codes of ethics (Dickson, 1995). When confidentiality exists, it allows the client to freely express concerns and discuss sensitive issues with professionals without the fear that his or her information will be shared with individuals outside of the agency. Overall, some professions maintain that the process of helping a client is dependent on confidentiality. Without it, there can be no trust between the client and the professional. The *Ethical Standards of Human Service Professionals* explains the obligation to the client's confidentiality and privacy:

> **Statement 3**: Human service professionals protect the client's right to privacy and confidentiality except when such confidentiality would cause harm to the client or others, when agency guidelines state otherwise, or under other stated conditions (e.g., local, state, or federal laws). Professionals inform clients of the limits of confidentiality prior to the onset of the helping relationship. (Reprinted by permission of the National Organization for Human Services.)

In some instances, a practitioner might breach client confidentiality and this can result in legal actions against that individual. This might be the suspension of a professional's license to practice. In other instances, a breach of confidentiality doesn't lead to a legal action, but it does harm the client–practitioner relationship. A breach of confidentiality typically happens because practitioners are careless. Here's a real example. I was working in a large medical center and was on my way to lunch. I decided to catch the elevator and as I was riding down to the ground floor I overheard two surgeons talking about a case. A woman next to me looked at me and then shook her head in disgust. The two surgeons continued a very graphic and demeaning conversation about their patient. Without warning, the woman next to me started shouting at the two surgeons for talking about their patient in a public elevator. It came to light that the surgeons had been talking about her child! Was this an act of breaching confidentiality? Yes it was! There is no excuse for this insensitive and unprofessional behavior. Discussions about clients should occur behind closed doors and not in public spaces or at home. That's right; you shouldn't be talking about clients with your spouse or loved ones.

THE LEGAL CONCEPT OF PRIVACY   **Privacy** is a key legal concept (statutory and constitutional) that is observed in both health and human services. There are at least three types of privacy—but the one that is relevant to your work with clients focuses on privacy as a legal right that protects clients from the government's unauthorized disclosure of their personal information, records, or files (Dickson, 1995). The client owns the privilege to determine the time, circumstance, and the amount of personal information that can be shared or withheld. However, there are limitations to a person's autonomy with respect to privacy because the law may forbid or regulate a range of human conducts (e.g., viewing child pornography or child abuse), which does not make privacy an absolute right.

Before a practitioner or agency can release a client's personal records, the client must give informed consent. Giving informed consent means that the client understands the consequence for releasing his or her personal information and records to a third party and willingly authorizes such a release. Agencies typically have informed consent forms and have procedures about how to complete the form with the client. What happens if you don't have informed consent from a client? If informed consent is not obtained and the client's personal information is released, this could lead to legal actions against a professional and the agency in which he or she works. The *Ethical Standards of Human Service Professionals* explains your responsibilities for client records:

> **Statement 5:** Human service professionals protect the integrity, safety, and security of client records. All written client information that is shared with other professionals, except in the course of professional supervision, must have the client's prior written consent. (Reprinted by permission of the National Organization for Human Services.)

THE LEGAL CONCEPT OF PRIVILEGED COMMUNICATION Some professionals are legally protected from revealing a client's confidential information in court. The exception to this law is if the client gives consent to release his or her personal information. Protection under **privileged communication** laws are not an absolute legal right. Privileged communication is not granted in some jurisdictions, so you need to be aware of the legal statutes in your state to determine whether you are or are not covered under privileged communications. There are relatively few professions that have privileged communications in the United States. Box 3.4 lists the professionals that typically have privileged communications with their clients.

Currently, human services generalists (those with degrees in human services) are not in the class of professionals who are legally protected under privileged communications. In most states, the helping professionals who typically fall into this privileged class are licensed psychologists, social workers, school counselors, licensed professional counselors, and marriage and family therapists (Barbara & Sheeley, 1987). Other professionals who have been extended the status of privileged communication are attorneys, clergy, news reporters, and married couples. According to the legal scholar Dean Wigmore (1961), there are four conditions necessary for privileged communications:

> The communication is made in confidence with the understanding that it will not be divulged.
> Confidentiality is essential to the complete and acceptable maintenance of the relationship between parties.

Box 3.4	**Clients May Have Privileged Communications With:**

- Psychologists
- Social Workers
- Physicians
- Dentists
- Sexual Assault Counselors
- Domestic Violence Counselor
- Nurses
- Chiropractors
- Marriage and Family Counselors

The relationship between parties must be one that in public opinion should be diligently promoted.

The injury to the relationship that would result from divulging the communication must be greater than the benefit gained by divulging it.

An in-depth examination of the legal issues in human services practices is far beyond the scope of this book. However, you need to be aware that violations of the legal concepts we reviewed typically occur because professionals are careless or ignorant about the laws that protect client information. The *Ethical Standards of Human Service Professionals* points out that human services professionals have a responsibility to be aware of laws:

> **Statement 10:** Human service professionals are aware of local, state, and federal laws. They advocate for change in regulations and statutes when such legislation conflicts with ethical guidelines and/or client rights. Where laws are harmful to individuals, groups, or communities, human service professionals consider the conflict between the values of obeying the law and the values of serving people and may decide to initiate social action. (Reprinted by permission of the National Organization for Human Services.)

You cannot plead ignorance of the law. Therefore, take the time to learn and understand the legal concepts appropriate to your profession.

Managing Permanent Legal Records

Documenting and record keeping are important skills that take time to master. Each contact that you have with a client typically needs to be documented. A client's records serve to inform team members and other professionals outside of your agency about what has been done with the client. The things that you will document depend on what your job is and what your agency requires you to put into the client's record.

Documenting can come in the form of individual service plans, process notes, and progress reports. In the realm of record keeping, many agencies have a full complement of standard forms that need to be completed on each client. A client's file typically contains the following forms: intake, consent, referrals, and requests for services. Despite the type of paperwork you have, it must be done, and done correctly, if clients are to be served effectively.

THE CLIENT'S FILE A practitioner's documentation about a client and standard forms comprise the client's file, which is considered a **permanent legal record**. Therefore, anything that a practitioner writes should be written with a ballpoint pen and not a pencil, because it can be altered. In many agencies, the client's file has a place for notes. Typically entries into a client's file should be an informative summary of what has occurred between you and the client. The purpose of the meeting will determine what the focus of the entry will highlight. Here is a list of different notes that could be put into a client's file:

1. **Progress note** outlines how the client is progressing with different objectives that have been set out.

Client-Related Values & Attitudes

Understanding and Mastery: Confidentiality of information.

Critical Thinking Question: Human services practitioners are currently not legally protected under the privileged communications laws in most states. Yet the human services profession values maintaining the confidentiality of client information. What would be a good argument or rationale for granting privileged communications status to practitioners who hold a human services degree?

• •

2. **Process note** is a detailed note taken of an interview. Typically the complete client and practitioner conversation is recorded. These notes are then used as a teaching tool by a practicum instructor with the student. If process notes are to be included into the client's file, they should be summarized.

3. **S.O.A.P. note** (an acronym for subjective, objective, assessment, and plan) is a type of documenting that is typically used in medical settings. The components are as follows: S = the subjective component is a brief statement written about the client's major complaints; O = objective component is used to record physical or psychological findings, vital signs, and lab results; A = assessment component where a summary is written about symptoms and a list of possible diagnosis are offered; P = plan component includes professional records of what they intend to do for the client, which might include referrals, changes in plans, advising, or education initiatives.

Despite what type of written note you make in a client's file, strive to make accurate and informative notes. Use good grammar and check your spelling to ensure that you are accurately communicating the information you want others to have. A sample page from a client progress note is shown in Exhibit 3.1. Examine both entries and determine what's right and what's wrong.

What is right with the first entry on the Client Progress Notes page? In the first entry, Kim Scott dated her note and then explained what she and the client worked on. This was followed with an explanation about another planned objective. Her note was well written and had no apparent spelling errors. Finally, the entry was signed with Ms. Scott's signature followed by her degree and job title. Please note that all spaces left in the entry were filled with a straight line so no other entry could be made within this note at a later date.

What's wrong with the second entry on the Client Progress Notes page? First the full date is missing. Second, the entry doesn't explain what type of referral was made, and there is no other information about what occurred during the client contact. His note is not well written and has some spelling errors. Spaces are left open on the entry

---

EXHIBIT 3.1

Sample Client
Progress Notes

Client Progress Notes

January 15, 2014   Today I met with Ms. Dalloway and she said that the plan we had _____

devised was working. What she meant by working is she wrote her resume. _____

Then she went to the job skills workshop in her neighborhood and got more advice _____

about how to improve it. We reviewed her planned objectives and she will now work on _____

sending out the resumes to employers. Kim Scott, BHS, Human Services Generalist _____

Example of the second chart entry
January 2014 Referral made for Dalloway. She was a pain about the hole thing.

I think she needs a shrink. Belter be fass getting one.   John Walters, AA so anyone could make an unauthorized entry within the note. The note also reflects that Mr. Walters has some strong opinions about the client. Personal opinions should never be entered into a client's file; they are not relevant. Finally, John Walters only put his degree behind his name and not his job title, so we have no idea what his official capacity is in the agency.

Why have we done this exercise? If this client's file is subpoenaed for court, you want to have a coherent and informative entry for the court to review. You also need to be aware that clients can get access to their files. Therefore, there should be nothing in the file that would hurt, humiliate, or disrespect the client's humanity.

You have been given an example of the mechanics of making a handwritten entry, but you might be required to make entries in a secured agency computer. When using a secured computer, never give another staff member your login. Never let someone else enter your electronic notes. Precautions should be taken to ensure that your notes are protected from others tampering with them. Yes, the use of technology has created a growing concern about privacy and protection of client information. Yet technology is here to stay, and it can be a powerful tool for human services practice.

CASE MANAGEMENT TECHNOLOGY   In general, the nonprofit human services sector has been behind the technology curve compared to the private and public sectors. To be effective, human services practitioners and their agencies must stay abreast of innovative technologies. There have been efforts to integrate and coordinate human services since World War I, but the results have been sparse and disappointing. As a result, nonprofit human services organizations have often been blind to the efforts of other organizations. This blindness makes everyone less effective at addressing growing social problems such as poverty, hunger, child abuse, and elder care. Problems of society are becoming more complex, and innovative technology can be used to support the endeavors of groups working for the social good.

If you haven't already done so, consider finding case management software that will help you and your organization function more effectively on behalf of your clients. To get a sense of how case management software works, *Social Solution* has free software—named ETO-1—for independent human services practitioners who are providing direct services. The ETO-1 software helps the practitioner track his or her work and outcomes with clients. The software can create client contact databases, track basic client demographics, and track client service delivery. Social Solutions is basically giving individual practitioners an opportunity to test their case management software before considering making a larger financial investment. More advanced software will allow a practitioner to monitor the client's progress toward an optimal level of living and autonomy.

Go to the web link for **Social Solutions** to learn more about case management software.

Case management software could help an agency maximize every operational dollar. In other words, it can make an organization more efficient and effective. For example, the software can capture data about the current state and progress of each client. Assessments can be created to measure a client's financial literacy, activities of daily living, or threat to personal safety. Supervisors, managers, and administrators can run reports with collected data to get a sense of what is and is not working in the organization. This knowledge allows for informed adjustments to be made to increase the effectiveness of client services. There are numerous add-ons available to the software such as programs that utilize billable services, classroom training, or client job matching. Case management software has a flexible configuration, which allows the same software to support different types of human services programs. This could promote a strong community-based collaborative among agencies using similar software. The cost of case management software for an organization will depend upon the usage, the design, and the size.

Although technology can save you time with your work, you still must know how to manage your time in the office. You can keep track of your time by using a calendar and appointment book that you write in (low tech). There are also hundreds of different calendars and appointment books in electronic formats. The electronic formats can be accessed on your cell phone, tablet, or computer. Use whatever calendar and appointment system that works best for you. However, make sure you record all meetings, tasks, and appointments on one calendar. I'm old fashioned and still use a pocket-sized calendar and appointment book because it fits in my purse and I can readily get my hands on it. The page setup allows me to enter each activity on the day and time it's going to happen and I can see everything in one glance. Many of you will have mobile phones with a calendar and appointment application that connects all your electronic devices and simultaneously sends your entries to each device. However, I would caution you to be careful never to put a client's full name into your personal calendar to ensure the client's identity is protected. Is there a learning curve with new software? Yes. It takes time to learn new technology and it takes time for people to learn a different method for getting their tasks done, but the time has come and there is no turning back.

Case Study: General Intake Interview

At this juncture, we will use the intake interview to illustrate the interviewing process that you have examined previously. In the context of a human services setting, an intake interview will occur when a client is attempting to get services from your agency. Among helping professionals, intakes are often considered the least glamorous activity in direct services. However, you should consider the intake interview as the most important contact because it is a critical entry point for the client into the human services system. During the intake interview, the client should be experiencing the greatest warmth and humanity from the different professionals who are attempting to get them the appropriate services. Moreover, professionals should hail clients for their courage to ask for help and should reward clients with a positive response. At this critical time, professionals should be making things better not worse for clients seeking help.

Step 1—Building Rapport With the Client

People seeking help are often confused, frightened, and apprehensive about coming to a formal agency. The prospective client's first encounter with an agency is a critical moment for the agency representative to make a lasting impression with the client. That first encounter occurs when a prospective client undergoes an intake interview. This interview can be a stressful experience for many clients. The practitioner should take steps in the intake process to alleviate stress of the client, which is done by building rapport with a client. Rapport simply means having a harmonious relationship in which individuals understand each other's feelings or ideas and communicate well. Building rapport will serve you well in all types of interviews, of course.

There are a number of simple things that help to build rapport between the client and human services practitioner. First, practitioners should introduce themselves and give a brief explanation about who they are. This should be brief, respectful, and precise: "Good morning, Mrs. Dalloway. I am Ms. Woolf and I am the intake coordinator for the center." In American culture, it is customary to shake hands when greeting someone, but practitioners should be mindful of their body language. A firm handshake and smile from the practitioner demonstrates respect and desire to comfort the client.

Second, when practitioners address an adult client they should use the client's surname (e.g., Mrs. Dalloway). New adult clients should not be greeted by their first names until they give permission for the practitioner to do so. However, in the case of children it would be appropriate to address them by their first name. Names are very personal, and so it is no small matter. For instance, when an older African American woman (we will call her Mrs. Dalloway) came to my office for counseling services, I always addressed her as Mrs. Dalloway. One day I noticed that Mrs. Dalloway was agitated, so I asked what the problem was. She indicated that another member of the treatment team called her by her first name, which she felt was disrespectful. Because of the rapport I had built with my patient she was able to communicate her discomfort to me. I was able to inform the team member about the issue. Mrs. Dalloway would later tell me she felt disrespected because the early racism in the country had denied her the personal dignity for so many years.

A third way to build rapport is to demonstrate concern for the client. For instance, the practitioner could ask the client if he or she had any trouble finding the agency or any problems with parking (if that is relevant). If the practitioner is working in a region where people are dependent on mass transit, it would be wise to have bus and train schedules handy or have the number of a taxicab company available. Once again, without words the practitioner's behavior demonstrates that he or she values the client's time. In the same vein of demonstrating concern, the practitioner should ensure the client is physically comfortable. The client could be offered the restroom or a bottle of water before initiating the intake interview. You might be thinking, Is this all really necessary? Yes! All these small gestures convey to clients that you respect their humanity.

Another rapport-building strategy is when the practitioner takes a short period of time to engage the client in small talk before the intake. Engaging in small talk shows the human side of the practitioner and demonstrates that this formal meeting is all about business. When will you have time to do this? As you have more experiences in the process of building rapport with clients you will be amazed that much of what we just reviewed can be done in a matter of minutes. Many of you will see clients back to back and might only get a break when it's time for lunch. So it is important to learn how to make the world slow down for just a moment as you create a safe space for your clients to share their woes. Your job is to obtain client information, but you will get more information if you create a welcoming environment.

Step 2—Asking the Client Basic Questions

Once the practitioner and client are ready, the interview begins in earnest. In the case of an intake interview, the practitioner will first explain (a) what the agency does and does not do, (b) what it typically takes to qualify for services, (c) what the fees are for service, and (d) whether there is financial assistance. Then the practitioner will give an explanation about the intake process, such as how long it will take, the type of information that will be asked of the client, and what follow-up there will be. The practitioner also explains what type of information can and cannot be held in confidence. Human services generalists do not belong to the class of helping professionals who are protected under the privileged communications statutes. So be very clear about confidentiality with your clients.

The purpose of the intake interview is to get the prospective client's personal information to determine if the agency is a good fit or offers the appropriate services for that person. Intake interviews can run between 30 and 60 minutes. Typically, an intake interview has a structured format because all prospective clients are asked the same series of questions. An intake interview that is structured is easier to do than an unstructured intake that involves asking open-ended questions. In truth, it takes a lot of practice to be an effective interviewer regardless of the interview format.

In an intake interview, the practitioner will usually be asking a set of standard closed-ended questions that require only a short response from the client. The challenge of doing any interview is getting the most accurate and complete information from a client. Period. However, be prepared, because you never know what questions might cause a client distress. For example, during an intake I asked the client about her income level. I watched as the client nervously twisted in the chair. She wouldn't give me a straight answer. Then I recalled what I had learned in graduate school about questioning clients. When it comes to getting people to reveal their true income versus their personal problems, more will be apt to talk about their problems rather than their income. So be prepared and open to a broad range of responses from clients when asking them questions, because being interviewed can be a stressful situation for many clients.

Because of practitioners having limited work time, they must work smart. So during the intake interview the practitioner should immediately record the client's responses on the agency's intake form. This practice of recording leaves nothing to the practitioner's memory. When a practitioner takes notes during any interview, he or she must be aware that the client may regard note-taking as impersonal and distracting. To preserve the rapport, the practitioner should explain why he or she needs to take notes during the intake. Typically the practitioner explains the need to record the client information at once, which ensures that it is accurate. The practitioner doesn't want rely on his or her memory to recall information after the interview. Even though the practitioner writes during the interview, he or she should make every effort to have eye contact with the client, especially when questions are asked. After the practitioner records the client's responses, a brief summary of the written responses should be read back to the client. Then the client is given the opportunity to tell the practitioner if the recorded material is accurate.

There is no standard intake form used by all agencies, but intakes are required to have similar categories that capture client information such as who the client is, what type of problems he or she might have, and what he or she needs in terms of services.

Intake forms will vary according to the needs of a particular agency. For instance, an emergency shelter might focus on information about the client's employment history, past housing stability, and illegal drug use, but a child intake would focus on the child's family system, educational progress, and medical history. The following are demographic information categories that might appear on an intake form:

1. Date of intake would be the initial contact (e.g., 20 December 2013) should be recorded on the intake form. If there is no place for the date to be recorded on the intake form, as sometimes happens, place the date in the margin of the form to ensure that it is clear when the information was obtained from the client.
2. Basic client information would include name, birth date, age, race or ethnicity, religion, gender, marital status, local and email addresses, home and cell numbers. Demographic information about the client is routinely obtained during the intake process, but there should be a reason for collecting specific information. For instance, an agency that offers services to immigrants might have an intake that includes questions about the client's primary language, country of birth, and immigration status. Great care must be taken with respect to the type of personal information collected; because once it is recorded it could unintentionally jeopardize your client. An agency's records are considered legal documents and can, in many instances, be subpoenaed by a court of law (Dickson, 1995). So don't record extraneous information or unsubstantiated rumors because this kind of information may be called into question if the records end up in court.

If the client is unable to give accurate demographic information during the intake process because of a languages barrier, physical disability, or because the client is a minor, it might be necessary to have a family member, interpreter, or legal guardian present during the intake process to ensure that all vital information is accurately and completely obtained. In this instance, confidentiality is set aside to ensure that the most accurate information is gathered on behalf of the client.

Step 3—Asking a Client Difficult Questions

This step in the interviewing process is when more difficult questions are asked. It is typically difficult to get clients to talk about personal and sensitive problems with a total stranger. The following are examples of other intake information categories:

1. **Reason for seeking services.** The client is asked to briefly describe the problem and to explain both internal and external stressors that might play a role in creating the problem. The client's problem statement should include an explanation of what caused the problem, what services are being sought, and what the client hopes to achieve as a result of receiving services.
2. **In-depth information about the problem.** Getting the client to accurately describe his or her problem is not as simple because during the intake process a client can be stressed, fearful, and uncertain about seeking help. It is important to give the client time and space to gather his or her thoughts. Remember that the process of getting intimate or sensitive information from a client requires that the practitioner be sensitive, patient, and empathetic. If the client is unable to get started, the practitioner might want to ask some probing questions to move the client along, by using the when, how, where, what, and why questions listed:
   - When did you start experiencing the problem?
   - How often or long has the problem been occurring?

- Where did the problem begin and are there external causes?
- What do you think caused the problem?
- Why do you think the problem persists?

3. **Health and social information.** The intake form might have a health and social component, which is sometimes referred to as a psychosocial component. This information category could include questions about the client's general health, mental health history, occupational status, and religious/spiritual information. In recording this information, use descriptive, not diagnostic, language. Stick to the client's terminology if possible. If a client reports hearing voices, write "the client talked about hearing voices," not "the client appears to be schizophrenic"! It is beyond the human services generalist's scope of practice to make medical or psychological diagnoses. Definitive diagnoses are made by licensed professionals (e.g., physician, psychologist, or clinical social worker). Human services practitioners may be asked by their agencies to give their impressions of a client's observable behaviors. The ability to accurately report a client's behavior is extremely important and that information should be brought to the attention of the appropriate team to ensure that the client receives the right services.

Step 4—Closing the Interview Sensitively

After the intake form is completed, there usually is a place on the form for the client to sign and date. It is the practitioner's responsibility to conclude the interview in a sensitive and humane manner. During the closing, the practitioner will quickly but calmly summarize what has occurred during the intake interview and reassure the client his or her information will be secured. Finally, as in all good interviewing situations, the practitioner closes the intake interview in the same manner as it was begun.

Before the client leaves the interview, the practitioner will check to make sure that the correct client contact information such as phone number, email, and address has been recorded. The practitioner will impress upon the client the importance of having the correct contact information, which will allow the agency to do a follow-up with the client in a timely manner. Follow-up after an intake is typically done to directly inform the client about the status of his or her application for services. The practitioner will make a note about the client's preference of how to be contacted. Typically, an agency will not leave a message in any form (voicemail, text message, or email) because the client's privacy can't be ensured. If the client insists that the practitioner leave a message, that should be recorded on the intake form and a unit supervisor should be immediately made aware. Let me tell you a cautionary tale. A young Asian college student came to my agency seeking services. She explained to me that her family system was very patriarchal, which meant that her father and brothers typically monitor her movements in and around the community. The only freedom she had was when she went to work and to school. On the job she met a young man and secretly started dating him. After sometime she decided to begin a sexual relationship with him. But soon after, she discovered he was HIV positive and she too became infected. If it was discovered my client had been infected due to having premarital sex, she risked alienation from her family and community. Imagine the problems you would create by leaving a phone or electronic message that could be accidentally picked up by this young woman's family members. In our electronic savvy culture, it is all too easy to forget this rule, but an important rule is: Don't leave messages and make sure you have the correct contact information so you directly speak with, and only with, the client.

Now that the intake is done, look over the intake form to ensure it is completed. If there are additional comments about the client, these notes should be directly entered into the file. Client notes should not be taken on a separate piece of paper or an electronic tablet because this necessitates additional time (which most of you won't have) for transferring information back into the client's file. Furthermore, client notes should be directly recorded into the file to ensure privacy and confidentiality. Many agencies will not allow practitioners to take client notes or files out of the agency. So if you have fallen behind with your record keeping that means you'll be stuck at work until it's done. To avoid working more, work smart, which means working efficiently. Client notes should be brief, relevant, and capture the essentials of what was done with the client. I know you might be thinking: Why not just record the interview? Using an electronic recording device might seem like an option. But generally, tape or video recording an interview introduces numerous legal complexities. Therefore, many agencies won't allow interviews to be electronically recorded because of concerns for client privacy and confidentiality. So in many instances, you are going to be left with pen and paper or an onsite computer system to record client information.

This case has focused on the intake interview, but the principles apply to all kinds of interviews. Build rapport; start with basic questions; move to more difficult questions; take careful notes; close the interview sensitively; and write your client notes promptly.

Summary

Interviewing is an important human services practice. To be a good interviewer, the practitioner must genuinely like people. An interview is a purposeful exchange of information and occurs between a practitioner and client. Different types of interviews are done in different settings. In a human services setting, interviews are conducted by the practitioner during intake, to facilitate case management, or in the community and political arena. Interview formats can be unstructured, semi-structured, or highly structured; each is designed to elicit different kinds of information from the client. Regardless of the interview format, it is essential that the practitioner builds rapport with the client. Rapport building is important in the interviewing process because it makes the client feel accepted and safe in the presence of the practitioner. Afterward, the practitioner can more easily engage the client in a purposeful exchange by asking questions, listening, and observing while gathering client information. Client information divulged in the context of the interview creates legal and ethical obligations for the practitioner. As a result, a practitioner is legally or ethically obligated to warn a third party of an imminent threat from his or her clients—known as the duty to warn. In addition, a practitioner is legally or ethically obligated to maintain client confidentiality and privacy, plus manage and protect the client's legal records.

Assess your analysis and evaluation of this chapter's content by completing the Chapter Review.

Section Two

· ·

Organizational Service

The human services generalist needs to know and understand how organizations function (Woodside & McClam, 2011). Everyone working in an organization contributes to its overall success and its failures, and it is important for practitioners to acquire knowledge and skills that will help them work more efficiently and effectively in organizations.

The chapters in this section are designed to help you build a foundation in human services practices, which focuses on organizational service. Chapter 4 describes the rationale for the creation of the nonprofit sector in the United States and examines the structure and function of nonprofit organizations. Chapter 5 provides an overview of management theories and approaches commonly used in the human services industry. These theories and approaches will help you understand how organizations are managed from the executive suite down to the front line. In addition, you will examine how to manage volunteers so that the work of the organization can get done. The chapter also explores diversity in the workplace. Chapter 6 introduces the practice of fundraising and the importance of developing and maintaining viable income streams so that an organization can continue doing social good. The equally important practice of supervising volunteers in fundraising initiatives is also discussed. After completing the chapters in this section, you will have a foundation in organizational service that you can use in public agencies and nonprofit human services organizations. It is also hoped that you will understand that the scope of your practice expands beyond just serving individual clients and that human services is really about service in a much broader sense.

CHAPTER 4

Nonprofit Structure and Function

· ·

In a competitive business market with shrinking financial resources, human services practitioners need knowledge about the nonprofit sector, nonprofit structure, and how the nonprofit operates. Why? Because most human services organizations are nonprofit entities. In this chapter, you will examine the history of nonprofits in the United States and the rationale for having tax-exempt organizations. This material is followed by an examination of the federal guidelines for nonprofits. You will then explore how nonprofit human services organizations function, how diversity issues are managed in the workplace, and how external forces influence these entities. With a greater understanding of how the nonprofit sector functions, you will have a better opportunity for advancing the mission of the human services organization.

The Evolution of the American Nonprofit Sector

In the post-American Revolutionary period, the Old World system of politics, social order, and welfare were abandoned and replaced by a new American colonial society. English law was replaced with new American laws founded on the premise of a strict separation of church and state and limited government control over individual citizens. Because of the spirit of individualism and liberty in America, citizens took a hands-on approach to finding solutions in their communities. Typically, community members established and worked in voluntary associations that provided for the public good. In colonial America, there were no pre-existing social barriers or rigid government, and so **voluntary associations** could freely embark on their charitable mission with limited involvement from the central governmental authorities. Over time, these organizations became the only providers of education and social welfare (Anheier, 2005). In the 1830s, Alexis de Tocqueville, a French historian, wrote about his observations of American voluntary associations:

> In the United States, political associations are only one small part of the immense number of different types of associations found there. Americans of all ages, all stations in life, and all types of disposition are forever forming associations. There are not only commercial and industrial associations in which all take part, but others of a thousand different types—religious, moral, serious, futile, very general and very limited, immensely large and very minute. The Americans combine to give fetes, found seminaries, to build churches, to distribute books, to send missionaries to the antipodes. Hospitals, prisons, and schools take shape in that way. Finally, if they want to proclaim a truth or propagate some feeling by the encouragement of a great example, they form an association. (De Tocqueville, 1832/2006, p. 513)

It is believed that when a complex society incurs significant changes in its economic and political system, there will be a need for the establishment of voluntary associations (O'Neill, 2002). Voluntary associations serve as protectors of democratic rights and freedoms of citizens, and they also serve as instruments of social coordination to offset the power of the government (Frumkin, 2002). A strong democratic society is dependent on social connections, civic engagements, and voluntary associations (De Tocqueville, 1832/2006). Without those connections, a society would be filled with public apathy toward civic affairs, which would lead to the concentration of power in the government.

Whatever the reason for the existence of voluntary associations, be it missionary fervor, the desire to influence policy, or a means to advocate for human rights, the associational infrastructure became a fundamental part of early American society. Later in history, the early associational infrastructure became the foundation on which the modern nonprofit sector would be built.

Legal Motivations for the Modern Nonprofit Sector

In 1894, the U.S. government offered the first income tax exemption to corporations and associations involved in religious, educational, or charitable activities (Fremont-Smith, 2004). Initially, few organizations working for the public good would register with the Internal Revenue Service (IRS) as a tax-exempt charity. Those that did file for tax-exempt status were typically large charitable and philanthropic foundations headed by people such as John D. Rockefeller and Andrew Carnegie. Large charitable foundations became tax-exempt organizations because they provided public services.

Because of legal loopholes in the tax shelter laws, many large foundations took advantage of the tax exemption to shelter vast business fortunes of their parent corporations. When the government discovered how corporations were sheltering their money, the federal tax shelter laws were amended to close these loopholes. As a result, new charity laws were drafted that allowed wealthy individuals to engage in large-scale philanthropy (Hall, 2005) while preventing them from sheltering their estates. These new laws created public concern because it gave a small group of wealthy philanthropists power and influence over charitable organizations, social culture, and public policy.

In 1929, the American stock market crashed and resulted in the Great Depression. During the Depression, there was mass economic collapse and high unemployment throughout the United States. Private charitable organizations, without the help of government, attempted to handle the basic needs of people who had been put out of work. However, the demands of the poor and destitute quickly exceeded the resources of charitable groups. By 1930, most charitable organizations closed their doors and never reopened.

Franklin D. Roosevelt took office during the depths of the Depression. Within the first couple of years of his presidency, Roosevelt had legislation passed to fund massive public work projects and implement major tax reforms, in an effort to reenergize the economic market. The tax reforms helped to redistribute the concentrated wealth of the richest citizens through progressive income and estate taxes (Hall, 2005). All in all, there was virtually no tax impact on average American citizens. Yet the new taxes served as a powerful incentive for the wealthy citizens to engage in large-scale charitable donations. Donations could be listed as a tax deduction and allowed wealthy citizens to avoid tax penalties.

In 1942, Congress authorized a new progressive income tax for corporations and individuals as a way to generate revenue for World War II and international peace efforts (Friedman & McGarvie, 2003). Unregistered nonprofit organizations soon began registering with the IRS as legal nonprofits. Being a legal nonprofit meant that the bulk of the organization's revenue would not become a tax liability, which allowed nonprofits to build their revenue base.

New tax policies resulted in the growth of the nonprofit sector. However, by the mid-1940s, many state governments began pushing for greater supervision of charitable activities in nonprofit organizations. States began requiring nonprofit organizations to register and submit an annual financial report to the state attorney general's office. However, nonprofit administrators in most states disregarded the request for registration and submission of their organization's financial records, the reason being that state governments could not legally compel nonprofit organizations to comply. Greater compliance for submission of financials began only after the revision of the Internal Revenue Code, which threatened revocation of an organization's tax-exempt status if the nonprofit failed to submit its financials (Fremont-Smith, 2004).

The Birth of 501(c)(3) Organizations

In 1954, Congress redrafted the Internal Revenue Code with more specificity about the classification of nonprofit organizations and the type of tax exemption that these organizations were eligible for. The part of the redraft of interest to the development of nonprofits is the **Internal Revenue Code section 501(c)(3)**. The 501(c)(3) organization was redefined as:

> [C]orporations, and any community chest, fund, or foundation, organized and operated exclusively for religious, charitable, scientific, testing for public safety, literary, or educational purposes, or to foster national or international amateur sports competition (but only if no part of its activities involves the provision of athletic facilities or equipment), or for the prevention of cruelty to children or animals, no part of the net earnings of which inures to the benefit of any private

shareholder or individual, no substantial part of which is carrying on propaganda, or otherwise attempting to influence legislation (except as otherwise provided in subsection (h), and which does not participate in, or intervene in (including the publishing or distribution of statements), any political campaign on behalf of (or in opposition to) any candidate for public office.

Why should you be concerned with section 501(c)(3) of the Internal Revenue Code? Because the majority of human services organizations are 501(c)(3), and you should be knowledgeable about this category of organizations. Organizations in this category are involved in activities such as religion, education, charity, science, or literature, public safety, national or international amateur sports competitions, and prevention of cruelty to children and animals. By the 1950s, the number of 501(c)(3) nonprofit organizations continued to increase, but so did large wealthy charitable foundations. Wealthy business owners were again using their foundations to avoid taxation. This practice resulted in new congressional investigations of these foundations and other tax-exempt entities between 1952 and 1969 (Hall, 2005). The federal government also began to take a closer look at the financial activities of nonprofits.

Under Senator Joe McCarthy, who headed the Un-American Activities Committee, citizens and all types of organizations came under government scrutiny. During the McCarthy era, congressional committees such as the Cox Committee (established in 1952) and the Reece Committee (established in 1954) investigated large charitable and philanthropic foundations to determine whether they were financially supporting "subversive" activities or attempting to unduly influence social legislation. However, by the late 1950s, McCarthy's investigations lost momentum because the federal government became absorbed with other issues at home and abroad. As a result, congressional committees quickly wrapped up their investigations of philanthropic foundations and concluded that they were not involved in un-American activities (Fremont-Smith, 2004; O'Neill, 2002).

In the early 1960s, the federal government seemed to be interested only in general oversight of nonprofits and their tax status. New and more enforceable tax codes such as the Tax Reform Act of 1969 were put into place. The 1969 law was considered a historic milestone in the regulation of nonprofits. The four key provisions of the Tax Reform Act (a) place strict limitations on the administration of foundations, (b) impose new sanctions for noncompliance, (c) enforce more aggressive tax penalties, and (d) make individuals rather than foundation responsible for fines for profiting from self-dealing (Salamon, 2002).

The Filer Commission

In the 1970s, the IRS became interested in how taxation affected private charitable giving to nonprofits. A privately initiated and funded citizen's panel called the Commission on Private Philanthropy and Public Needs—also known as the Filer Commission—began collecting data about charitable giving in the United States.

The Filer Commission—named after its chairperson John H. Filer—sought to study philanthropic-giving patterns, understand tax effects on private giving, and determine where the majority of charitable dollars were channeled to in the nonprofit sector. After an in-depth study, the Commission made recommendations to the general public, nonprofit sector, and Congress about how to strengthen and make more effective the practice of private giving. The Commission's recommendations were summarized in a report titled *Giving in America: Toward a Stronger Voluntary Sector* (1975) into four broad statements:

1. The voluntary sector is a large and vital part of American society, more important today than ever. But the sector is undergoing economic strains that predate and are generally more severe than the troubles of the economy as a whole (p. 9).
2. Giving in America involves an immense amount of time and money, is the fundamental, underpinning of the voluntary sector, encompasses a wide diversity of relationships between donor, donations and donee, and is not keeping pace (p. 13).
3. Decreasing levels of private giving, increasing costs of nonprofit activity and broadening expectations for health, education and welfare services as basic entitlements of citizenship have led to the government's becoming a principal provider of programs and revenues in many areas once dominated by private philanthropy. And government's growing role in these areas poses fundamental questions about the autonomy and basic functioning of private nonprofit organizations and institutions (p. 16).
4. Our society has long encouraged "charitable" nonprofit activity by excluding it from certain tax obligations. But the principal tax encouragement of giving to nonprofit organizations—the charitable deduction in personal income taxes—has been both challenged from some quarters in recent years on grounds of equity and eroded by expansion of the standard deduction (p. 17).

Over a two-year period, the Filer Commission sponsored approximately 85 studies that focused on various aspects of nonprofit activities. The Commission's work highlighted that nonprofits had the capacity to perform an assortment of social welfare activities in communities throughout the United States. Policy makers wanted to be more responsive to social changes in the United States and so they began to (a) reconsider the scope of governmental oversight of nonprofits, (b) redefine the nonprofit sector, and (c) redraft nonprofit laws.

Over the next several decades, adjustments were made to nonprofit laws as a result of various social and political events. For example, nonprofit civil rights organizations that sought greater civil liberties for people of color, the poor, and women were soon recognized for their importance by the government. As a result, the Internal Revenue Code section 501(c)(3) redefined the nonprofit sector by adding a new category of tax-exempt organization. This new category covered organizations that worked to promote social welfare to lessen community tensions and deterioration. It also included organizations that worked to eliminate prejudice and discrimination while defending human and civil rights. In addition, during the first years of the 21st century, the threat of domestic and international terrorism caused the government to modify laws concerning nonprofit organizations involved in disaster relief. After the terrorist attacks on the World Trade Center in 2001, President George Bush signed legislation that allowed public charities and private foundation to make a one-time payment to victims or their families by using a reasonable and objective formula for distribution of funds (Fremont-Smith, 2004). Distribution of funds to victims would not be based on their prior living expenses, so as to ensure equitable assistance to all victims. Furthermore, the law does not require victims who receive qualified disaster relief payments to report it as income, which makes the payment tax free.

Features of Nonprofit Organizations

We will now return our focus to nonprofit organizations in the United States. U.S. nonprofits have three essential features that you will examine: (a) participation in the organization is voluntary, (b) revenues are not paid to stakeholders or owners, and (c) there is no definitive organizational ownership and accountability (Frumkin, 2002; Hasenfeld, 1992).

> **Voluntary Participation:** In the United States, volunteers and paid staff freely participate or work in the management and operations to deliver services or products to clients. Federal laws prohibit payment of excessive wages to staff working in a nonprofit. This wage limitation doesn't mean that paid employees should work for menial salaries. To ensure that nonprofit wages are within an allowable range, it is best to consult a nationally published compensation survey for nonprofits (Silk, 2005) such as the Watkins Uniberall Nonprofit Compensation Survey. Salary ranges vary from state to state.

> **Revenues Not Paid to Stakeholders or Owners:** A nonprofit's revenues are obtained by engaging in noncommercial activities that are related to their exempt purpose (Silk, 2005). These revenues cannot be paid to advance the wealth of any stakeholders associated with the organization. This limitation for handling revenue is referred to as a nondistribution restriction. One exception is that a nonprofit can make grants to individuals, groups, and organizations if the grant is used for proper charitable purposes.

> **No Definitive Organizational Ownership and Accountability:** There is no key ownership of the nonprofit organization, and no one person is legally accountable. Nonprofits are governed by a voluntary board of directors which serves multiple interest groups such as the community, donors, clients, management, and staff.

Box 4.1, IRS categories for 501(c) organizations, lists all the different types of organizations that comprise this category. However, we will only examine the essential features of both 501(c)(3) and 501(c)(4) organizations because most human services organizations fall within these two categories.

The Essential Features of a 501(c)(3) Organization

An organization can apply for the 501(c)(3) IRC tax-exempt status if it is organized for purposes such as religious, charitable, literary, educational or scientific activities, or testing for public safety. To be considered a 501(c)(3) organization, there are formal guidelines called the IRC 501(c)(3) "organizational tests," which outline what an organization must do to be considered exempt. Each organizational test has a long list of activities the organization can engage in. The three tests that must be passed to qualify are (1) the organizational test, (2) the political test, and (3) the asset test. You should know that it is not a simple process to qualify as a 501(c)(3) organization.

If you are attempting to create a nonprofit, you need to be knowledgeable about nonprofit laws. For instance, there are things a 501(c)(3) can and cannot do such as the following:

1. Can pay reasonable salaries for services to further the organization's mission.
2. Can offer services or products for reasonable noncommercial fee.

Box 4.1 IRS Categories for 501(c) Organizations 83

501(c)(1)—Corporations Organized Under Act of Congress (include Federal Credit Unions)

501(c)(2)—Title Holding Corporation for Exempt Organization

501(c)(3)—Religious, Educational, Charitable, Scientific, Literary, Testing for Public Safety, to Foster National or International Amateur Sports Competition or Prevention of Cruelty to Children or Animals Organizations

501(c)(4)—Civic Leagues, Social Welfare Organizations, and Local Associations of Employees

501(c)(5)—Labor, Agricultural, and Horticultural Organizations

501(c)(6)—Business Leagues, Chambers of Commerce, Real Estate Boards, etc.

501(c)(7)—Social and Recreational Clubs

501(c)(8)—Fraternal Beneficiary Societies and Associations

501(c)(9)—Voluntary Employees Beneficiary Associations

501(c)(10)—Domestic Fraternal Societies and Associations

501(c)(11)—Teachers' Retirement Fund Associations

501(c)(12)—Benevolent Life Insurance Associations, Ditch or Irrigation Companies, Telephone Companies

501(c)(13)—Cemetery Companies

501(c)(14)—State-Chartered Credit Unions, Mutual Reserve Funds

501(c)(15)—Mutual Insurance Companies or Associations

501(c)(16)—Cooperative Organizations to Finance Crop Operations

501(c)(17)—Supplemental Unemployment Benefit Trusts

501(c)(18)—Employee-Funded Pension Trust (created before June 25, 1959)

501(c)(19)—Post or Organization of Past or Present Members of the Armed Forces

501(c)(21)—Black Lung Benefit Trusts

501(c)(22)—Withdrawal Liability Payment Fund

501(c)(23)—Veterans Organization (created before 1880)

501(c)(25)—Title Holding Corporations or Trusts With Multiple Parents

501(c)(26)—State-Sponsored Organization Providing Health Coverage for High-Risk Individuals

501(c)(27)—State-Sponsored Workers' Compensation Reinsurance Organization

501(c)(28)—National Railroad Retirement Investment Trust

3. Can solicit tax-deductible donations from the public.
4. Can publish public educational material and sell it at cost.
5. Can publish a balance analysis of public issues with remove to debate.
6. Can lobby to protect budgetary appropriations.
7. Can testify on proposed legislation if formally invited in writing by a government committee.
8. Cannot take political positions or be involved in political campaigns.
9. Cannot discriminate on basis of race, nationality, or ethnicity.
10. Cannot overly engage in activities unrelated to your tax-exempt purposes.
11. Cannot pay profits to individuals (i.e., non-distribution of profits).
12. Cannot lobby to influence legislation except at an insubstantial level or must choose to file a 501(h) form.

Human Systems

Understanding and Mastery: Organizational structures of communities..

Critical Thinking Question: Human services practitioners function in an array of organizations and seek to understand their structure so that they may work effectively. According to the Internal Revenue Code, a 501(c)(3) organization can only lobby to influence legislation at an "insubstantial" level. What would constitute an insubstantial level of influence? Find out how the IRS defines "insubstantial." What sorts of influence can you think of that might be ambiguous? What should an organization do to decide whether it can or should engage in such an activity?

The Essential Features of a 501(c)(4) Organization

If a 501(c)(3) organization finds itself involved in advocating and lobbying rather than in providing charitable and service activities, it might be necessary for the organization to change its tax-exempt status to a 501(c)(4) to safeguard its nonprofit status. A nonprofit organization that engages in lobbying as a means to influence specific legislation and is using more than 20% of the organizational efforts and money on political activities should be registered as a 501(c)(4) tax-exempt organization. According to the **Internal Revenue Code section 501(c)(4)**, this type of organization

> [P]rovides for exemption of civic leagues or organizations not organized for profit but operated exclusively for the promotion of social welfare. Local associations of employees, the membership of which is limited to the employees of a designated person or persons in a particular municipality and the net earnings of which are devoted exclusively to charitable, educational, or recreational purposes.

The 501(c)(4) designation means that donors cannot take a tax deduction for contributions to this type of organization. The organization will usually not be exempt from sales tax and will not qualify for postal rate reductions for the organization's mailings.

You should be able to discern the differences between 501(c)(3) and 501(c)(4) nonprofit organizations to ensure that the organization you work for does not violate the Internal Revenue Code. Violation of these tax codes could be a costly mistake for the organization. So it would be advisable to consult a lawyer with an expertise in nonprofit tax-exempt laws if a question arises about the organization's status.

The benefit of being a 501(c) nonprofit is that these entities have a limited or no tax burden. However, to get a federal tax-exempt status, an organization must apply for it with the government, which involves fitting certain criteria and filling out lots of paperwork.

How Nonprofits Get Tax-Exempt Status

An organization must apply for federal tax-exempt status with the IRS to be considered a legally tax-exempt entity. Those who have positions of responsibility in a nonprofit organization should be aware of the IRS category under which the organization has registered. It is important to know the organizational category to ensure that you are in compliance with the Internal Revenue Codes. A nonprofit organization that is not in compliance risks losing its tax-exempt status, and without tax-exempt status, a nonprofit could lose essential revenue necessary for paying staff salaries, keeping programs running, and paying for general operations.

Nonprofit activities are not limited to charitable works, education, or community development. The nonprofit sector is composed of a diverse group of organizations such as social services organizations, philanthropic foundations, educational institutions, health organizations, museums, and ballet companies. It is important to look closely at the 501(c)(3) and the 501(c)(4) designations because these two categories account for approximately 70% of all registered nonprofits. Because, as a human services practitioner you will probably work in a 501(c)(3) or an 501(c)(4) organization, it is important you understand their essential features (Box 4.1 lists other types of 501(c) entities).

The Roles of Nonprofit Human Services Organizations

In general terms, human services organizations exist for the "social good," and their goal is to enhance human wellbeing and welfare while seeking no profit (Frumkin, 2002; Hasenfeld, 1992; Schmid, 2004). Over the years, the power of these organizations has been demonstrated by their ability to function in socially ambiguous situations and to operate under constantly changing public policies. Nonprofit human services organizations continue to provide social services even when the government has abandoned its most needy citizens (Piven & Cloward, 1993). Moreover, these organizations continue to serve as a safety net to individuals and communities in need.

Human services organizations comprise 17.5% of the nonprofit sector and are primarily involved in direct service to all types of people (Anheier, 2005). Approximately 1.8 million nonprofits are registered in the United States. It is estimated that there are more than 1.2 million nonprofit entities registered as either 501(c)(3) or 501(c)(4) (Fremont-Smith, 2004; O'Neill, 2002). No accurate count of nonprofits exists, because the IRS does not require certain types of nonprofit organizations to register, such as (a) religious organizations, (b) organizational affiliates, and (c) organizations with annual incomes less than $5000 (Friedman & McGarvie, 2003; Frumkin, 2002; O'Neill, 2002).

In terms of economic power, at the start of the 21st century nonprofits accounted for 5–10% of the gross domestic product (GDP). The GDP is an annual economic measure of the market value of all products and services produced in a country. Currently, the paid earnings (i.e., revenues) in the nonprofit sector account for about 6% ($281.9 billion) of the total U.S. business market (Anheier, 2005). These revenues come from three different sources: private fees, public sector payments, and private giving. Here is an interesting fact: 501(c)(3) organizations are worth billions of dollars in the open market. Also, nonprofit human services organizations maintain the majority market share in the delivery of social and welfare services (Anheier, 2005; Frumkin, 2002). What does all this mean? This means that the human services industry is a major economic powerhouse in the United States.

Some believe that because nonprofit human services organizations put greater emphasis on the wellbeing of the client as opposed to making profit or serving a government authority, they are better suited to perform direct service (1997; Schmid, 2004). Currently, there is much interest in the scope, structure and finances of human services organizations (Austin, 1988; Drucker, 2003). Yet, in light of the growing interest and importance of these organizations what remains vague is how these organizations are defined.

Defining the Function of Human Services Organizations

According to some nonprofit scholars, vagueness about what human services organizations do makes it difficult for organizations to work together (Zins, 2001). This vagueness also makes it hard for social policy makers to evaluate or assist many human services organizations and support their work (Salamon & Anheier, 1997; Schmid, 2004). Furthermore, at a time when there is a greater demand for accountability of human services organizations from external funding sources and other stakeholders, having a clear definition of the organizational function is important.

In a study of human services organizations, it was shown that three common themes defined their function: (a) they function as providers of services to people in need;

(b) they function to protect, maintain, or enhance the personal wellbeing of recipients of services by defining, shaping, or altering their personal attributes; and (c) they function to address basic human needs of people through policy creation and programs development (Zins, 2001). In general, the three functional definitions of human services organizations are not concise in terms of what client needs are addressed or what type of client is being helped.

Another way to define human services organizations focuses on whether they take a minimalistic approach to human needs or an optimal attempt to address larger issues of life stability. The minimalistic approach focuses on such things as basic food and shelter. However, in the larger picture, human needs include housing, recreation, education, and psychological welfare. This is no small issue, especially when an organization is trying to define what it is doing for clients. Some organizations clearly aim to address basic human needs and take a minimalistic approach to service delivery; they address only necessary conditions required for basic human existence (Zins, 2001). One familiar organization that takes a minimalistic approach is the social welfare system. Social welfare agencies provide clients with an allowance for basic material benefits such as food, shelter, and job training. This approach is theoretically geared to cause service recipients to move toward work that will make them self-sufficient (Cheng, 2002).

In some instances a minimalistic approach makes it impossible for service recipients to comply with institutional rules and policies designed to move them to self-sufficiency (Grigsby, 1998; Hawkins, 2005). A poor single father with three small children who is receiving social welfare benefits is required to take a job, which typically pays minimum wage, to qualify for the benefit (this is called "workfare"). However, under the minimalistic approach, the combined wages and benefits are still insufficient to allow him to pay for childcare and transportation. Thus, the job actually reduces his total income. As a result, he does not achieve self-sufficiency and his family may sink further into poverty.

On the other hand, a human services organization that addresses human needs by using an optimal service approach promotes the overall quality of life for clients (Zins, 2001). In other words, an optimal approach goes beyond offering the client basic needs (e.g., food, shelter, and job training) by fulfilling the client's non-basic needs (e.g., leisure, recreation, and environmental protection) to help the client achieve a decent overall human existence. For example, a human services agency helps a poor single mom and her two school-aged children move to housing in a middle-class neighborhood outside the city. The family's new housing is in walking distance to the mother's job and the children's school. This means that the mother doesn't initially need a car or other transportation to get to work. The children are enrolled in an after-school program, and issues of safety are no longer a problem. The children's mother knows where her children are and can pick them up on her way home. To ensure the family is thriving in this new environment, the agency makes sure they have signed up for food stamps, and the family is assigned to a local doctor who will take Medicaid. When school is out for summer vacation, the children qualify for free enrollment to a summer camp, which is paid for by the township. Which parent do you think will more likely escape the poverty cycle? You should be getting a sense of how important it is for an organization to have a clear definition of what they are and how they do things.

Organizations also need to be concerned about defining who is being helped by the services that are offered. According to Zins (2001), there are two service approaches that organizations can adopt. Service could be offered using a "differentiated approach," which means targeting vulnerable populations (e.g., the disabled, inmates, mentally ill, and the poor). Or service could be offered using a "general public approach," which means targeting general populations (e.g., retirees, students, and consumers) by helping them maintain their current level of functioning.

Overall, when human services organizations are not clear about the target population they are servicing and which human needs are being met, it may impair the development of better social policies, service designs, and program assessments. In some instances, an organization could lose its funding if its mission and programs don't meet the expectations of external funding groups. Armed with an understanding of what the organization does, who it serves, and how it helps clients allows organizations to clearly explain to external funding sources what the organization is all about.

If you work outside the United States, it is also important to know how nonprofits function in other countries. We will now examine from a cross-cultural perspective how the nonprofit sector is defined because it could impact the way you work in an international setting.

Defining the Nonprofit Sector: A Cross-cultural Perspective

The nonprofit sector has different meanings in different countries throughout the world. Terms used to describe the nonprofit sector seem to imply different functions, but they are used interchangeably, which leads to faulty assumptions about what these organizations actually do. Salamon (2002) lists and defines the various terms used for organizations that function outside of the government and the private sector in different countries:

1. **Philanthropic sector:** Used in the United States, the United Kingdom, and Japan to describe private individuals and foundations that make donations (money, property, or securities) to an array of organizations.
2. **Social Economy (or Economie Sociale):** Used in France and Belgium for a broad range of nongovernmental organizations such as cooperatives, savings banks, and mutual insurance companies. The four main characteristics of these organizations are (a) they serve members, (b) they have independent management, (c) they use a democratic decision-making process, and (d) they practice social distribution of income.
3. **Nongovernmental organization (NGO):** Typically used in developing countries to describe organizations engaged in promoting economic and social development at the grassroots level. NGOs are run by volunteer groups or organizations and are not affiliated to any government. They provide services to individuals in domestic and international locations. NGOs are also involved in advocating for human rights, protecting the environment, and promoting economic and social development, often at the grassroots level. To get a sense of the size of the NGO community, go to the online NGO directory WANGO (www.wango.org).
4. **Voluntary sector:** Used primarily in the United Kingdom to describe organizations that are run in part by volunteers. In some instances, there is paid staff and management.

You should also be aware of other terms used for the nonprofit sector, such as associational sector, charity sector, eleemosynary sector, independent sector, third sector, nongovernmental sector, and tax-exempt sector. Each of the terms listed emphasizes some relevant feature about what the sector does or where the sector exists in relationship to the government and private sectors. To reiterate, the terms used to describe human services organizations that function outside of the government are often used interchangeably.

According to Salamon and Anheier (1997), there is no common global definition for the nonprofit sector because countries around the world have different social, political, and economic factors that shape their nonprofit sector. The United States probably has the clearest definition and concept of a nonprofit sector because of the Internal Revenue Codes that define what it is and is not. The United Kingdom, which comprises Northern Ireland, Wales, England, and Scotland, has an ongoing problem with having a singular definition for a nonprofit because each country has different laws and tax systems. However, the U.K. nonprofit sector is considered separate from the public and private sectors. The United Kingdom typically refers to its nonprofit sector as a "voluntary sector," and the voluntary sector has nonprofit organizations that engage in the delivery of services to individuals within communities.

In Germany and France, the concept of a nonprofit sector is less developed. Nonprofit organizations in these countries are tied closely to government in complex ways that makes their operation quite different from those in the United States. Italy also has a less formal nonprofit sector but operates in three distinct spheres: public, secular, and within the Catholic Church.

In some countries, the concept of a nonprofit sector conflicts with the sociopolitical structure. For instance, Sweden's highly developed welfare system makes the nonprofit sector unnecessary because the state provides for citizens who are unable to care for themselves. In countries in the former Soviet Union, there is only a nascent nonprofit sector. Many Soviet citizens are mistrustful of formal agencies because the former communist government used some organizations as instruments for social control. Yet in Hungary, also a formerly communist-run country, the nonprofit sector is evolving in a new political landscape under a democratic parliamentary republic.

In East Asia, countries such as Japan have neither a nonprofit sector nor laws that grant their formation. However, Japanese communities do have charitable organizations—known as *koeke hojin*—that can receive a tax benefit if the government determines that the organization serves a valid public service. In Southeast Asia, Thailand has a small nonprofit sector that is carefully monitored and regulated by the government. Their nonprofit sector is slowly developing within the region.

In India, the concept of nonprofit organizations (NPOs) has to be considered in context of the country's complex political economy and its long history of voluntarism. Voluntarism dates back to 1,500 B.C. and has been integral to Indian society (Salamon & Anheier, 1997). Even when India came under British rule in the late 1800s, local organizations remained involved in voluntary efforts for social development throughout the country. However, in the 1940s it would be Mahatma Gandhi—one of the most well-known leaders of Indian nationalism—who would promote a voluntary movement to develop all aspects of life for common Indians. Gandhi successfully mobilized people across India to fight for their independence from Britain.

After India's independence in 1947, two predominant types of Indian nonprofits were established: one was the Gandhian NPOs (involved in development and empowerment) and the other was the religion-based NPOs (involved in welfare and empowerment). The Gandhian NPOs worked with the new Indian government for the country's overall development. These organizations were financially funded by the government. Currently, voluntary agencies—under the acronym VOLAGs—is the term commonly used in India to describe the voluntary sector, which serves the developmental interests of a broad swath of the population.

If you hope to effectively practice in cultures or countries outside of your own, it is essential that you remain mindful of the differences that exist among nonprofits throughout the world. Remember, there is no universal concept or definition for what is referred to in the United States as the nonprofit sector.

Summary

While charitable organizations have been operating in the United States since the country's inception, the modern nonprofit came into existence only about 60 years ago. The Internal Revenue Code classified some organizations as nonprofits if they engaged primarily in social welfare, did not seek to make profit, and did not become involved in politics. When classified as a nonprofit, an organization gains tax exempt status. Currently, the majority of human services organizations are considered 501(c)(3) or 501(c)(4) nonprofits. Both types of nonprofits are guided by laws that tell them what they can and cannot do, and human services professionals must understand these legal requirements. There is no international agreement about what constitutes a nonprofit organization. Nonprofit sectors outside of the United States function in accordance to their social, political, and economic establishments.

Even within legally recognized nonprofit organizations, the scope of services provided may vary widely, from help with basic human needs to assistance with full integration into society. Scope of service significantly affects the way a human services organization will interact with other organizations, policy makers, and external funding sources.

Human Services Delivery Systems

Understanding and Mastery: International and global influences on service delivery.

Critical Thinking Question: To practice in nonprofits in countries outside of one's homeland, a human services practitioner must focus on global influences on service delivery systems. Therefore, the practitioner needs to be aware from a global perspective how nonprofit organizations are perceived in their own countries. From a cross-cultural perspective, list several factors that influence how nonprofits function in different countries. Then determine which one factor among those you listed might create the greatest limitation in the delivery of human services.

Assess your analysis and evaluation of this chapter's content by completing the **Chapter Review**.

Human Services Management and Supervision

· ·

The goal of nonprofit human service organizations is to provide the highest quality client service consistent with the resources that have been entrusted to them. While the study of management is typically associated with for-profit enterprises whose goal is to maximize profit, the practices are essentially the same for nonprofit organizations. Indeed, learning about the management of human service organizations is essential if nonprofits are going to effectively compete and survive in a competitive business market (Brody, 2005; Drucker, 2005). Good management practices are also necessary to protect the funds and assets of nonprofit human service organizations and are necessary for the efficient, effective, productive, and beneficial functioning of these organizations.

So you need management knowledge and skills to help your organization. The study of management means learning how to facilitate and supervise human interactions within a work environment to bolster effective and efficient products or services. In this chapter, you will examine the work roles of the board of directors, administration, management, and volunteers of nonprofit human services organizations. (Staff roles are not discussed because they are too varied across nonprofit organizations.) In the later part of the chapter, there is a discussion about workplace problems and managing diversity in the workplace.

The Nonprofit Hierarchy

A **nonprofit hierarchy** exists to guide the execution of an organization's mission. Having a hierarchy implies that the majority of power is held by people in the upper levels of an organization. Figure 5.1 is a chart of a

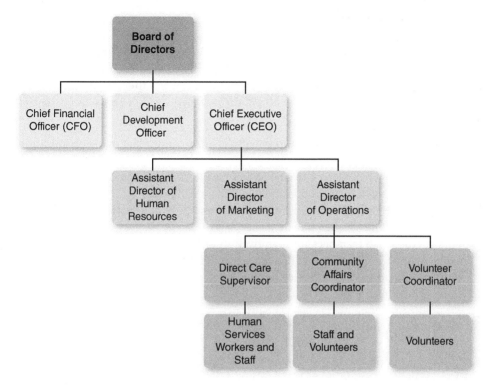

FIGURE 5.1
Nonprofit Organization Hierarchy Chart
Courtesy: vertex42.com
Google Images

typical nonprofit's organizational hierarchy, which illustrates the different positions held by people in a human service organization. This hierarchy also represents the chain of command (who reports to whom) that exists in most organizations. To work effectively you must be mindful of working with your immediate supervisor. Practitioners who are new to organizations sometimes violate the chain of command and find themselves in hot water. When the established chain of command is appropriately used, it ensures an orderly process for addressing problems and concerns of workers at all levels of the organization.

The Board of Directors

In a nonprofit organization, a group of volunteers—called **trustees**—serve on the board of directors. Trustees on nonprofit boards serve without compensation, which means they derive no financial benefit for their work. As the top leadership, the board advances the organization's mission and vision, but the board does not oversee the day-to-day operations of the agency: That is the job of the executive director.

CREATING A BOARD   Boards range in size, often depending on the size and complexity of the organization, and states may mandate a minimum number of board members. Nonprofit governance research suggests an ideal of 9–11 trustees (Renz, 2010). Each trustee appointed to the board should bring some special knowledge or skills (e.g., in business, law, education, politics, lobbying, or program planning) that will help advance the mission of the agency. The board should also include community members and clients who are served by the agency because they bring insight about the community and the agency's effectiveness. Also, the board should include (if possible) members from different socioeconomic classes, races, ethnicities, gender, sexual orientations, and people with disabilities.

Historically, nonprofit boards in the United States have been disproportionately controlled and run by white men from the upper class (Kettner, 2014). The rationale for having a board with a mixed demographic is that it brings a more balanced representation of concerns, insights, and approaches, which can help the agency be more effective. A board should be carefully put together, because in the end they can make or break the organization. To have an effective board, the members need these six competencies (Chait, Holland, & Taylor, 1996):

1. **Contextual:** Board members comprehend the norms and values of the organization that they govern.
2. **Educational:** Steps are taken to ensure that members are educated about the overall organization, board roles, responsibilities, and performance.
3. **Interpersonal:** Board members create work teams and a culture that fosters cohesiveness and collective welfare.
4. **Analytical:** Board members are cognitively aware of both subtle and complex problems and remain open to different perspectives to finding solutions.
5. **Political:** Board members develop and maintain healthy relationships with key stakeholders.
6. **Strategic:** Board members engage in a strategic approach to the organization's direction and future.

THE DUTIES OF THE BOARD   Being a trustee on a board requires a significant commitment. A board meeting is not a social event but an occasion where a group of people collectively work to advance the objectives and goals of the agency. Thomas Wolf (1999) summarizes the general duties of board trustees:

1. Determine the organization's mission and set policies for its operation, ensuring that the provisions of the organization's charter and the law are being followed.
2. Set the organization's overall program from year to year and engage in longer range planning to establish its general course for the future.
3. Establish fiscal policy and boundaries, with budgets and financial controls.
4. Provide adequate resources for the activities of the organization through direct financial contributions and a commitment to fundraising.
5. Select, evaluate, and, if necessary, terminate the appointment of the chief executive officer (CEO).
6. Develop and maintain a communication link to the community, promoting the work of the organization. (p. 48)

FOUNDATION DOCUMENTS   If a board is going to determine the organization's mission, set operation policies, and ensure the charter and laws are followed, then every board member should have knowledge of the following three foundation documents: (a) articles of incorporation, (b) bylaws, and (c) personnel manuals. If the organization is established and has been operating for some time, board members won't be involved in the creation of the foundation documents, but they will be involved in editing and reviewing all foundation documents.

The first foundation document, the **articles of incorporation**—also known as the charter—outlines the operating framework of the agency and gives reasons for its existence. Why would an organization incorporate? When a nonprofit organization becomes incorporated, it is considered a separate legal entity that is equivalent to a separate legal person. As a separate legal entity or person, the incorporated nonprofit organization can enter into contracts, acquire debt, pay taxes, and be sued. In addition, once an organization is incorporated, executive officers, employees, and volunteers are protected from legal liabilities in most cases.

The trustees on a board should retain a lawyer to create and complete the paperwork necessary to become legally incorporated within their state. Because the process of incorporating is fairly complex, it would be prudent to hire a lawyer who specializes in incorporation and knows the laws of the state in which the organization resides. If the organization doesn't have the funds to hire a lawyer, the board should reference books to get general information about the process of incorporation. Books about incorporation will give the board a step-by-step description about how to incorporate the organization and include copies of relevant legal forms for incorporation.

The second foundation document that board members should be knowledgeable of is the operating constitution for the organization—called the **bylaws**. The bylaws outline the general operation and identify board officers, term limits, meeting protocols, board duties, committee formation, elections of officers, and voting. Finally, a board should be knowledgeable about the organization's **personnel manuals** that cover policies and procedures in the organization. In fact, there should be two separate personnel manuals, one created for board members and the executive director and the second for staff and volunteers.

OTHER BOARD RESPONSIBILITIES   To carry out the general duties described previously, every board member should be involved with planning time-bound objectives and goals for the organization. The objectives should clearly state what will be accomplished by the organization and when program goals are met. With objectives and goals in place, the board can make an assessment about the organization's overall effectiveness and efficiency.

Another major duty of a board deals with establishing fiscal policies and boundaries, with budgets and financial controls. Therefore, the board must develop, approve, and monitor the organization's annual budget to ensure there is adequate fiscal control and projected expenses are covered. The board is also responsible for submitting reports to tax and regulatory agencies. It is extremely helpful to have a board member who is knowledgeable and has the skills to use tax software (e.g., Turbo Tax) so that tax forms can be submitted and tracked. It is the responsibility of a board to make sure tax returns and other legal documents are filed in a timely manner. Government audits are rare (Silk, 2005), but it is best to stay on the right side of the law.

Another major duty of the board is to provide adequate resources to organizational activities through direct financial contributions and a commitment to fundraising. All board members should support their agency by making an annual donation. Why? The act of donating signals to funders and prospective donors that the board has a high level of commitment to the organization's mission, which is backed with their own money. A board member's cash donation should, of course, be within his or her financial means. When a board member doesn't have money to donate—due to poverty or other circumstances—he or she can contribute additional time and personal material contributions to assist with fundraising.

All board members should also be involved in at least one fundraising activity such as proposal writing, letter campaigns, cultivating prospective donors, or planning fundraising events. A board member's involvement in these activities signals to prospective donors, staff, and the community that the works of the organization are worth advancing with their donations and time. In larger nonprofits, fundraising falls under the scope of a development office. Typically, a development officer (Figure 5.1) will oversee the fundraising activities in the organization, but this does not free board members from their fundraising obligation. Boards are the major fundraisers within a nonprofit organization. Without the income stream from fundraising, many organizations will close. In Chapter 6 you will learn about fundraising strategies that will help your organization thrive.

EDUCATING BOARD MEMBERS To get a high level of commitment from board members, they have to be educated about what it means to be on a board. Prospective board members need to be educated about being on a board to clarify what they will be doing and the time needed. When things are planned out and organized, people are more apt to want to get involved and stay involved with an organization.

New board members should have a formal orientation, at which time they are given the following:

1. Ring binder that contains copies of the articles of incorporation
2. Bylaws
3. Mission statement
4. Formal organizational chart
5. Summary of budget reports
6. Personnel handbooks
7. Summary of projects completed and proposed

Updated documents should also be in the possession of the existing board. New board members should be thoroughly briefed about issues and concerns of the organization and be given a clear explanation of their duties. New board members should also be informed that if they fail to carry out their prescribed duties they can be discharged from the board. Carrying deadweight—members who do nothing—on the board serves no purpose and burdens the trustees who are committed and willing to work for the organization. There should be continuing education for all board members to ensure they have the whole picture of the organization and the opportunity to develop their knowledge and skills to be an effective governing body.

New board members should definitely be made aware of their legal accountability and legal liability, because board members can be sued. As a result, the president of the board or the organization's lawyer needs to inform new members about the appropriate liability insurance they should obtain. This **liability insurance** is carried to ensure that board members' personal assets cannot be attached to settle a financial claim against the organization.

SARBANES-OXLEY ACT It is also important for trustees to be aware of laws that will affect their practice. Because nonprofit boards are legally accountable as stewards of the agency, many are voluntarily complying with the *Public Company Accounting Reform and Investor Protection Act of 2002*—known as the **Sarbanes-Oxley Act (SOX)**. This legislation is designed to create greater accountability of nonprofits and publicly traded corporations with respect to governance, financial disclosure, and public accounting. The legislation also protects the interests of stakeholders and employees.

Box 5.1	Sarbanes-Oxley Legislation Relevant to Best Practices for Nonprofits

Title II.	Auditor Independence
Title III.	Corporate Responsibility
Title IV.	Enhance Financial Disclosures
Title VIII.	Corporate and Criminal Fraud Accountability / Document Preservation / Whistleblower Protection
Title IX.	White-Collar Crime Penalty
XI.	Corporate Fraud and Accountability

Currently, only two SOX regulations are legally required of all nonprofits: (a) whistleblower protection for employees who report illegal activities occurring in the organization and (b) document preservation, which prohibits the destruction and falsification of organizational records or documents that are to be used in an investigation (Jackson, 2006). Nonprofit boards also follow other SOX regulations to guide them in the best practices for governance and management. See Box 5.1 for the list of Sarbanes-Oxley legislation that is relevant to best practices for nonprofits.

The Chief Executive Officer

The board's job is complex as trustees ensure that the charitable mission of the agency is suitable and accomplished efficiently and effectively. The trustees serve as a governing body, and they have little time for much else. So the overall operation of the agency is left to the **CEO**. Upper administration in large nonprofits could have three equally powerful top administrators such as a CEO, chief financial officer, and a chief development officer (Figure 5.1). An effective CEO possesses knowledge and skills to oversee the complex affairs of organizations.

CEO COMPETENCIES   The **Competing-Values Model** outlines four distinct competencies needed in the management of a human services organization (Quinn, 1988):

1. ability to mobilize and motivate personnel to work toward organizational goals,
2. ability to monitor and coordinate staff, oversee fiscal issues, and create reports to assure internal and external consistency in communications,
3. ability to effectively and efficiently produce services that are geared toward market demands, and
4. ability to be driven by goals and objectives.

Effective CEOs are mindful of being "board-centered," which means they cultivate a respectful, communicative, and interactive relationship with the board (Herman & Heimovics, 1991). CEOs need the support of their boards to do their job. In a nonprofit hierarchy, this upper echelon of administrators would report directly to the board, but in a medium or small organization, there usually is only one top administrator and that would be the CEO. Despite the size of the organization, the CEO answers directly to the board of directors and receives his or her assignments from the board. In other words, the CEO works for the board and can be fired by the board. If a CEO appears to be running the board of directors, he or she is acting beyond the scope of his or her job.

The CEO takes the role of administrator, which means handling the day-to-day operations, implementing policy, promoting organizational continuity, monitoring financial performance, and interfacing with the public. A CEO also must take the role of an innovator who facilitates adaptation and change. For example, as the human service industry faces increased competition for limited resources, the leadership of nonprofits is finding new approaches (e.g., rebranding, interactive market campaigns, and consumer-driven services) to take a larger market share from for-profit organizations.

A CEO who is supportive of a "change culture" allows for open discussions about ideas, proposals, and options for revision and greater autonomy for people working in the organization. Change is necessary to keep a human service organization vital, but the process comes with predictable resistance that normally is followed by slow acceptance of changes (Austin, 2002; Brody, 2005). Therefore, CEOs need to possess the ability to advocate their visions to employees and have the ability to be persistent through the change process in order to reach organizational goals.

In the public, the CEO is the face of the organization and speaks for the organization. The CEO's public persona shapes the community image of the organization. Board members should be very careful about whom they pick for the top administrator's position. While in the public sphere, a CEO may be busy securing new money sources, interfacing with external stakeholders, and making the organization visible to the community. Because many nonprofits are fiscally susceptible to external forces, it is crucial that a CEO goes outside of the organization to procure funds, recruit personnel, and appeal to the general public. In turn, some CEOs spend little time on the internal operations of the organization because they are engaged in the external business of the organization to ensure it remains solvent and relevant to the community it serves.

As a CEO interfaces with the community, he or she must become adept at working with special interest groups. Influential special interest groups can procure resources and/or make substantial donations to an organization. As a result, these groups often have great influence in their communities and need to be embraced by the leadership of nonprofit organizations (Brody, 2005).

Managers and Supervisors

If the board of directors is involved with overseeing the mission, fundraising, and legal matters and the CEO is overseeing the operations while also interfacing with the public, then who is running the organization? Who is getting the work of the organization done?

THE ROLE OF MIDDLE MANAGERS The **middle manager** (e.g., assistant director) is directly involved with the internal functions of the organization. In other words, the middle manager oversees the key operational components of the organization such as personnel, payroll, facilities, services/deliverables, and clients/customers (Robbins & Coulter, 2009). Other duties of the middle manager include creating a work environment that allows workers to report what's going on in the organization and what's going on with clients. This information helps the middle manager to make needed adjustments to ensure that the work of the organization is being done. Moreover, the manager must be open and responsive to subordinates to create an open work environment.

With respect to who reports to whom, the middle manager's subordinates (e.g., direct care supervisor or volunteer coordinator) report directly to him or her, and the middle manager reports directly to the CEO, which puts the middle manager in between the CEO and the subordinates. As a result, the middle manager is pulled to do the bidding of upper administration and pulled to help lower management satisfy workers on the frontlines. In some instances, the needs of the administration and subordinates are very different; this makes the job of the middle manager difficult.

SUPERVISORS ON THE FRONTLINE   **Supervisors**—also known as line managers—oversee the work of direct-service workers, general staff, and volunteers to ensure the work of the organization is being done (Robbins & Coulter, 2009). The supervisor's role is to help, educate, guide, and motivate all workers. Administrative duties of a supervisor include doing appraisals of staff work performance, determining rewards for work performance, and initiating the termination of unsuitable employees (Kettner, 2014). The supervisor also monitors client or customer feedback to ensure service delivery is effective and efficient.

Metaphorically speaking, the supervisor is in the trenches and sees what's going on at the frontlines. In turn, supervisors are the ears and eyes of management but they are also the mouth of line workers. As the mouthpiece, the supervisor advocates for his or her subordinates to ensure they have the tools and resources to do their jobs in the field. However, the supervisor is accountable to a middle manager, and the direct-service workers, general staff, and volunteers are accountable to their supervisor.

Management Theories, Models, and Approaches

Over the past several decades, the management of human service organizations has become a critical issue (Hong, 2011). Yet in these organizations it has been traditional to promote hard-working direct-care practitioners into supervisory or management positions. The transition of these practitioners into supervisory or management positions can be fraught with many problems (Brody, 2005) that are caused by the lack of training, developmental support (Nolan & Johnson, 2011), and little to no management knowledge. When newly promoted practitioners attempt to manage or supervise work groups without management knowledge, the result, all too frequently, is a disagreeable work environment. Sadly, human service organizations have often been criticized for work environments that need better management (Austin, 2002; Brody, 2005). In poorly managed organizations, the staff experience work overload, role ambiguity, low annual salaries, decreased employee job satisfaction, and high turnover rates (Hong, 2011). If human service organizations are going to have better work environments, it is essential that administrators, managers, and supervisors working in these systems learn management theories and approaches so that they collectively create better work environments.

We will examine four management theories that have been widely used in public, for-profit, and nonprofit organizations. The first two are the "classic" theories of scientific management and bureaucratic management—both of which, as we will see, have significant limitations. Despite these limitations, they are deeply ingrained in many organizations, and it is important to understand how they work. We will then move on to two more modern theories, total quality management (TQM) and management by objectives (MBO), which have real promise as models for human service organizations.

Classic Management Theories

Scientific management theory and the rational-legal bureaucracy model brought significant benefits to the management of 20th-century businesses, and they are still used in great many an organization, but as we shall see, they have attracted a good deal of criticism as well.

SCIENTIFIC MANAGEMENT THEORY   **Scientific management** is also known as Taylorism because the theory was first formulated by Frederick Winslow Taylor (1856–1915). Taylor was a mechanical engineer who believed that management should be based on true science, defined laws, rules, and principles that could be applied to all types of human activity (Kettner, 2014). He believed that managers who used scientific management in industrial and manufacturing establishments could find solutions to inefficiency in labor productivity that was unattainable with less systematic management (Taylor, 1911/2001). The major objective of scientific management is to secure the maximum prosperity (riches) for the employer in tandem with the maximum prosperity (wages) for each employee.

According to Taylor (1911/2001), scientific management theory has four guiding practices. The first practice involves gathering a body of scientific data about motion studies and time studies of workers doing their assigned jobs. Managers would use these data to create rules, laws, or mathematical formulas that would be calculated into the scientific training and development of workers. This training and development would help workers achieve maximum efficiency in their jobs so that they could safely work faster and be more productive. As a result, by maximizing the efficiency of workers, society could (the theory claimed) eliminate the fundamental causes of unemployment and poverty.

The second practice under scientific management involved engaging in the scientific study of the worker so that employers could determine desirable traits. Then the study results of desirable work traits could be used in the future selection of workers. This scientific information could also be used to create appropriate training of new workers that would lead to a "better class of work," which would match the workers' natural abilities. The third practice was the systematic administration of concrete incentives (e.g., higher wages or demotions depending on job performance) because they could be used to change work behaviors (e.g., work faster).

The final practice under scientific management involved the division of labor between workers and managers, which was based on an individual's education and mental capacity. For instance, managers were considered a group with greater mental capacity and education; therefore they should be given more workplace responsibilities such as (a) developing a scientific understanding of each activity of the worker, (b) planning how workers were to complete their tasks, (c) offering aid to workers with their tasks, and (d) having direct contact with workers.

Overall, scientific management was based on the premise that everyone was working for the same end and would share in the results. The work environment would be democratic, which ensured all members would do their part or risk being reported. Moreover, there would be greater efficiency from workers and greater cost effectiveness in the workplace, which would increase an industry's profitability and increase wages and job opportunities for workers.

SCIENTIFIC MANAGEMENT THEORY LIMITATIONS   The scientific management theory was one of the earliest attempts in the 1900s to scientifically analyze the work process (the example often used was loading pig iron on a rail car) with motion and time studies across different industries. However, within two decades of its birth, the theory became obsolete. It was revealed that there was little reliable empirical data to support concrete results such as efficiency and cost effectiveness in the workplace (Stewart, 2006). Also, from a humane perspective, scientific management was criticized as an unequal management approach that gave the manager full control of how, when, and where work would be done.

Yet, many consumer product manufacturing industries around the world (e.g., the U.S. meat industry, clothing factories in India, and Chinese manufacturers of durable products) still function under quasi-scientific management. In addition the surgical nursing (Wigens, 1997) and human service industries (Hasenfeld, 1992) continue to dabble in neo-scientific management with varying degrees of success, despite the fact that scientific management has not been proven to be effective.

RATIONAL-LEGAL BUREAUCRACY MODEL   The term *bureaucracy* may well bring to mind the image of a large organization or government agency bogged down by complicated rules and regulations. Let's explore where the concept of bureaucracy came from.

Max Weber (1864–1920), a German philosopher and political economist, made an analysis of modern state institutions and determined that they functioned as rational-legal bureaucracies (Kettner, 2014). From this perspective, it is assumed that the organization is a purposely designed entity that has clear goals (Hasenfeld, 1992). Furthermore, the bureaucratic model—like the scientific management theory— emphasizes authoritarianism, objectivity, predictability, practicality, and technical competence (Robbins & Coulter, 2009).

There are two distinct components to the **rational-legal bureaucracy model**. First is the rational component of the model. A rational organization has an internal division of labor and well-defined work positions, and the distribution of authority is formal and hierarchical. The second component of the model is legal. An organization that is described as being legal means it has objective rules that are universally applied to things such as position assignments, distribution of authority, and rights and duties connected to each position. In other words, a rational-legal bureaucracy exists when the organization functions with explicit goals, and workers' behaviors are determined by formal role definitions within the context of the organization.

Weber's analysis of state institutions revealed three elements that were prevalent in functioning bureaucracies. The first element is that regular activities are distributed as fixed official duties among subordinates working in a bureaucracy. The second element is that some people are given authority but function under a strict set of rules that guide how they get subordinates to complete their official duties. The third element is that bureaucratic institutions use a systematic approach for the regular and continual fulfillment of official duties and execution of rights that go with each position. Therefore, designated positions can only be filled by individuals who have the regulated qualifications an institution has specified.

RATIONAL-LEGAL BUREAUCRACY MODEL LIMITATIONS Bureaucracies tend to become rigid and may focus too much attention on the rules of the organization and away from the organization's mission. An organization's responsiveness may suffer and individual practitioners may find that they are prevented from using their professional judgment because of the dominance of bureaucratic uniformity. According to Hasenfeld (1992), the rational-legal model, when used in human service organizations, impeded the ability to respond to changes in external rules and funding, produced disagreement about goals, and was unresponsive to a variety of unanticipated needs that led to informal arrangements and considerable confusion. In short, the benefits of this model—identifying a clear goal and organizing to achieve it—may create conditions that make flexibility and change very difficult.

Modern Management Models: TQM and MBO

There are two promising alternatives to the scientific and bureaucratic models. These two modern empowerment management approaches have great promise for the human service industry. They are described as *empowerment models* because they give management and workers an opportunity to have input about the operations in an organization. Every approach or model has some limitations; so even with these models, carefully consider whether they are appropriate for use in your organization.

TOTAL QUALITY MANAGEMENT W. Edwards Deming, an American statistician, developed **total quality management** (TQM) in 1945. What is total quality management? TQM is a consumer-driven model of management. The focus of TQM is on continuous improvement, which is responsive to the needs and expectations of external customers and internal consumers (e.g., employees, funders, and vendors) that use or interact with services or products in the organization (Robbins & Coulter, 2009).

The two essential elements of TQM are continuous improvement and responsiveness. To achieve continuous improvement, an accurate statistical measurement is done of every critical variable of work processes in an organization. Each variable is compared to a fixed optimal standard, which then helps the managers to identify and correct a specific variable (e.g., response time to client took 45 minutes) that fell below the fixed optimal standard (e.g., if optimal response time to client is 10 minutes) in the work processes. This statistical quality control is repeatedly done to ensure that continuous improvements are achieved and maintained.

In practical terms, employees and managers need to have basic statistical knowledge to perform a quantitative analysis of the collected data. From these data, the quality of services for multiple consumers such as clients, organizations, and communities can be determined. Defining quality with respect to service can be difficult because the lives of clients can have conflicting needs. The process of continuous quality improvement requires accountability from every employee in an organization (Deming, 2008). The other element of TQM is responsiveness. From a systems perspective, all functions such as work processes, employees, managers, and departments are integral to the success of the delivery of services. Success comes with managers and workers learning to adapt to continuous change. Change is constant in the life of an organization and that will always be a fact.

THE SLOW ADOPTION OF TQM In the 1980s, TQM was adopted by many in the American private and public sectors and was embraced as an empowerment management approach (Swiss, 1992). In the United States, TQM was initially used to manage factory assembly-lines, but later was used in public agencies (Swiss, 1992) and in nonprofit human service organizations (Martin, 1993). Scholars suspected that these organizations were motivated to use TQM as a way to improve organization efficiency and authority (Kennedy & Fiss, 2009). Despite the motives for adoption of TQM, it took great commitment to use this empowerment management approach because it necessitated change in the organization's culture, system, and the individual work performance of each employee (Bedwell, 1993). Change is a difficult process for people (Argyris, 1991; Coutu, 2002; Kegan & Lahey, 2001) and organizations (Ashforth & Fried, 1988).

MANAGEMENT BY OBJECTIVES Peter Drucker, a world-renowned business educator, first conceptualized "management by objectives" in his book *The Practice of Management*. **Management by objectives (MBO)**—also known as management by results—involves employees and management in a process where they create mutually agreed-upon objectives that will be used to achieve the organization's goals (Robbins & Coulter, 2009). According to Drucker (1954), MBO is a process of collaboration in decision making, goal setting, and defining objectives. Scholars describe MBO as an approach or technique (Halpern & Osofsky, 1990; McConkey, 1973; Rodgers & Hunter, 1992) that includes the following practices:

1. MBO calls upon employees and managers to collectively negotiate where to take the organization by establishing clearly defined objectives to reach a common goal.
2. It is a motivational program in which managers and employees have sufficient authority over their own efforts to achieve a common goal, which maximizes their motivation to work toward a common goal.
3. MBO is a coordinated approach in which employees' efforts are blended into a total team effort to achieve greater total results for the organization.
4. MBO is an objective feedback approach in which controls and feedback mechanisms are created so there is continuous review and revision of objectives and adjustments to work activities to continue advancement toward the goal.
5. MBO calls for evaluation that uses feedback on task performance to gauge the employees' progress toward achieving their objectives; rewards are contingent on each employee's level of achievement.

In practical terms, MBO is driven by an organization's mission. From the mission you should be able to determine (1) the business focus of the organization, (2) the clients who are served, and (3) the objectives that the organization is trying to accomplish (Tauber, 1983).

Research has shown that MBO is a good management practice that leads to greater productivity in the public sector, the private sector (Rodgers & Hunter, 1992), and the nonprofit sector (McConkey, 1973). However, MBO will only work when the organizational leadership accepts it in place of their hierarchy, which creates superior–subordinate relationships.

Overall, TQM and MBO are now commonly used by public and nonprofit managers in human service organizations (Austin, 2002; Hardina & Montana, 2011). These empowerment-oriented management approaches have improved the quality of client service, increased worker productivity, inspired innovation, and enhanced interpersonal relationships within the workplace. Unlike the classic management theories, newer empowerment-oriented management takes a team approach to business and expands the decision-making roles of non-administrative staff and clients in human services organizations.

> ## Administration
>
> *Understanding and Mastery: Supervision and human resource management.*
>
> ---
>
> **Critical Thinking Question:** The supervisor's role is to help, educate, guide, and motivate all workers. In some organizations a human service practitioner will supervise a volunteer corps, which is an important human resource. What management theory or model (discussed in this chapter) might work best when supervising volunteers? Explain why the particular theory or model you have chosen would work better than another.

Practical Supervising Approaches

In this section, we will look at reports of *practice wisdom*. Practice wisdom is based on a practitioner's experiential activities in the field. For example, a manager could write an article or book about supervising approaches that he or she felt advanced the work of an organization. Practice wisdom is not supported by empirical studies, yet practice wisdom does offer you an insight into what practitioners are doing in the field. So imagine you have just been promoted to the rank of supervisor: What practical supervising approaches might you want to know? As a new supervisor, you might want to know how to orient workers on the job, how to teach workers on the job, and how to be a good leader.

ORIENTING WORKERS ON THE JOB Orienting new employees to a work unit takes a lot of time and effort. A comprehensive employee orientation involves relaying a tremendous amount of organizational information to the new employee. As a result, the supervisor doing an employee orientation must be prepared to give a comprehensive overview of the organization. During an orientation period, the supervisor should make sure new employees are given an orientation that would include (Sand, 2005)

1. an explanation of the organizational hierarchy,
2. overview of the organization's policies and procedures,
3. explanation of the laws that apply to the work done in the agency, and
4. information about the scope of the job and required duties.

Furthermore, the supervisor should be prepared to cover the history of the organization, explain the mission, describe the clients served, and explain roles of the board of directors, CEO, management, and different units in the organization. When possible, the new employee should also meet other employees and clients who are receiving services from the organization. A proper welcome into an organization makes new employees feel valued and gives them a sense of how people are collectively working toward the organization's goals.

TEACHING ON THE JOB The supervisor is also a teacher and instructs subordinates about their jobs. When a supervisor teaches workers about their jobs, he or she has to have knowledge of job descriptions and how job duties are done. Therefore, it is important that a supervisor knows how to communicate clear instructions to subordinates about how to perform their assigned duties (Brody, 2005). In the process of teaching subordinates, there needs to be a clear procedure for problem solving so that workers can resolve problems in a timely fashion (Sand, 2005).

Because supervisors are accountable for their subordinates' work performances, they need to keep abreast of worker activities by having regularly scheduled meetings with each subordinate (Kettner, 2014). It is important for the supervisor to make time to meet formally and informally with staff so that they have an opportunity to know their supervisor (Brody, 2005). Benefits of these meetings are that the supervisor learns about the strengths and weaknesses of each worker and can help staff improve job performance. An important part of supervision is to help staff improve job performance and identify positive examples to follow.

A supervisor creates the work culture in the unit. It is important for the supervisor to make sure that subordinates feel that they can ask for help to improve job performance and ask for help when they have made a mistake. Workers learn from their mistakes, but if they are covered up, the opportunity to learn is lost (Cannon & Edmondson, 2001). So supervisors must create a learning environment in which subordinates will feel they can be honest about their work performance and learn to be better workers.

LEADING THE UNIT   As the leader of the work unit, the supervisor must remain aware that he or she serves as a role model to workers in the unit. To successfully lead, a supervisor should engage every worker in an adult-to-adult relationship. In this relationship, both parties are respectful of the other's dignity, knowledge, skills, and time (Kettner, 2014). The supervisor must also be a good listener and empathetic to workers, yet keep a focus on quality job performance of workers (Brody, 2005). Moreover, a good leader builds team spirit in the work unit, helps workers understand the organizational goals, builds staff support, and actively seeks workers' innovative ideas to improve the organization's productivity.

As the staff collectively works toward the organizational goals, the supervisor will monitor them to ensure they stay on course. The supervisor helps workers meet work standards created by the organization by coaching and motivating staff to efficiently and effectively get their work done (Nolan & Johnson, 2011; Sand, 2005). To know whether workers are meeting standards, a supervisor will have to do performance evaluations. Evaluations are typically outlined in the organization's policies and should be done in a consistent manner (Kettner, 2014). Some of you might feel uncomfortable with the concept of doing an evaluation of another person, but you need to understand that performance evaluations are important to the organization for several reasons. First, a performance evaluation is used to give feedback to workers and can help improve their work performance. Second, the evaluation can help determine which workers are doing unsatisfactory work. Third, with the data collected from a performance evaluation the supervisor can determine whom to give or withhold rewards. Finally, if an organization has to terminate a worker who is underperforming, having performance evaluations will support that action.

Terminating a person is not a pleasant task. Yet a supervisor must show strong leadership by addressing and resolving problems in his or her work unit. To allow a nonperformer to remain in the work unit ultimately means impeding the collective work progression toward the organizational mission (Drucker, 2005). If the supervisor is involved in the termination of a worker in the unit, that worker, whether they are a paid staff member or a volunteer, should be terminated in a manner that preserves his or her dignity.

Managing Human Service Volunteers

Volunteers are an important part of the work team in human service organizations. Yet there is a growing resistance among professionals about volunteers functioning in a professional capacity, addressing complex social issues with clients, and taking time away from paid staff (Austin, 2002). Simply, professionals perceived volunteers as a threat to their status, time, and authority (Netting, Nelson, Borders, & Huber, 2004). Despite professional resistance to utilizing volunteers, the simple fact is, the nonprofit sector has become dependent upon the unpaid labor provided by volunteers (Drucker, 2005; Wolf, 1999). Volunteer services are worth approximately $239 billion per year, which makes these individuals an important financial asset to the nonprofit sector (Netting et al., 2004).

Creating a Volunteer Program

Each year a quarter of the American population volunteers, and on average a volunteer spends 50 hours in an organization (Bureau of Labor Statistics, 2012). Volunteers come with a broad range of backgrounds, skills, knowledge, and experience, which sometimes matches or even surpasses the paid staff. Volunteers with these types of backgrounds can be used by an organization to perform multiple functions. Overall, volunteers and paid staff collectively work toward the organization's goals.

Nonprofits are uniquely dependent upon volunteers because they play a vital role in the optimal functioning of the nonprofit sector (O'Neill, 2002) in roles such as service providers, fundraisers, program planners, policy makers, and community organizers. However, many nonprofits don't harness the productive labor of volunteers and have dysfunctional volunteer programs. If nonprofit organizations hope to keep their volunteers, they must develop policies that promote volunteer roles, define volunteer positions (Netting et al., 2004), and give volunteers meaningful job duties (Sand, 2005). These organizations need to create innovative volunteer programs and then effectively manage volunteers like paid staff. Seven actions have been identified that are essential to creating an effective volunteer program (Brundney, 2010; McCurley, 2005):

1. Identify reasons for having volunteers by doing a needs assessment.
2. Involve staff, volunteers, and clientele in designing the volunteer program.
3. Integrate the volunteer program into the organizational structure.
4. Make systematic efforts to recruit the right type and number of volunteers.
5. Design volunteer job descriptions with meaningful duties.
6. Have volunteer protocols for orientation, training, and supervising.
7. Make formal efforts to evaluate and recognize the work of volunteers.

IDENTIFY REASONS FOR SEEKING VOLUNTEERS   Before an organization begins to recruit volunteers, it must determine the reasons for seeking volunteers. A needs assessment can be used to help an organization determine where volunteers might be helpful (McCurley, 2005). The management of an organization must consider what type of volunteer they need and will work well for them. For example, some human service agencies sought volunteers who were baby boomers (people born between 1946 and 1964) because 70% of their clients belonged to that demographic group (Nashman, Morrison, & Duggal, 2008). These volunteers were valuable to the organization because they brought their experience, money, and network capabilities for recruiting skilled peers.

GETTING BUY-IN FROM STAFF   If you are hired to be a volunteer coordinator who is to start a new program, there are several things you need to know. To implement a volunteer program, you need buy-in (or support) from the paid staff whose job duties will be directly affected by your new program. If you don't have buy-in from this group, the volunteer program will likely be undermined by paid staff because they will perceive that their rights and job security are being threatened by the presence of volunteers (Brundney, 2010) or by your program.

Working from the bottom of the organizational hierarchy is the best strategy to get a new program under way. In other words, you will work at the grassroots level to cultivate interest, educate, and seek feedback from staff. You want to get the new program integrated into the organization, so staff should be asked for input about plans to build the volunteer program. The staff can give you realistic assessments of what is needed on the ground (Sand, 2005), and staff can explain how and where volunteers can be used most effectively. When the staff has a hand in creating a program they will be less likely to sabotage their own efforts.

You will also need to get buy-in from the administration. Typically administration has limited power over staff, but they do have the power to create a positive work environment that is open to change (Beer, Eisenstat, & Spector, 1990) and open to having a new volunteer program in the organization. When the administration has had a say in the building of a program, they too will make it easier for you to implement your program.

WORKING TOWARD PROGRAM INTEGRATION   To ensure that a new volunteer program is fully integrated into an existing organization, the program should have a definitive structure and organizational plan. Paid staff members need to know who will be responsible for managing volunteers. Having procedures and structure helps clarify to everyone in the workplace the expectations and limitations with respect to each worker's job and duties (Brundney, 2010).

RECRUITING VOLUNTEERS   Some people will volunteer spontaneously while others need to be recruited. According to the United States Bureau of Labor Statistics (2012), the volunteer rate rose from 26.3% to 26.8 % in the year ending September 2011. This new percentage equates to 64.3 million individuals volunteering in an organization at least one time between September 2010 and September 2011. The percent of people who volunteer remained virtually the same over the succeeding six years.

To successfully recruit volunteers, you need to understand their motivations. For instance, people are motivated to volunteer if the time commitment is short, because they have little time to offer (McCurley, 2005). People are more likely to volunteer if they know an organization will support them in their volunteering role. Because organizational support is perceived as respect, this makes working for this type of organization more desirable (Galindo-Kuhn & Guzley, 2001). People are less likely to volunteer for a high status organization, because they feel additional volunteers are not needed. People are less likely to volunteer for organizations when they have "undesirable" clientele such as the mentally ill, homeless, or sex workers.

With an understanding of what causes people to volunteer, you need to make motivational appeals to bring people in (McCurley, 2005). As in all good advertising, a motivational appeal must be tailored in a manner to appeal to a specific volunteer population. To successfully recruit volunteers, you also need to know where to find them. New volunteers can be recruited by peers who are already working for the organization, and volunteers can be

Explore Volunteer Match to view an example of an Internet-based referral system for nonprofit organizations.

recruited through direct advertising or via an Internet-based referral nonprofit organization like Volunteer Match.

Even though your organization might be in need of volunteers, you want to make sure you get the right person. Be selective and recruit the right type of volunteers to avoid personnel problems before they start. Seek out the people who have the skill set, and also be clear about people's motivations for wanting to volunteer. So make sure that the job is in line with what has motivated a person to volunteer (e.g., the accountant wanted to do something that put her in contact with people because she had no desire to work in an office anymore).

CREATING A VOLUNTEER JOB DESCRIPTION   Part of recruiting is offering people meaningful jobs in the organization. As the volunteer coordinator, you will have to create a list of volunteer jobs. Each job will need to have a detailed outline of general duties, time needed to do the job, and the knowledge and skills needed to do the job.

The ideal way to create a job description is in a small group that has individuals who are knowledgeable about (1) the organization's mission and goals, (2) the jobs that can best be done by volunteers, and (3) how the volunteer program will guide and support new volunteers. Does it take more time to create a job description in a group? Yes. But you are more likely to develop a better job description if the group includes a volunteer supervisor, line worker, and a client that the agency serves.

Good job descriptions are hard to produce, so instead of explaining how to do it in the abstract, you should try to create one with a small group in your class. Box 5.2 lists the critical elements found in a job description. In your group, discuss what traits and skills you would be looking for in a volunteer for an organization a member might work in.

After you have created a volunteer job description answer, the following questions: What was the easiest part of developing the job description? Using the job description, could a volunteer do the job you have described? Is there something in the job

---

Box 5.2   **Elements of a Job Description for a Volunteer**

1. General Volunteer Job Description

2. Role Description or Title

3. Person to Report to/Supervisor

4. Major Activities and Key Outputs

5. Work Hours and Work Location

6. Knowledge and Skills

7. Benefits

description that would motivate the volunteer to become involved with the organization? Would the skill set outlined in the job description result in attracting a small or large applicant pool? Are the major activities and key outputs measurable in the event you wanted to evaluate a volunteer's performance at a later date?

Supervising Volunteers

A major part of the volunteer coordinator's job involves the ongoing supervision of volunteers. To be an effective coordinator, you need to possess flexibility, people skills, heightened responsiveness, and commitment to the volunteer program (Carlsen, 1991). Supervising paid staff is similar to supervising volunteers because you must orient them to their jobs, train them to do their jobs, and lead them in the workplace.

VOLUNTEER ORIENTATION   Volunteers should be made to feel welcome in their work unit and the organization. The volunteer coordinator should make great effort to know why new volunteers have come to the organization. Volunteer assignments should match the person's interests. During the formal orientation, they need to be given a clear and straightforward explanation about the importance of their role. Each volunteer should be oriented to his or her unit and be introduced to staff members with whom he or she might be working. It is also important that volunteers realize that the work done by the organization is accomplished when people work as a team. Volunteers should be shown how their contribution of time and money are advancing the organization's mission and goals.

The volunteer orientation should mirror the staff orientation. This means the volunteer coordinator has to painstakingly review all aspects of the organization, operations, and goals. You will also need to conduct a risk management audit of volunteers to ensure that clients (especially vulnerable service populations) are not at risk while in the presence of volunteers (Forsyth, 1999). If you are wondering why a risk management audit is necessary, consider what happened to the administration of the Boys Scouts of America. At the time of this writing, the Boys Scouts of America has been accused of allegedly giving volunteers access to children without proper supervision, and some volunteers have been accused of child molestation. This case should make any supervisor pause before letting a volunteer have access to clients without checking first. Supervisors need to be cautious and prepared to scrutinize volunteers before they get access to clients. Only when the risk management audit is done can you determine the level of supervision that is appropriate for a volunteer, which is done for the wellbeing of the clients.

During the orientation, volunteers need to be made aware that nonperformance in their job can result in their termination. Yes, volunteers will need to be terminated. An organization is within its legal right to dismiss a volunteer who is inappropriate or unable to do his or her assigned task. However, before a volunteer is terminated, check with the human resources department to make sure that the right procedures are followed. A volunteer should be terminated in a manner that allows his or her dignity to remain intact.

VOLUNTEER TRAINING   A volunteer training program should be designed to help volunteers develop new skills. For instance, volunteers who desire to work directly with clients could be trained to do active listening or to engage in cross-class partnerships to assist clients out of poverty. The volunteer coordinator should make every effort to find volunteers the jobs that match their interests and skills. Then volunteers are trained to do the job that they have been assigned. Use the volunteer's job description to review the tasks, the time to complete tasks, and where the task will be done. Make sure that volunteers know who they report to if there are problems with an assignment, if their time commitment has changed, or if they are not happy in the volunteer position that they have chosen.

Training takes time and effort from staff. If the staff becomes dependent on volunteers to complete certain tasks, it is very disruptive to a work unit if they fail to show. It might be better to give volunteers short-term commitments to ensure they can complete the assignment. Volunteers have multiple obligations in their lives, and the coordinator should appreciate that those personal obligations are just as important.

LEADING VOLUNTEERS IN THE WORKPLACE   Once volunteers are working at completing their tasks, it is important for the coordinator to coach and encourage them to maintain or increase the quality of their work. Make effective and efficient use of volunteers by being clear about what specific tasks the volunteer will be doing. All volunteers should be given a work performance review so the coordinator knows whether they are capable of doing the assigned job. Volunteers need feedback (just as staff) from the coordinator so they can make adjustments to their work performance if necessary. Supervision also means being aware of volunteers' job assignments, work performance, scheduling, and problems.

Volunteer meetings need to be held so everyone is brought up to speed about what is and is not going on inside of the organization. This meeting can be used not only to update volunteers but also as a time for problem solving. Volunteers also need recognition for their dedication, loyalty, and work for the organization. To make sure the volunteers are recognized, the volunteer coordinator should design a program within the organization and the community that highlights the work of volunteers in company newsletters and local newspapers. Individual volunteer recognition from the coordinator can be made through emails, personal handwritten letters, a parking spot for volunteer of the month, or awards given at a special events dinner. All of these things are important to people who volunteer.

Is there more to supervising and managing than what has been outlined in this chapter? Yes! But there is enough information here to get you started. If you consider the management of people and groups as a skill, then you have to accept that it takes time and effort to develop this skill before you become proficient.

Managing Diversity in the Workplace

Many human service organizations' missions focus on social justice and equity and in turn their workers labor to empower clients. It would be conceivable that these same organizations would be equally devoted to creating work environments that were just, equitable, and empowering for their workers. However, it might surprise you to know that human service organizations have not had the best work environments. These organizations have admirable missions that are humane and community minded, but they have problems that mirror those found in other work environments. Some of those problems deal with managing diversity in the workplace.

Gender Issues

Let's review gender issues from a historical and sociopolitical perspective. In the United States, women's traditional role focused on taking care of the home and children. However, the role of women would be transformed during World War I when industrial factories lost their male labor pool to the armed forces. This void in the labor pool gave women the opportunity to work outside of the home.

Women were encouraged by patriotic government advertising to leave their jobs in the home and join the workforce to support the war effort. Large numbers of women took jobs in factories that provided for the first time round the clock daycare. Women worked in jobs that had been traditionally reserved for and held by men. At the same time that World War I efforts were focused on securing democracy in Europe, other efforts were being advanced by women's groups to secure greater democratic rights for women in the United States.

Shortly after the war ended, progressive women's groups successfully pushed for the 19th Amendment to the United States Constitution, which was ratified in the summer of 1920. The 19th Amendment prohibits citizens from being denied the right to vote based on their sex, and this right cannot be denied or reduced by the United States or any state. For the first time in U.S. history, women were given the right to vote!

Although women were granted the right to vote, this did not radically change women's traditional roles. It was not until the 1960s that the Women's Movement ignited one of the biggest social movements in U.S. history. American feminists directly challenged the status quo and sought greater equity in all spheres of life for women, especially in the workplace (Brownmiller, 1999).

Watch the PBS 3-part video series titled **"Makers: Women Who Make America"** to learn more about the Women's Movement and the difficulties women experienced and continue to experience in the workplace.

Because of the social and political influence of the feminist movement, the role of women began to change. For example, more women were working outside of the home, and employers had to contend with having the influx of women in the workplace. However, across the board employers were less than accommodating to women in the workplace. Because of employer resistance, new federal laws had to be created such as the Equal Pay Act of 1963. This Act requires employers to pay women and men equally for doing the same work. Simply, equal pay for equal work! The Equal Pay Act was followed by the Civil Rights Act of 1964, which prohibited discrimination against women, racial, ethnic, national, and religious minorities.

With federal legislation in place, you would think the workplace would have eliminated discrimination, prejudice, and sexual discrimination, but that is not the case, even in the modern day work environment. President Barack Obama signed new legislation to rectify the process of fighting against pay discrimination. The first legislation that President Obama signed into law was the Lilly Ledbetter Fair Pay Act in 2009. This federal law amends Title VII of the Civil Rights Act of 1964 by altering the statute of limitations for filing an equal pay lawsuit regarding pay discrimination in the workplace.

So have things changed for women in the workplace? More importantly, do women have equal job opportunities and get equal pay? Currently, for every dollar men make, women make only seventy-seven cents. This difference in pay over a lifetime of work translates in the loss of thousands of dollars for women. There still are few women who head multinational corporations (Sandberg, 2013). Women are the largest employee group in the human service industry, but few women occupy positions in administration, management, or lead boards in nonprofit human service organizations

(Joslyn, 2009; Nagada & Gutierrez, 2000). So the glass ceiling (that invisible barrier between lower-level and upper-level jobs) has only been slightly cracked, and only a few women slip through. The women who do slip into the upper ranks of their organization are often put in the position of having to continually prove to others that they are deserving of an upper-level position. For the moment, women's upward mobility into leadership positions in the workplace seems to have stalled (Sandberg, 2013).

Women's lives are also complicated by social norms of marriage. In a traditional marriage (between a woman and man), the woman is expected to multitask as she cares for the children and completes the chores to keep her home running. Some describe this additional work as the woman's second shift (Hochschild & Machung, 2012). In the traditional marriage with children, women are left to figure out the work–life balance, while many husbands and traditional organizations turn a blind eye to the reality of family commitments.

If you want organizations that are just, equitable, and empowering, then the leadership must be prepared for organizational change. There is no magic; there is only commitment to change. So the organization that embraces change will serve its workers and clients better.

Race Issues

Race problems are real, and they invade our lives, our jobs, and the world we live in. Let's review race issues in the workplace from a sociopolitical perspective to begin to get a sense of how racism affects human service organizations.

The mission of many nonprofit human services organizations embodies the ideology of social justice and equity for individuals who lack the means to achieve it independently. It would then follow that the leadership of these organizations would be sensitive to groups that have experienced injustice and inequity in all spheres of life such as the workplace. However, few racial minorities head or manage nonprofit human service organizations (Joslyn, 2009) even though minorities comprise a large portion of the personnel pool (McNeely, 1992). Yet when the issue of racial and ethnic barriers is broached with boards of directors and upper-level administrators (who are predominantly white and male), they perceive this line of questioning as a personal attack (Nagada & Gutierrez, 2000). Often minority human services workers frame the problem of being barred from boards and upper levels of administration in a racial context, which creates racial tensions within organizations (Peters & Masaoka, 2000).

The few racial minorities who do have career success and move into upper management are faced with extreme challenges because their career success is dependent upon adoption of the symbols, language, and beliefs of the dominant culture (Nagada & Gutierrez, 2000). As minorities (and for that matter women) ascend into positions of power, they are pressured to conform to the dominant cultural norms. This results in cultural marginality, which does irreparable damage to racial minorities as they negotiate between their own culture and the dominant culture. In turn, some minorities in upper-level management become isolated because they have no personal or political support.

Compliance to the informal and formal cultural norms keeps the status quo intact and reduces the anxiety of the dominant group (Katz, 1989), but these norms are the basis of employment barriers. When women and other minority groups are excluded from upper-level management and boards, this exclusion impedes the overall functioning of human services organizations. Without women and other minority groups physically present in board rooms and executive suites, the problem of racism and sexism will probably be overlooked. It is incumbent upon human service leadership to remain aware of complex diversity issues and change diversity management policies and practices (Harvey & Allard, 2012).

Disability Issues

Disability problems are sometimes not covered in diversity discussions, but it is unequivocally a diversity issue that must be managed in the workplace. Globally, there are over 600 million individuals with a disability that was acquired through a disease process, physical injury, or by some other cause (Robinson, West, & Woodworth, 1995). In the United States, there are approximately 56.7 million people living with some type of disability (Brault, 2012), and a large percentage (14 million) of those people are in the workforce. Disability issues are everyone's issues. At any point and time, you or any other person could become disabled, and anyone could instantly become part of this growing minority group.

Disabilities movements, though relatively new, have affected many changes in the American society. Disabled citizens have organized into political and social organizations throughout the country and have been fighting widespread discrimination (Pardeck, 2005) As a result, advocates in the disabilities movement have also been working to get equal access to employment, education, housing, and all the amenities in their communities. To learn about the disability movements in the United States, go to the PBS link and preview the Independent Lens video titled *Like an Emancipation Proclamation for the Disabled*.

Watch the PBS Independent Lens video titled *Like an Emancipation Proclamation for the Disabled* to learn about the U.S. disabilities movement.

The ideology of human service organizations centers on social justice and equity for individuals who can't achieve it for themselves. Yet people with disabilities, like other minority groups and women, are often denied employment opportunities or advancements in human service organizations (Nagada & Gutierrez, 2000). The Americans with Disabilities Act of 1990 (ADA)—the country's first comprehensive civil rights law—prohibits discrimination of the disabled in employment, telecommunication, public accommodations, and public services. In addition, the ADA addresses the needs of people with disabilities.

ADA defines disability as a physical or mental impairment that substantially limits a major life activity. There are groups of different titles of the ADA, but we will examine only Title I—Employment. Title I of the ADA states that an employment agency or labor organization cannot discriminate against a qualified individual with a disability, which applies to job application procedures, hiring, job advancement, and job training. ADA was amended in 2008 to restore the intent and protections of the original Act of 1990.

To learn more about the ADA legislation and its amendments go to the following links:

Americans with Disabilities Act of 1990

ADA Amendments Act of 2008

The failure to manage diversity problems in the workplace means discrimination and sexual harassment will continue unchecked. Addressing diversity is beyond the scope of this book, but that doesn't mean you can't do something now. At the individual level, you can take time to learn about the history of the women's movement and the history of race relations in the United States from books and documentaries. You can also take time and self-reflect about your beliefs, values, and practices. Be honest with yourself and remember no one is perfect. If you wish to contribute to positive change, begin by taking the time to understand the complex dynamics of diversity. Managing diversity is an important human services practice, and you've got to get it right for the sake of clients and the people you work with.

Self-Development

Understanding and Mastery: Awareness of diversity.

Critical Thinking Question: In human services organizations, some practitioners will face problems related to managing diversity. In the human services profession, awareness of diversity issues is critical to the practitioner's overall practice. Diversity awareness should enable practitioners to promote a work environment that is just, equitable, and empowering to both workers and clients. Imagine you are working in a human service organization that focuses on poor women's issues in rural America. While working in the organization you learn that men typically are not advanced into the upper ranks of management. How might you go about creating change in such an organization, which would lead to less discriminatory practices in the workplace?

Summary

Possessing knowledge and skills to manage a human service organization is essential if nonprofits are going to effectively compete and survive in a competitive business market. The process of managing focuses on how to manipulate an organizational system and its workers to bolster effective and efficient products or services. To manage a nonprofit organization, it is essential to understand how its organizational hierarchy works. First, there is a board of directors comprised of volunteers who serve as the top leadership to advance the organization's mission and vision through activities such as fundraising. Second, there is the CEO or director who answers to the board and oversees the day-to-day operations of the organization and interfaces with the service community and other stakeholders. Middle managers are directly involved with the internal functions and oversee the key operational components of the organizations such as personnel, payroll, facilities, services or deliverables, and clients or customers. Finally, supervisors oversee the work of direct-service workers, general staff, and volunteers to ensure the work of the organization is being done.

Human services administration and management have the benefit of classic management theories and TQM and MBO models to support their practice. Not all management theories and models work equally well in the human service workplace. However, human service organizations are in need of better management to create better work environments, especially for their volunteers. Volunteers are the life's blood of the nonprofit sector, and there are management strategies to recruit, train, and retain this group of workers in nonprofit organizations. In addition, management must also learn how to handle diversity issues in the workplace to ensure all workers and volunteers are treated fairly despite gender, race, or their disability status.

Assess your analysis and evaluation of this chapter's content by completing the Chapter Review.

CHAPTER 6

Fundraising in Human Services

· ·

The overall growth of the nonprofit sector has been bolstered by government financial support. This support is given to nonprofits in the form of grants, contracts, and fee-for-service agreements (Salamon, 2002), and it is the largest source of revenue for the nonprofit sector (O'Neill, 2002). Many nonprofit organizations have become overly dependent on government financial support because they have failed to develop other income streams to maintain their organizational operations. Sometimes nonprofit organizations even move away from their missions in order to get or keep their government funding. This shift away from one's original mission is called **mission drift** (Anheier, 2005; Austin, 2002).

When a nonprofit organization is financially dependent on a single external funding source for the majority of their operations, it inadvertently gives the external funder a lot of influence and power over the organization. To avoid undue influence of an external funder—like the government—some nonprofit organizations won't take external funding. As noble as that may sound, this leaves these organizations in a constant battle to remain financially solvent. However, there is an alternative way to develop new funding streams, which can be done through fundraising.

Fundraising is an organized management function for raising capital by soliciting money from private citizens, businesses, government agencies, and foundations so that an organization can carry out its mission-related activities (Ozdemir, Altinkemer, De, & Ozcelik, 2010). In nonprofits, fundraising is the primary method used to generate

Chapter Outline

income that supports day-to-day operations, staff salaries, and programs (Hager, Rooney, & Pollak, 2002). However, many nonprofits have no development officer or staff dedicated to fundraising. As a result, nonprofit human service organizations, especially smaller ones, are not effectively utilizing fundraising strategies to generate revenue. Also, many organizations continue to use old fundraising approaches despite the changes in demographics, socioeconomics, and technology (Miller, 2009).

Fundraising Strategies

When staff or volunteers are asked to engage in fundraising, they typically dread doing it because they feel it is equivalent to begging for money (Burnett, 2002; Lysakowski, 2005). Their misgivings about fundraising are often sparked by a lack of knowledge about the process. However, when people understand the many different fundraising strategies, it can transform their negative perceptions of the process.

Fundraising is a process that is backed by in-depth research. Fundraising research covers topics such as the psychology of giving (Bell, 2009), building effective fundraising teams (Stephens, 2004), identifying insufficient fundraising approaches (Jacobs & Marudas, 2006), and developing compelling fundraising letters (Bekkers & Crutzen, 2007). In addition, there is a wealth of practical fundraising information that can be described as practice wisdom. Both empirical and practice wisdom literature contain information that can expand one's knowledge and skill set in fundraising.

Relationship Fundraising

Let's examine three promising fundraising strategies. We will start with relationship fundraising, which is a donor-centered approach. This means the fundraiser focuses his or her attention on creating a relationship with a prospective donor before asking for a pledge, donation, or gift. How does it work? According to Ken Burnett (2002), an expert fundraiser, **relationship fundraising** is based on these concepts:

1. Donors give to people and not to an organization.
2. Donors need to be inspired to give with clear and consistent messages.
3. Fundraisers who are also donors have greater insight into why other donors give.
4. Fundraisers must be knowledgeable about donors.
5. Fundraisers must recognize who should be asked for a donation.
6. Fundraisers should appeal to the donor's emotions by sharing passionate stories.
7. Fundraisers must be compassionate and appreciate a donor's perspective.
8. Fundraisers should establish a friendship with donors before asking for donations.
9. Fundraisers must properly and thoughtfully thank those who donate.
10. Fundraisers need to be clear about how donations are used.
11. Fundraising should be framed as an opportunity to be involved with a cause rather than an opportunity to ask for donations.

With those concepts in mind, let's examine what it takes to become a good relationship fundraiser. People who make the best relationship fundraisers are committed, knowledgeable, and have had a long-term relationship with the organization. Having a relationship with the organization only partially prepares a person to go out to do this type of fundraising. Fundraisers must also be dedicated to learning about their prospective donors.

Prior to a meeting with prospective donors, a relationship fundraiser will learn all that he or she can about the donors. Learning about prospective donors can be accomplished by engaging in qualitative and quantitative research. Surveys, questionnaires, or interviews can be conducted with prospective donors to determine their primary giving motivations, beliefs, values, and attitudes. In addition, a computer search of public records could be done to develop donor demographics data. With donor data, fundraisers can determine who is more likely to make a substantial donation to the organization.

Once the fundraiser has identified prospective donors—known as prospects—the next step is to begin building relationships with these donors. Prospective donors who are most likely to give are called by the fundraiser who arranges a series of face-to-face meetings. During the initial meetings, the fundraiser's primary focus is to build a relationship with the prospect. This can be done by the fundraiser sharing compelling stories that demonstrate his or her genuine commitment to the organization's cause. In turn, the prospective donor is also encouraged to share his or her stories. After multiple person-to-person contacts, a relationship begins to form between the fundraiser and the prospective donor.

To solidify the newly formed relationships, the fundraiser makes sure that the prospective donors are continually provided with compelling organizational materials about the cause. Prospects are also kept informed about important topics and activities of the organization in a timely manner to keep them connected. Because the hallmark of relationship fundraising is honesty and transparency, prospective donors are also updated about the organization's finances and how past donations have been used.

Discussions about donations—referred to as the "ask"—are entered into once a relationship exists between the prospect and fundraiser. With a sense of connection between the two parties, the fundraiser makes an appeal for money or major gifts. The objective of relationship fundraising is to make prospects feel connected and passionate about the organization's mission in order to maximize donations in the long term. With the right donor, a relationship fundraiser can solicit extremely lucrative gifts for the organization (Burnett, 2002).

Strategic Fundraising

Strategic fundraising is another approach that can be used to develop revenue for an organization. Strategic fundraising is a mission-based approach (Warwick 2000), which means the organization's mission is critical to the process of setting fundraising objectives and goals, but there is much more to this fundraising strategy. There are five steps to strategic fundraising (Rice & Keller, 2011):

1. Evaluate the present situation of your organization.
2. Determine your organization's fundraising opportunities.
3. Use benchmarking to compare your organization with other organizations.
4. Establish goals for your organization based on the mission.
5. Design a fundraising plan.

Implementing strategic fundraising first involves conducting a comprehensive analysis of the organization's fundraising activities. This analysis should include an overview of current supporters, fundraising needs, and the fundraising program's growth or decline (Rice & Keller, 2011). The analysis should shed light on the organization's fundraising capacity, immediate funding needs, and where the organization can solicit new funds. The data from this comprehensive analysis are incorporated into a long-term fundraising plan.

The second step in the process is assessing the organization's fundraising opportunities. This assessment is done to determine what activities the donors support and where the donors come from (i.e., public or private sectors). The donor information should also illuminate what fundraising activities have attracted prospects and what will maintain current donor giving.

Because fundraising is costly, organizations must determine whether it pays to continue certain types of fundraising activities. Therefore, an assessment must be done of the organization's financial health by evaluating the organization's revenue and expenditures as they relate to their fundraising activities. This evaluation will help an organization identify what fundraising activities give the best return on time, energy, and money spent.

The third step in strategic fundraising requires that the organization compare and measure its outcomes against organizations that are similar in size, activities, donor pool, and so on. This comparison will allow the organization to measure its fundraising impact, donor support, growth, and return on investments. This measure is considered benchmarking and gives an organization a sense of how successful it is in comparison to peers and its own goals. Remember, functioning in a silo is not good business strategy, so to remain competitive in the fundraising arena organizations must be aware of what is going on in other organizations.

The fourth step of strategic fundraising involves setting goals and creating a plan. Before goals can be set, an organization needs to review its program needs and fundraising potential (e.g., have personnel, funds, and time to do the planned activities). Annual goals should include operational goals, monetary goals, and activity goals (Rice & Keller, 2011). These goals should be based, in part, on the organization's strategic plan. A strategic plan is a blueprint to guide an organization's future actions. The plan must be compatible with an organization's interests, limitations, and strengths (Brody, 2005). To get a sense of what a strategic plan is, review Box 6.1.

Box 6.1	**Strategic Plan Components and Process**

Components:
- Mission statement
- Vision of the organization over a three- to five-year time span
- Objectives and goals to be completed in three to five years
- Internal strengths and weaknesses of the organization
- External opportunities available to the organization
- External threats to the organization
- Critical issues to the organization
- Actions for each critical issue and timeline
- Key stakeholders are identified to be accountable for each critical issue

The final step of strategic fundraising involves creating a plan that incorporates all that has been learned about the organization's operational challenges, current and prospective donors, prior plan failures, more effective fundraising strategies, and what other organizations have done. The plan is a collaborative effort among active members of the organization and should prioritize objectives and goals that focus the organization.

The fundraising plan should outline the coordinated activities and spell out the goals to be achieved. This will keep staff and volunteers involved. The plan must also outline a fundraising strategy that considers the organization's potential for growth, which takes a balanced approach to the use of its resources, time, and energy. In addition, the organization's budget should be used to determine the appropriate fiscal allocations to achieve the strategic fundraising goals.

A fundraising plan should not be a static document; therefore, the plan needs a built-in feedback mechanism. With continual feedback, a plan can be adjusted, but this can happen only if the feedback is frequently collected and reviewed. After a review of the feedback, the plan can be modified to keep it significant.

You've Got Mail: Email Marketing

One of the most cost-effective ways to reach donors and prospective donors is through email marketing (Sargeant & Shang, 2010). **Email marketing** can be done with announcements, newsletters, event invitations, or other types of notifications. In the electronic marketing realm, there is much to know about keeping an email list updated, limiting email sent to donors, and avoiding spam filters. If an organization hopes to effectively use email marketing for fundraising, it needs to know there is a steep learning curve before the potential of the software can be realized. In other words, staff using new marketing software must be given time to learn how it works.

Once staff members are trained to use the email marketing software, they can begin to manage email communications to the donor base much more efficiently. Despite having powerful software on hand, staff must carefully compose and edit written materials before they are electronically sent from the organization.

Email marketing software can be programmed to target different types of supporters so the entire donor base will not be inundated with unnecessary emails. Similar software also allows the organization to collect information about people who come to the site. This information can be compiled and used to add to the existing database of prospective donors. Email marketing software can be used to advance a fundraising campaign, but a discussion of the complexities is beyond the scope of this book.

Other Online Fundraising

Technology has revolutionized communication among people in the United States and around the world. **Social media** usage, for example, has become a very important communication strategy among U.S. nonprofit charities (Barnes & Mattson, 2009). Organizations using social media (e.g., Facebook) for fundraising have successfully generated higher financial returns compared to traditional mailing campaigns (Finch, 2009). Yet some nonprofits are not utilizing the full potential of fundraising technology using social-media networks to inform people or to get people involved (Waters, Burnett, & Lucas, 2009).

Large nonprofits have been quick to incorporate new fundraising technology. This technology has allowed them to reach donors and prospects via their websites, which are enhanced with online-giving interfaces (Hogan, 2012). Conversely, small nonprofit organizations have been slower to adopt new fundraising technology. This reluctance to use fundraising technology might be due to a fear of change, but the current reality is that organizations using online fundraising strategies are experiencing revenue growth.

Approximately 5% ($14.7 billion) of the total charitable giving in the United States is now done online (Sargeant & Shang, 2010). This fact makes it important that organizations have an online presence. Furthermore, prospective donors are suspicious of nonprofits that have no website or email (Hitchcock, 2004). That suspicion will likely result in fewer donations because an organization without a website can't be taken seriously.

AN EXAMPLE OF A FUNDRAISING WEBSITE: The Operation Gratitude website is a good example of a website with an effective fundraising component. Operation Gratitude is a nonprofit organization that sends care packages to U.S. military personnel throughout the world. Operation Gratitude's mission states:

> Go to the website of **Operation Gratitude** to see an example of a nonprofit website.

> Operation Gratitude seeks to lift morale and put smiles on faces by sending care packages addressed to individual Soldiers, Sailors, Airmen and Marines deployed in harm's way, to their children left behind, and to Veterans, Wounded Warriors and First Responders.

—Used by permission of Operation Gratitude, Inc.

Carolyn Blashek, the founder and current board president of Operation Gratitude, has graciously offered the Operation Gratitude website for you to examine and learn from.

What attracts donors to a nonprofit website? In a study of fundraising websites, five elements were identified that attracted donors to a nonprofit's website: (a) accessibility, (b) accountability, (c) education, (d) empowerment, and (e) interaction (Sargeant, West, & Jay, 2007). When you examine the Operation Gratitude website, the element of accessibility is apparent. On each page of the organization's website, donate buttons are readily accessible. There is no need to click half a dozen links to a place where the donor can make a donation: The buttons are visible in the upper right side of the webpages. Donations can be made online with a credit card, by mail, with securities or stocks, through a vehicle donation, or a used cell phone donation, or people can purchase products from the Gratitude Store or the Official eBay auction site. Every purchase helps Operation Gratitude raise funds so they can send more care packages to military service members. Thus, donors can make donations by various methods with relative ease, which is an attractive feature of this site.

With respect to the education element, the home page has two links: one is "About Us" and the other link is "Programs." These links will take a prospect to news clips, videos, and other information about the organization. If a prospect has the time, he or she can be thoroughly educated about the organization's activities. Having comprehensive information about an organization allows a prospect to be educated and informed, which helps a person make an informed decision about donating.

Empowerment is another essential element that attracts people to a fundraising site. Operation Gratitude has a "Contact Us" webpage that lists all of its social media sites (Facebook, Twitter, and LinkedIn). Prospects can use these social-media feeds to communicate with staff or other donors. As a result, a prospect, donor, or volunteer has the opportunity to contribute to the conversations that are occurring on different social media sites. Having the opportunity to share thoughts or suggestions can be an empowering act.

Interaction is another element that attracts people to a fundraising website. Operation Gratitude's social media sites allow for person-to-person interaction. If you look at the online discussions, you will observe that many people are involved. In addition to online interaction, Operation Gratitude's homepage contains links titled "Get Involved" and "Volunteer." Off the electronic site, donors and others have the opportunity to participate in a full range of activities such as writing letters to service members, community projects, or working on special fundraising events. These events also allow people to interact, but more importantly they appear to keep people engaged with the organization.

The last element to examine is accountability, which means being legally responsible or answerable to someone (in this case the donor). To get a sense of how Operation Gratitude is accountable to its donors, on the home page a prospect can click "About Us." This link takes the prospective donor to an assortment of information about the organization. One pressing question that prospects have about donations is where the donations are going. Operation Gratitude's website contains easy-to-read reports that explain how donated funds and resources are used. If a prospect has additional questions, there also is a "Contact Us" link for general information. Plus emails are provided to specific divisions and officers in the organization.

We have looked at a website that appears to contain elements designed to attract donors, but if a prospect wants an outside view of an organization, there are fundraising watchdogs that can provide additional information about a registered nonprofit. Online intermediaries such as GuideStar or Foundation Center are nonprofit organizations that serve as fundraising watchdogs (Hogan, 2012). They provide searchable databases that contain information about millions of U.S. nonprofits, including their missions, programs, outcomes, governance, fundraising, and other fiscal practices. The information from these databases (such as IRS 990 form that is filed by a registered nonprofit) can help donors make informed decisions about their giving (Ozdemir et al., 2010), and when there is proof that donations are effectively being used by an organization, donors are more apt to give.

> Review information about a registered U.S. nonprofit go to any of the following fundraising watchdogs' websites: *Guide Star: Foundation Center*. Locate a nonprofit human service organization's IRS 990 form; what information from that form would help a donor decide to give to that organization?

Fundraising: A Human Services Practice

It is becoming a trend in nonprofits to hire full-time fundraising professionals—also known as **development professionals** (Burnett, 2002). Typically, a development professional engages in growing the donor base, writing grant proposals, managing fundraising activities, and overseeing the board of director's fundraising efforts to ensure they are fulfilling their primary fundraising obligations to the organization (Alexander & Carlson, 2005).

Approximately 63% of nonprofits have no full-time development professionals (Hager, Rooney, & Pollak, 2002). Nonprofits that hire development professionals typically task them only with grant writing. Some believe that grants can offer an organization a large income stream compared to other fundraising activities.

Should a development professional spend the majority of his or her time writing grants? To answer that question, consider the following facts about charitable giving in the United States. Charitable contributions are distributed among the following types of organizations: (a) human services, (b) education, (c) environment and wildlife, (d) public and society, (e) arts, (f) culture and humanities, (g) international, and (h) religion (Burnett, 2002). In Table 6.1, contributions made to these organizations are listed in descending order with respect to the amount contributed (Giving USA, 2012).

In 2011, contributions made to nonprofits by different sources included individuals ($217.79 billion), foundations ($41.67 billion), bequests ($24.41 billion), and corporations ($14.55 billion). For the past six years, on average, approximately 5% comes from corporations, 10% comes from foundations, and 80% of private donations come from individuals. The majority of individuals donating money are from the middle- and working-class income brackets (Klein, 2004).

The answer to the question of whether a development professional should spend the majority of his or her time writing grants would be, No! If 80% of donations come from individuals (who are middle class and working class), it is statistically more probable that an organization will generate more revenue by targeting individual donors than philanthropic foundations. So, if grant writing is not generating enough revenue for the organization, it might be time to refocus fundraising efforts that go after donor dollars.

Many human service organizations have only a single development professional, but fundraising events of the kind identified in Table 6.2 require a dedicated group of people. Volunteers can be used to supplement a small development staff. Volunteers can work in a full range of fundraising events. In fact, fundraising is the main activity of 11% of women volunteers and 8.9% of men volunteers in the United States (Bureau of Labor Statistics, 2012). Successful fundraising campaigns are run by volunteers in many nonprofits (Lysakowski, 2005).

Table 6.1	Contributions by Type of Recipient Organization During 2011
Organization Type	**Contributions**
Religion	$95.88 billion
Education	$38.87 billion
Gifts to foundations*	$25.83 billion
Human services	$35.39 billion
Public-society benefit	$21.37 billion
Health	$24.75 billion
International affairs	$22.68 billion
Arts, culture, & humanities	$13.12 billion
Environment & animals	$7.81 billion
Foundation grants to individuals	$3.75 billion
Unallocated	$8.97 billion

*Estimate developed jointly by Foundation Center and Giving USA

Table 6.2	Fundraising Events and Activities

Type of Event	Explanation of the Activities
Annual Fund	This type of event is planned by an organization each year as a way to grow their donor base and solicit regular donations to be used for daily operations of an organization and its programs.
Capital Campaigns	This type of campaign occurs every ten years in the life of the organization and is used to raise money for a specific project that has a fixed budget and timeline so an organization could purchase a building, property, or equipment.
Direct-Response Fundraising	This type of fundraising is an interactive process that addresses donors through different advertising media in which the organization's mission or cause is explained. People are asked to be involved with the cause and are solicited donations that can be made via the organization's toll-free number, email, or webpage.
Disaster Fundraising	This is an appeal made to help victims of a specific man-made disaster (house fire or war) or a natural disaster (hurricane or flood). Disaster appeals are often made via direct-response television advertising.
Endowment	This is a permanent fund that is invested, and a portion of the annual dividends (income) is used for the organization's operations or other specific purposes. Primarily, it is used for the perpetual upkeep and benefit of the organization.
Foundation Fundraising	Foundations exist to support nonprofit organizations. Foundations have a request for proposal, which involves nonprofits applying for their grants. A request for proposal is then judged to determine if it will or will not be funded.
Major Gifts Fundraising	These gifts are solicited from donors or businesses willing to give a relatively large donation in comparison to the average donations made to a fundraising campaign.
Mobile Giving	This type of giving is done via cellular phone by texting a specific word provided by an organization making the appeal, which is then sent to a specific phone number that is also provided by the organization.
Planned Giving	This type of donation involves a donor making a gift of their assets via bequests, trusts, annuities, which require legal documentation. If the gift is made when the donor is alive, it is conveyed by a trust. If the gift is made through the donor's will, it comes from their estate. Other terms used for this type of donation are legacy giving, gift giving, or deferred giving.
Sequential Fundraising	This involves securing a substantial gift first to build some momentum to get others to make donations.
Special Events Fundraising	This includes a wide range of activities that have a theme for a specific audience. Special events include activities such as auctions, dances, walks, wine tasting, or gold tournaments, which are all designed to raise money for a cause via direct donations, underwriters, ticket sales, or purchase of merchandise and services.
Sustainer Programs	This type of program is also referred to as monthly gifts. Donors may spread their donations over a period of time (e.g., year) and give the organization a regular amount of money each month, which are used to supplement the annual fund.
Telemarketing Fundraising	This direct-response fundraising activity involves making calls via a landline to solicit prospects or active donors. Donations can be made with credit card.

Recruiting and Managing Fundraising Volunteers

Chapter 5 includes a discussion of ways to integrate and supervise volunteers in a human service organization, but **fundraising volunteers** are in a special class all by themselves. In a human service organization, it is a good idea to put a volunteer coordinator in charge of volunteers of all kinds, but it is especially appropriate for fundraising volunteers. If volunteers have no experience in fundraising, they will need to be trained and supervised. Supervision of volunteers encompasses the activities of recruiting, training, and retaining. Moreover, supervision of fundraising volunteers has special challenges.

Recruiting Fundraising Volunteers

Volunteers are customarily recruited through an extensive organizational network that includes board members, management, staff, and active volunteers (Burnett, 2002), but recruiting volunteers to be a part of a fundraising campaign can be a major challenge.

So who makes a good fundraising volunteer? Some believe that volunteers who are committed to the mission of the organization are more apt to make effective fundraisers (Lysakowski, 2003) because committed volunteers can effectively transmit their enthusiasm and relay compelling stories, which makes it easier for them to solicit donations from prospectives (Burnett, 2002). Moreover, committed volunteers who are also donors feel empowered to ask others for donations because they have a sense of great moral authority (Stephens, 2004). In terms of recruiting, committed volunteers might be the first group of people to recruit for fundraising events. However, this pool of volunteers might not yield enough people. As a result, it might be necessary to recruit people from outside of the organization.

WRITING A VOLUNTEER JOB DESCRIPTION In general, the process of recruiting fundraising volunteers necessitates doing a comprehensive labor requirement analysis. This analysis will help a volunteer coordinator determine what activities are suitable for volunteers to have in a fundraising event (Wymer & Sargeant, 2010). This analysis will also be instrumental to the process of creating volunteer job descriptions.

A job description should be clearly written so an applicant can clearly comprehend what work duties are required and what goals are to be accomplished (Pecora & Austin, 1987). Some argue that writing a job description is labor intensive because it requires multiple redrafts of the document (Wolf, 1999). Overall, a good job description might result in attracting the right person to apply to be a volunteer for the organization (Wymer & Sargeant, 2010).

You might think writing a job description isn't hard. Let's test your skills at writing a job description for a fundraising volunteer. Go back to Table 6.2 and pick one fundraising event you would hire a volunteer for, and then write the job description in a group. The group should have four or five people. The group must use the six headings in the job description outlined in Box 6.2. All group members must agree about the job description that will be produced by the group.

TRAITS OF THE IDEAL VOLUNTEER Ideally, you want to recruit fundraising volunteers who are passionate about the organization's cause and committed to the campaign. You want new recruits who are willing to work set hours and take directions graciously, but there are other things that must be considered. Recruiting volunteers for a fundraising campaign also involves searching for individuals who genuinely like people, because fundraising encompasses working directly with the general public and donors. Volunteer fundraisers must also be able to effectively communicate. The rationale for wanting volunteers with effective communication skills is

Box 6.2 **Job Description Outline** 123

- **Role Description or Title:** Provide appropriate job title but don't use volunteer in the job title.

- **Person to Report to/Supervisor:** Specify the job title of the person the volunteer will report to and support to be given.

- **Major Activities and Key Outputs:** Outline tasks to be fulfilled and measures used to estimate job performance.

- **Work Hours and Work Location:** Describe expected hours to be worked and where the work will be done.

- **Knowledge and Skills:** Outline both formal and informal education that might be necessary.

- **Benefits:** Outline expenses that would be reimbursed and types of rewards or stipends available.

that they can clearly explain the mission and activities of the organization, which is necessary because, in truth, they are going to be sales people for the organization, and you want volunteer fundraisers who can recognize or intuitively know which donors will donate. When recruiting fundraising volunteers, you want people who can listen to others. The rationale for wanting volunteers who can listen to potential donors is that it makes prospects feel they are heard and accepted. In turn, prospects are more likely to share personal information about their finances and future plans that will financially benefit the organization. Overall, volunteers must understand that they are considered professionals who are engaged in a business relationship with donors (Burnett, 2002).

The recruiting process is the time to ascertain whether a recruit is trustworthy and appropriate for the intended work. First, can the recruit be trusted with clients' personal information? You will have to explore whether recruits demonstrate good judgment and value honesty in business. Even though these traits are hard to assess, having volunteers with these traits leads to successfully building an effective fundraising team (Stephens, 2004). Finally, you must determine whether a recruit is appropriate to serve. Some states might require a criminal background check if the volunteer will come in contact with the general public. Consider doing a criminal background check even if it is not required in your state. It's better to be safe than sorry, especially if your organization deals with a vulnerable service population such as the elderly.

Administration

Understanding and Mastery: Recruiting and managing volunteers.

Critical Thinking Question: A human services practitioner who works in the development office may have to use volunteers to supplement his or her staff for fundraising. Explain why recruiting volunteers for fundraising would be different from recruiting volunteers for general organizational activities. Write a job description for a fundraising volunteer that would reflect the personal characteristics needed to do fundraising.

Orienting Fundraising Volunteers

Orientation of new fundraising volunteers should be a formal process where a volunteer is given an orientation packet that includes a volunteer handbook, fundraising campaign information, an organizational chart, and material to carry out a specific fundraising campaign. Another way to acquaint volunteers with the organization's in-house fundraising activities is to have them open and respond to incoming mail for two days (Burnett, 2002). Why? This activity gives volunteers a bird's-eye view of why the public supports or doesn't support the organization. Volunteers will quickly learn about all the different people and businesses that the organization comes in contact with.

Fundraising volunteers are commonly chosen because they have had a long-term relationship with the organization and are acquainted with the organization. Don't assume they understand the fundraising operations of the organization. This group might not need a general orientation to the organization, but they will need an orientation to the fundraising process.

Training Fundraising Volunteers

In the role of supervisor, you will motivate and guide subordinates to get the work of the organization done. Volunteers will have to be trained to do their job. Let's examine two fundraising activities that volunteers might need to be trained for.

DONOR DATABASES Doing research is an important skill in the context of fundraising because you can learn about prospective donors. Prospect research should be a skill taught to fundraising volunteers, but it is often not taught in nonprofit organizations. Prospect research is a mixture of activities that help reveal a prospective donor's interests, goals, and donating ability in relationship to an organization's goals and funding needs (Alexander & Carlson, 2005).

The first step to training volunteers to do prospect research deals with teaching them about different electronic databases that can be searched for information about a prospect. Many of you, for instance, are adept at retrieving a person's phone number and address on the Internet. However, there are many electronic sites that will yield personal information about a person. For example, volunteers can be taught to mine social media sites (e.g., Facebook or LinkedIn) and electronic public records (e.g., property records) for information about prospects, but you have to put the collected data somewhere. These data have to be entered into a donor database.

A **donor database** is necessary to a nonprofit organization that hopes to generate long-term revenue (Burnett, 2002). If volunteers are going to be entering data into the database they must be trained. As with any new software, it takes time to learn how to use it. There are numerous software packages such as Community Impact Online Data Manager, Convio Fundraising Software, DonorPerfect, or Idealware, to name a few. These software packages have programs to set up different types of databases to

1. track donors and other constituents' information,
2. streamline fundraising management tasks,
3. income analysis of donations,
4. track pledges from donors,
5. track and summarize gift types, amounts, and restrictions,
6. track matching gifts and honorariums,
7. track donors, volunteers, and memberships, and
8. support volunteers throughout the grant management process.

At a minimum, the database should track donors' name, address, donation amounts, and other communications. Because there are multiple fields for donor information within a database, it is possible to do individual screening. This screening allows the database to generate personalized direct mailings, control the number of times donors are contacted, and respond appropriately to donors' wishes, desires, and needs. Managing donor information is a daunting task, but a good database system can effectively record all fundraising activities (Alexander & Carlson, 2005).

DONOR QUESTIONNAIRES   Other prospect research can be done with questionnaires. Questionnaires can be used to collect a broad range of information from prospects or current donors, but creating a good questionnaire is hard. Construction of a questionnaire involves considering its length, complexity, and what type of information needs to be generated. Construction of this instrument also includes creating questions that accurately get the information desired—which is known as validity—and consistently yield similar information from each respondent—which is known as reliability. In Chapter 3, we examined the complexity of creating questions, differences among question structures, and how different questions generate different types of information. It takes a lot of time and money to put a good questionnaire together; if possible find a volunteer who is experienced at constructing this type of instrument, or seek help from people at a local college or university who have experience constructing questionnaires.

Volunteers can be used to do a large mailing of questionnaires to donors and they can handle the returned questionnaires. It is labor intensive to manage returned questionnaires because each one has to be opened. Then the information from each questionnaire has to be entered into a database. Once the data are entered into the database a statistical analysis can be performed. If your organization is lucky you might have a volunteer with a statistical background to help you interpret the collected data.

DONOR INTERVIEWS   Donor research can also be done by having volunteers conduct interviews. Volunteers can be trained to do a variety of interviews. Unstructured interviews could be conducted during an informal meeting at a coffee café with a group of supporters. During an unstructured interview, the volunteer has the opportunity to gather information about what it will take to get the donor to make a donation or gift to the organization. Volunteers can also be trained to do face-to-face interviews, which will return in-depth information from the donor (Box 6.3). Once again, rich data from the interviews must be analyzed by someone who has the expertise in qualitative analysis if you hope to get usable information about your donors. Doing face-to-face interviews is labor intensive and can become costly because the volunteer may have to travel to meet each person for the interview. It would be cost-effective to have volunteers conduct an interview that is in close proximity to their homes. In Chapter 3, you can review the different interview formats and the how to do an interview.

USING A RANGE OF GIFTS TABLE   More volunteers involved in the organization's fundraising campaigns translates into more representatives who can personally ask other people for donations (Alexander & Carlson, 2005). However, volunteers have to be trained

Information Management

Understanding and Mastery: Utilizing research findings and other information for community education and public relations and using technology to create and manage spreadsheets and databases.

Critical Thinking Question: A human services organization doing fundraising needs to have a donor database if it hopes to generate revenue. Practitioners obtain donor information through interviews and research but need some organized means of storing and retrieving donor information. First, research software packages designed to organize donor information such as Community Impact Online Data Manager, Convio Fundraising Software, DonorPerfect, or Idealware. Second, explore how such software works and find out how much the software costs. Finally, carefully craft a proposal to persuade a group of human service administrators about the importance of having donor database software.

Box 6.3	A Face-to-Face Interview with a Nonprofit Fundraiser

Rachel Yurman, Director of Foundation and Government Relations for the nonprofit Boston Ballet—an organization that sponsors a number of community-based arts programs—offered some practical insight into different research methods that can be used to find out where donation money is. In her organization, the membership base often makes generous donations, and revenue is generated from ticket sales and the ballet school. Typically, small human service organizations don't have a membership base that donates money; they have only direct services to generate revenues. Rachel suggested to first look for money in your local community government. It is important to research the people who head the different agencies or departments that have been targeted. Learn where they put their money and find out what procedure is needed to ask for a donation. This whole process can also be done at the state level, but it might be prudent to start locally and see what it takes to get the attention of local government officials. Have volunteers collect information from the local government website about the different departments or agencies:

- Find the names and phone numbers of contact people.
- Find the programs the organization is eligible to ask for monies.
- Go to organizations doing work similar to yours and look at their donor list.
- Build a relationship with business leaders in the community.
- Check national clearinghouse websites such as Foundation Center to determine what local affiliates are making donations to organizations similar to your own.

To get to the information on the Foundation Center website, you must become a member. There are different levels of membership, so the more you pay the more information is made available. Is it worth it? Yes! This membership is a good investment for a human service organization that is interested in fundraising.

to make a face-to-face solicitation. If you are in charge of training volunteers to ask for donations and gifts, it is important to have a sense of what approach will best work for your organization. There is not a one-size-fits-all approach to fundraising. Yet all volunteers asking for a donation must be taught about the organization's mission and cause. They also need to be taught about donation amounts that the organization is seeking in order to reach its fundraising goal.

During a volunteer training, it is useful to review a Range of Gifts Table (Table 6.3) to illustrate why certain amounts are asked of donors. There is nothing arbitrary about fundraising; everything is done for a reason. For example, with a Range of Gifts Table

Table 6.3	Range of Gifts Table			
Human Service Organization $4 Million Goal				
Number of Gifts	Size of Gift	Total at Level	Cumulative Total	Cumulative Percent (%) of Goal
2	$200,000	$400,000	$400,000	10%
3	$100,000	$300,000	$700,000	18%
10	$50,000	$500,000	$1,200,000	30%
30	$30,000	$900,000	$2,100,000	53%
50	$10,000	$500,000	$2,600,000	65%
300	$2,000	$600,000	$3,200,000	80%
Many under	$2,000	$800,000	$4,000,000	100%

there is a clear target so a fundraising team can decide where to focus their efforts. If the focus is on securing 300 donors who can each make a $2,000 gift during one fundraising event, the team knows that translates into $600,000. The fundraising team has a sense of what they are working toward and what will be left to do. Maybe it would better, for instance, to split their efforts and go after one large gift and spend more time cultivating donors who can make donations that amount to less than $2,000. Whatever strategy used, the Range of Gifts Table clearly outlines the number of gifts needed and their amounts, which creates a series of steps to reach the $4 million dollar goal.

Fundraising volunteers may know what size gift to ask for from prospects, but they also need to be able to explain the organization's budget and how donations have been or will be used. We will use the Operation Gratitude website again to understand an organization's budget and to track where donations go.

On the home page of Operation Gratitude, click the link "About Us" in the pull-down box, then click "Financial Reports and Information." That will give you the organization's financials. The reports available are (1) Statement of Financial Position, (2) Statement of Activities, (3) Statement of Functional Expenses, and (4) Statement of Cash Flows. Examine the Statement of Activities and Statement of Functional Expenses (Tables 6.4 and 6.5) to get a sense of where the organization obtains its revenues and how the organization spends its money.

Table 6.4	Operation Gratitude Statement of Activities.
Statement of Activities for the Year Ended December 31, 2011	**Unrestricted**
SUPPORT AND REVENUES	
Contributions	$ 2,004,470
Net realized and unrealized loss	(7,520)
Interest income	190
SUBTOTAL	1,997,140
Donated goods for distribution	10,792,153
Donated advertising	985,371
Donated management services	564,143
Donated use of facilities	200,000
Donated food service for volunteers	25,960
TOTAL SUPPORT AND REVENUES	14,564,767
EXPENSES:	
Program services	10,297,150
Management and general	440,864
Fundraising	315,637
TOTAL EXPENSES	11,053,651
INCREASE IN NET ASSETS—UNRESTRICTED	3,511,116
NET ASSETS, DECEMBER 31, 2010	4,916,887
NET ASSETS, DECEMBER 31, 2011	$ 8,428,003

Source: Used by permission of Operation Gratitude, Inc.

Table 6.5	Operation Gratitude Statement of Functional Expenses.			
	Program Services	Management and General	Fundraising	Total Expenses
Goods delivered	$ 7,700,650	–	–	$ 7,700,650
Advertising	603,716	201,238	201,238	1,006,192
Salaries and Outside Services	703,914	178,445	114,019	996,378
Postage and Shipping Supplies	954,906	–	–	954,906
Rent	200,000	–	–	200,000
Supplies and Donated Food Services	65,708	–	–	65,708
Professional Fees	–	34,858	380	35,238
Equipment Rental	26,884	–	–	26,884
Repairs and Maintenance	14,726	–	–	14,726
Depreciation	14,050	–	–	14,050
Project and Office Administration	3,274	7,579	–	10,853
Travel	9,322	–	–	9,322
Merchant Fees	–	6,713	–	6,713
Insurance	–	5,949	–	5,949
Telephone and Internet Services	–	4,536	–	4,536
Taxes and Licenses	–	1,546	–	1,546
TOTAL EXPENSES	$ 10,297,150	$ 440,864	$ 315,637	$ 11,053,651

The statement of functional expenses reflected above includes non-cash expenses for donated goods delivered ($7,700,650), donated advertising and publicity ($985,371), donated salaries and outside services ($540,143), donated rent ($200,000), donated volunteer food services ($25,960), and donated legal services ($24,000). These amounts comprise approximately 86% of total expenses during the year. For the year ended December 31, 2011.

Source: Used by permission of Operation Gratitude, Inc.

UNDERSTANDING THE PURPOSE OF A BUDGET   Organizations have budgets for two basic reasons: One is to calculate what needs to be spent to advance their mission and the other is to determine how much income they need to raise to pay their expenses. According to Michael Seltzer (2001), an educator in nonprofit management, there are six important functions to budgeting:

1. Budgeting is a management tool.
2. Budgeting is a program tool.

3. Budgeting ensures there is enough money to operate.
4. Budgeting is a financial planning tool.
5. Budgeting controls expenditures.
6. Budgeting is a development tool.

The budget serves as a management tool that helps organizations to prioritize the programs they will fund. The organization uses the budget to determine what funds will be needed and to make logical adjustments to funding that match their available resources. Being cautious about budgeting and budget administration can allow an organization to move toward its goals and demonstrate to supporters and prospects that donations will be intelligently used and pay dividends (Seltzer, 2001). A budget should be a constant reminder to the organization about what is happening with their resources, when to anticipate expenditures, and when to expect income or cash flow (Table 6.6).

Having a budget helps the administrators monitor the organization's income compared to expenditures. Monitoring can be done daily, weekly, monthly, or yearly but must be done to ensure there are enough funds to advance the mission of the organization. When the administration is aware of the budget, it guides their financial practices

Table 6.6	Operation Gratitude Statement of Cash Flows.
Cash Flows Provided by Operating Activities	
Change in net assets:	$ 3,511,116
Adjustments to reconcile change in unrestricted net assets to net cash provided by operating activities:	
Depreciation expense	14,050
Non-cash contribution of investments	(5,491)
Non-cash contribution of fixed assets	–
Net realized and unrealized investment loss	7,520
Changes in assets and liabilities:	
Contributions receivable	(15,015)
Prepaid expense	1,663
Donated inventory	(3,218,431)
Accounts payable	(946)
CASH PROVIDED BY OPERATING ACTIVITIES	294,466
CASH FLOWS PROVIDED BY INVESTING ACTIVITIES Proceeds from sale of investments	153
CASH PROVIDED BY INVESTING ACTIVITIES	153
INCREASE IN CASH AND CASH EQUIVALENTS	294,619
CASH AT BEGINNING OF YEAR	1,264,156
CASH AT END OF YEAR	$ 1,558,775

For the year ended December 31, 2011.
Source: Used by permission of Operation Gratitude, Inc.

and gives them a clear understanding about the amount of support that must be generated from fundraising. It also is important that everyone has a general understanding of the organization's budget. This understanding will ensure that the organization is functioning above board. The nonprofit sector needs no more financial scandals!

Administration

Understanding and Mastery: Developing budgets and monitoring expenditures.

Critical Thinking Question: A budget serves as a management tool, and human services practitioners must understand how to manage organizational finances to ensure that client programs survive in a competitive business market. In a small group, conceptualize a fundraising event that might work for a small nonprofit organization in your community. Develop a budget for the proposed event, which most likely would include the cost of renting a site, food, insurance, etc. (put everything you can think of into that "etc."). Determine how many people will be needed to run the event and the cost of their time. How much will you have to raise to make the whole project worthwhile?

. . . .

THREE SOLICITATION APPROACHES   We will end our discussion about training fundraising volunteers with the examination of three approaches to soliciting prospective donors. First, training volunteers to do telephone solicitations is somewhat different than the other fundraising approaches you have examined. Telephone solicitation involves training volunteers to follow a phone script, which has relatively standard format. The volunteer reads the phone script, which includes how much to ask donors to give. The phone solicitation should be set up so that the solicitor asks for a base donation (e.g., $100) but can make suggestions of lower amounts of money if the prospect is not comfortable with the base donation amount.

You should be aware of the Do Not Call legislation (Box 6.4) because it does in fact allow tax-exempt nonprofits to call. Knowing this will help you explain to donors or prospects why that the organization is able to call even if they are on a "Do Not Call" list. If a person prefers not to be called by your organization you must respect those wishes. Period! Organizations that repeatedly call a person who has requested not to be contacted will create an enemy of that person.

Another solicitation approach is direct mail. Organizations use direct mail to educate large numbers of people about their cause and to solicit donations. Direct mail items can be brochures, leaflets, emails, or letters that are crafted to elicit an emotional response from the reader. What direct mail activities can volunteers train for? Volunteers can be trained to personalize direct mail by addressing envelopes with the names of donors or creating handwritten notes to people they know on the organization's mailing list. Personalized appeals are more effective in getting people to make donations to an organization, but it takes a lot more time to produce this type of mailing. Some organizations do a personalized appeal only to donors who have been faithful contributors.

Finally, volunteers can also be trained to work special fundraising events such as a silent art auction, a 5K run, or an annual donor appreciation dinner. Despite the size or type, special events are labor intensive and can be costly. Training volunteers for special events might involve teaching them how to solicit corporate sponsors or how to develop promotional materials. There are also less-glamorous activities such as selling tickets or helping with venue setup and breakdown. Overall, you must stress to volunteers that all fundraising tasks are essential and can affect the fundraising bottom line (Allen, 2000).

Retaining Fundraising Volunteers

Volunteer labor is a valuable financial resource to nonprofit organizations that are service providers (Salamon, 2002). Training volunteers costs money and time;

Do-Not-Call List

Has your evening or weekend been disrupted by a call from a telemarketer? If so, you're not alone. The Federal Communications Commission (FCC) has been receiving complaints in increasing numbers from consumers throughout the nation about unwanted and uninvited calls to their homes from telemarketers.

Pursuant to its authority under the Telephone Consumer Protection Act (TCPA), the FCC established, together with the Federal Trade Commission (FTC), a national Do-Not-Call Registry. The registry is nationwide in scope, applies to all telemarketers (with the exception of certain nonprofit organizations) and covers both interstate and intrastate telemarketing calls. Commercial telemarketers are not allowed to call you if your number is on the registry, subject to certain exceptions. As a result, consumers can, if they choose, reduce the number of unwanted phone calls to their homes.

Do-Not-Call Registry

You can register your phone numbers for free, and they will remain on the list until you remove them or discontinue service. There is no need to re-register numbers.

The Do-Not-Call registry does not prevent all unwanted calls. It does not cover the following:

- calls from organizations with which you have established a business relationship,
- calls for which you have given prior written permission,
- calls which are not commercial or do not include unsolicited advertisements, and
- calls by or on behalf of tax-exempt nonprofit organizations.

How to Register

For Consumers:

Subscribers may register their residential telephone number, *including wireless numbers*, on the national Do-Not-Call registry by telephone or by Internet at no cost.

Consumers can register online for the national Do-Not-Call registry by going to www.donotcall.gov. To register by telephone, consumers may call 1-888-382-1222 for TTY call 1-866-290-4236. You must call from the phone number you wish to register.

• •

Source: Federal Communications Commission http://www.fcc.gov/encyclopedia/do-not-call-list

therefore, retaining volunteers conserves the resources of nonprofits. As the supervisor of volunteers, it is essential to understand what factors support their long-term retention in an organization. It has been reported in fundraising research that when supervisors are trained to effectively communicate information that aids volunteers in their work on a fundraising campaign, volunteers are more likely to be retained (Lysakowski, 2005). Good supervision of fundraising volunteers also means understanding their personal needs, such as satisfying volunteers' scheduling preferences or job assignments (Falasca, Zobel, & Ragsdale, 2011). Moreover, when a job assignment is effectively done, a supervisor must give a volunteer recognition for a job well done. Volunteer recognition should be earned for specific duties and achievements. This will ensure that volunteers feel appreciated for their unique contributions to the organization (Schwab, 2011).

Overall, organizations will have to determine which fundraising approach works best. They must carefully weigh between the money spent on fundraising activities relative to the amount realized in net donations which equals actual revenue (Jacobs & Marudas, 2006).

There are a lot of fundraising resources to be aware of. Fundraising magazines and journals include

1. *Giving USA*
2. *Fund Raising Management*
3. *Advancing Philanthropy*
4. *The Chronicle of Philanthropy*

Professional and educational fundraising organizations that you might want to know about if you become a volunteer coordinator who oversees fundraising events would be

1. International Fund Raising Congress
2. Association of Fundraising Professionals
3. Council for Advancement and Support Education
4. Indiana University Center on Philanthropy
5. Direct Marketing Association

Summary

The nonprofit sector's growth has been bolstered by government financial support that comes in the form of grants, contracts, and fee-for-service agreements. However, when organizations become overly dependent on government financial support they sometimes have mission drift. Human service development, commonly known as fundraising, is the primary method used by nonprofits to generate income that supports day-to-day operations, staff salaries, programs, and many other things. Fundraising is backed by research and some of the more promising practices are *relationship fundraising* and *strategic fundraising*. In addition, there is an assortment of online fundraising approaches. Operation Gratitude's website serves as an example of an effective online fundraising vehicle for this nonprofit.

The largest contributions made to nonprofits come from individuals making private donations. Therefore, human service organizations would make good use of their time and resources by engaging in fundraising events that fit their needs and budget. Fundraising volunteers can be recruited and trained to effectively fundraise for an organization, but the organization must be committed to creating a sound volunteer program and having a coordinator who possesses the skill to supervise fundraising volunteers and retain them for the long haul.

Assess your analysis and evaluation of this chapter's content by completing the **Chapter Review**.

CHAPTER 7

The Essentials of
Advocacy

· ·

A Brief Overview of American Advocacy

Many of those who need services are unable to obtain them and therefore turn to human service professionals for help. Advocacy is thus the practice of seeking services for someone else. In a larger sense, advocacy extends to all efforts to achieve better conditions for individuals or groups who are underserved in society.

Advocacy for social reform as an organized practice in the United States is relatively new. One of the earliest efforts at social reform advocacy focused on child welfare. It was, perhaps surprisingly, not until the mid-1890s that a group of activists made organized efforts for social reform in this area. This period of organized social reform was called the Progressive Era, which went from the mid-1890s until approximately 1920 (Marten, 2005). One decade later, the Roosevelt Administration enacted laws and social programs that significantly aided women and children. The federal government over the upcoming decades would take a reluctant stance toward involving itself in social welfare.

Advocating for Child Welfare

Progressive activists felt that government responsibility should include positive social reform by promoting child welfare, creating a fair economy, raising everyone's standard of living, and using the nation's resources to solve urban social problems—just to name a few issues. Activists also sought to educate the public about social problems. For example, they initiated activities such as child-saving campaigns to educate the public about the horrific living conditions of poor children and youth (Herbert & Mould, 1992). They also educated the public about social problems related to unchecked immigration, growing economic inequality between the rich and poor, and the growing social chaos, all of which were affecting urban centers. Overall, although the interests of progressive activists throughout the country varied, all agreed that child welfare had to be addressed (Marten, 2005).

By the start of the 20th century—known by some in the movement as the "Century of the Child"—Americans started to become concerned about the treatment of children in their homes, workplaces, and in society. Americans' motivation to seek social reform, especially in the area of child welfare, was greatly influenced by middle-class values and beliefs. Middle-class Americans became actively involved in child welfare reform because they feared that poor children with no education or moral guidance would ultimately grow into adult criminals who would disrupt the social order (McGowan, 1983). Yet others became involved because they believed that all children deserved an ideal life. This ideal life for children would include nurturing mothers, parents who jointly cared for their children, and opportunities for education and leisure (Marten, 2005).

Child welfare was framed not only in terms of middle-class values but also as a women's issue. At the start of the Progressive Era, the federal government halfheartedly became involved in the social problems of children and women. It was not until 1912 that the first federal agency dedicated to child welfare was established—the U.S. Children's Bureau. The federal government mandated that the Children's Bureau investigate and report about matters specific to the welfare of children and their lives (Lindsey, 2004). However, from its beginning, the Children's Bureau was continually underfunded. Despite its underfunding, the Children's Bureau completed extensive research about child health, labor, and nutrition plus ran a community health education program.

Professional History

Understanding and Mastery: Skills to analyze and interpret historical data application in advocacy and social changes.

Critical Thinking Question: Advocating has become a professional responsibility assigned to human services practitioners. It is essential that practitioners aim to change the historical patterns of exclusion of vulnerable groups in all spheres of life. Look into the ways that historical events and past attitudes have been translated into modern day policies through advocacy and social change for a vulnerable group (other than children) in our society.

With little government involvement to help alleviate the social problems of children and women, much of the job fell to private citizens and organizations. So advocates for children, working independently of the government, sought stricter labor laws to protect children from the dangers they faced while working in mines, foundries, and textile mills. Progressive advocates also believed that working children should have greater opportunities for education and play.

Dedicated advocates for children's welfare continued to seek improvements through legislation, government support, and social consciousness, and by the end of the 20th century had achieved considerable success. Their efforts show the need for advocacy and the need for persistence, but their achievements should be an inspiration for all those who want to work for positive social change.

Advocating in the 21st Century

Currently, a number of professions maintain that **advocacy** is an important duty, so much so that it has been incorporated into professional ethical standards in several fields (Herbert & Mould, 1992; McNutt, 2006). Advocating is a professional responsibility assigned to nursing (Byme, 2006), human services (Woodside & McClam, 2008), social work (Herbert & Mould, 1992), and counseling (Hanks, 2005). Advocacy as a formal professional duty is a relatively new role for many professionals even though many have unofficially engaged in the process (Satterly & Dyson, 2005). Despite the widespread understanding that advocacy is necessary, the practice is not empirically supported nor is there a common understanding of what the process entails across different professions (Herbert & Mould, 1992). Models or theoretical perspectives about advocacy are not fully developed and do not entirely explain how advocacy works (Ezell, 2001). Nevertheless, helping professions such as human services value the concept of advocating for marginalized groups and individuals in need. In the *Ethical Standards for Human Service Professionals* (1996), one statement reflects the profession's commitment to advocacy.

> **Statement 16:** Human service professionals advocate for the rights of all members of society, particularly those who are members of minorities and groups at which discriminatory practices have historically been directed.

> —Reprinted by permission of the National Organization for Human Services

There is thus a great need for professionals who have the knowledge and skills to advocate for clients and communities (Ezell, 2001). Methodically learning about advocacy and acquiring advocacy skills is something of a challenge because there are few evidence-based advocacy approaches. Advocacy theories and models are often discussions about personal endeavors undertaken to address inequities on behalf of clients, an approach that can be noted in the literature from counseling (Astramovich & Harris, 2007), human services (Wark, 2008), nursing (Hanks, 2005), and social work (Dalrymple, 2004). Not surprisingly, advocacy practices are hard to isolate and hard to scientifically measure (Ezell, 2001). As a result, helping professionals must rely on practice wisdom to guide their advocacy practices.

Because advocacy requires persuasion, we will begin to examine practical approaches to advocacy with the study of rhetoric, the ancient art of persuasion. Knowledge about rhetoric and rhetorical practices will help you advocate for the kinds of change that fall under the scope of human services practice such as advocating for client services, client programs, or lobbying for legislative changes in human service policies.

Advocacy: The Process of Persuasion

The study of persuasion in the West goes back to ancient Greece, when the general public would listen to speeches that were intended to influence political and judicial decisions within the community. An interest in how these public speeches swayed individuals resulted in the study of persuasion in both written and oral forms. The ancient term for the art of persuasion is *rhetoric*. Greek philosophers such as Aristotle and Plato became fascinated with rhetoric and began to seriously study the process. The observations and suggestions about rhetoric from the earliest Greek and Roman philosophers are still studied and used by scholars in English, psychology, and communication sciences.

I first presented this material about the art of persuasion to my human services students in a community agency class. During the presentation, my students sat expressionless. I initially thought the material was boring or just simply too hard for them. To my surprise, the students loved it and wanted more! One student explained that she understood why her presentation to outside funders had failed. Others students were simply amazed that there were theories about persuasion and felt they would better represent their clients. As the semester progressed, I watched my students utilize rhetorical theory to create stronger arguments in classroom discussions and in their presentations. In fact, many students expressed that they were more confident about making an argument for change in their field placements and at their current jobs in the community.

There is nothing magic about the process of persuasion, but if you intend to be an advocate, understanding rhetorical theory is essential. We will start with an established rhetorical process that has been broken down to five steps:

1. First, search for persuasive ways to present information and make arguments. This search begins by analyzing the situation in which the oral presentation will be given (or, in the case of a written document, the conditions under which it will be read), followed by researching the case and the information and potential arguments for and against it.
2. Second, arrange the elements of the oral presentation (or written document) in a structure that is most likely to win over the audience. Structure, interestingly, has a powerful effect upon persuasion, so this is an important step.
3. Third, compose the oral presentation or document using appropriate, striking, and effective language—that is, applying principles of style.
4. Fourth, prepare to deliver the oral presentation by practicing and fine-tuning.
5. Fifth, deliver the actual oral presentation as a performance.

Each of these steps has its own complexities, of course, and there may not be a clear break between the steps; for example, new arguments may arise during the composition or practice stages. However, it is important that you take these steps seriously. Let's examine the five steps in more depth. As you go through the five steps, imagine you are advocating for a client or group in need.

First Step: Process of Analyzing and Researching to Make an Argument

First, you want to search for persuasive ways to present information and make an argument. This search begins by analyzing the situation in which the oral presentation will be given or in the case of a written document, the conditions under which it will be read. This analysis is followed by researching the issues and gathering information for the potential arguments for and against your case. You want to do a thorough analysis of the situation in which you are making your case.

As you prepare to make an argument, it is necessary to answer the following questions as precisely as you can (don't guess or generalize). What exactly are the conditions under which you will speak? Where will it be? How long do you have to speak? Who will be listening? Visit the venue if possible, so you get a sense of the physical setup of the place where you will be making your presentation. Observe how others present their cases in the same venue. Be prepared to make adjustments to the conditions: If you prepared a ten-minute presentation and are given only five minutes to speak, you must adjust. Speaking twice as fast is not a solution because it will simply make your presentation incomprehensible. If there is no projector to do a PowerPoint presentation, you should be prepared to continue your presentation without it. Moreover, as do your research, don't be surprised, and never make excuses if you do get surprised.

It is also critical that you do an **audience analysis**. The more you know about your audience the better. Who are they and where do they come from? What interests or constituencies do they represent? What positions do they hold about your proposition? What professional or personal considerations may lead them to hold those positions? What is their stake in your proposition? How is it relevant to them? What might they already know about it? Is it possible for you to interview some of them in advance to answer these questions?

As you begin to write your **argument**, a similar analysis is necessary. If there is a standard form for presenting your case (such as a government proposal), you must use it. If there is a length limit, observe it to the letter. If there are format guidelines, treat them as sacred and see if you can obtain samples of successful submissions. As you write your argument, think about the audience. Knowing your audience will (or should) affect the arguments you use (or don't use), the illustrations you choose, the way you explain the significance of your proposition, and even the language you use.

The substance of your argument depends upon having accurate and complete information to support your proposition. You may have to explain everything about your case to people who know nothing at all about it. For instance, be prepared with a history, all possible data and relevant statistical outcomes (with an account of the reliability of your sources), an explanation of the significance of the situation, costs incurred, other proposals connected to yours, and anything else you can think of.

Finally, what are the reasons that someone should support or adopt your proposition? What is its aim? How will it work? Will it achieve the stated goals? What will it cost? Who or what will it benefit? What are the drawbacks, the alternatives, the objections? It is vital to research the alternatives and the opposition, because if these are not addressed, you will be less persuasive.

Second Step: Process of Structuring the Presentation

You want to arrange the elements of the oral presentation (or written document) in a structure that is most likely to win over the audience. The structure of your argument, interestingly, has a powerful effect upon persuasion. An effective structure was developed by a Roman rhetorician named Quintilian (Box 7.2). He taught a five-part form of rhetorical organization that has stood the test of time. It can be seen today in the psychology of persuasion research, in suggestions for lawyers making final arguments, and in books on selling strategies.

The five-part form of rhetorical organization has the following components: introduction, narration, argument for your case, refutation of alternatives or objections,

---

Box 7.2 ▶ **Who is Quintilian?**

Quintilian was a Roman rhetorician from Hispania, which was the Roman name for the Iberian Peninsula (Bizzell & Herzberg, 2001). In English translations, Quintilianus was commonly referred to as Quintilian. He learned and modeled himself after his older mentor, Afer, who delivered speeches and engaged in legal pleading in the courts. The only existing work of Quintilian is a 12-volume textbook on rhetoric entitled *Institutio Oratoria* (referred to in English as the *Institutes of Oratory*) published around 95 BCE. This work deals not only with the theory and practice of rhetoric but also with the foundational education and development of the orator himself, providing advice that ran from the cradle to the grave.

and a conclusion. The *introduction* is supposed to do several things, such as capture the interest of the audience, show why they should care about the topic, why the topic is relevant and compelling, and outline what the speaker is asking them to do or agree to. The *narrative* then follows, providing the audience with the information they need to understand the problem at hand. The narrative should be purely informative, and its neutrality should make the audience feel that they are getting an unbiased view from a knowledgeable speaker. As a result, trust in the speaker increases and the audience hears the *arguments* the speaker has mustered in support of his or her proposal. The speaker's knowledge of the case and his or her ethical principles lead the speaker to tell the audience why some people oppose the solution, increasing the audience's trust and making them feel that the case has been thoroughly considered. The speaker then *refutes* the objections honestly and *concludes* by reminding the audience that this is a compelling issue and that they can act to make things better.

Now, let's break down the five-part form of rhetorical organization so you can better understand how to arrange an oral or written presentation. Again, the rhetorical organization has the following components:

1. *Introduction:* The first thing you say or write should captivate the audience. Modern formulations of rhetorical arrangement often call this the "attention step."
2. *Narration:* An explanatory section that establishes the situation in an informative or neutral way. Here you may give the history of the situation or describe the nature of the problem you propose to address.
3. *Arguments for your case:* Present the support for your proposition, in as much detail as time allows.
4. *Refutation of alternatives or objections:* Explain the reasons why your proposition is the best of all possible approaches and why the objections to it are wrong.
5. *Conclusion:* Return to the main reasons for accepting your proposition, the dangers of not doing it, and the results it will achieve if implemented. Finally, call upon the audience to act, if that is what you aim for.

MAKING THE INTRODUCTION   The purpose of the **introduction** is to get the audience interested quickly. Start with a story or with a startling fact, ask a rhetorical question (a statement that is formulated as a question but is not meant to be answered), or give a stirring quote. Avoid formalities, don't hem and haw—start as quickly and energetically as possible. Think about making a good first impression. The introduction is usually short, but much depends on the circumstances, so reflect on your audience analysis, consider what might be most interesting or relevant to them, and find a way to start there. The end of the introduction should state your proposition very, very clearly.

MAKING THE NARRATION   A good **narrative** section will follow smoothly from your introduction. Use your introductory human-interest story or startling fact as an opening for a historical overview or to recount the basic facts of the case. The information you give here may be support for your argument later (the statistics on domestic violence, for example, in an argument that women are affected by it more than men), but it is presented here purely in the guise of necessary informational background. Don't anticipate the arguments you will build on this information, but state it as an unchallengeable fact.

MAKING THE ARGUMENT   The **argument** section will be the longest and most complex section of your oral presentation or written document. Use your outlining skills to set up a strong internal structure for this section. If possible, your arguments should build upon one another, so start with arguments that serve as the foundation for later or more complex arguments.

The Greek philosopher Aristotle (384–322 BCE) identified three types of appeal in the presentation of an argument: logic, emotion, and character. Arguments that appeal to logic are founded on concrete data or statistics and are based on reason. They give solid evidence to back up claims. Arguments appealing to emotion (*pathos* is the Greek word for emotion) are those that try to generate emotions in the audience, whether sadness, fear, pity, joy, or excitement. For example, a politician telling an audience that his or her opponent will cut services to the elderly appeals to their emotions. Finally, arguments that appeal to ethos (*ethos* is the Greek word for character) attempt to persuade by calling attention to the writer's or speaker's character, making him or her appear credible. A speaker might, for example, tell the audience that he or she is a decorated veteran, a prominent member of society, or a renowned authority in the subject being discussed.

It seems obvious that an argument should be grounded in logic and that a speaker needs to appear trustworthy. However, emotional arguments are both important and legitimate. Audiences should be drawn into the human world of the case, especially in arguments that concern human services. The danger in emotional arguments is that they may appear to be sentimental and shallow. Yes, emotional arguments alone may give that impression. So the aim is to use all the kinds of argument together (logic, emotion, and character). Use emotional arguments to bring statistics and data to life, to draw the audience into the detailed effects that policies and services have on people and families and communities. Use striking language to show your passion and make memorable statements.

MAKING THE REFUTATION   A well-researched narrative section gives the sense that the speaker is objective and trustworthy as does a **refutation** section that states opposing arguments fairly and accurately. Both the argument and refutation sections depend upon sound logic and solid evidence.

Refutation must begin with an accurate and complete representation of the objections and possible objections to your argument. Not mentioning objections is actually quite dangerous! For instance, if somebody in the audience has an objection in mind (and you can bet somebody does), your failure to address it will seem like avoidance—even if the objection is fairly minor. Your avoidance of the objections to your argument translates into fear and dishonesty—and there goes your case! On the other hand, if you have considered the objections to your argument, you have the time to formulate your response—or you have the chance to get ahead of the objections by incorporating safeguards in your argument. You may even discover weaknesses in your argument that need to be addressed before you pursue it.

MAKING THE CONCLUSION   In the **conclusion**, you should assume that you have been successful with your argument. Be forceful about its worth and importance and the good it will do. Be clear about what you want from the audience—usually that they should do something like vote for your proposal or grant your request. If you used a striking story or fact at the beginning of the presentation, see if you can pick it up again and use it as a conclusion as well. Audiences love closure.

Too often, you have been taught to outline your papers or speeches and to organize them logically, where "logically" means grouping related subtopics. Unless you must follow a predetermined format for your oral presentation or written document, always try to use the five rhetorical components we have examined because it is memorable, flexible, and reliable. Rhetorical organization is geared to the psychological reactions of the audience as they hear or read each successive part of the presentation and has been proven to be persuasive.

Third Step: Process of Composing and Revising the Presentation

The third step in the process involves composing the oral presentation or document. Composing involves using appropriate, striking, and effective language. Composing also involves applying the principle of style. Good writing involves doing multiple revisions.

COMPOSING　To compose effectively, go back to the earliest stage of the process, the audience analysis and the speech-situation analysis. As you compose, you should keep your goals for the speech or written document firmly in mind. It's easy to get immersed in details of the argument or organization and forget your primary purpose—to persuade real people who will be listening to you or reading your words.

Reconsider your captivating opening: During your research and drafting, perhaps you came upon a story that is even more striking and powerful than the one you had in mind at first—or perhaps you have learned something about your audience that suggests a connection that will be more relevant and immediate to many of them. You may even want to revise or rephrase your proposition in light of information and arguments you have discovered. Make your proposition as precise as you can.

Be sure that you have a narrative section. This can be difficult to conceptualize if you have not done it before. Don't skip this section! As noted earlier, it is critically important in establishing the underlying facts and in persuading your audience that you are well informed. If you found in your argument section that you had to fill in a lot of background detail to make a point, try moving that information to the narrative section. You can then refer to it later in making your argument. This kind of repetition is very useful.

There are a number of ways to approach the argument and refutation sections to make them effective. You might, for example, begin with the negatives and refute them, or go back and forth from positive to negative arguments. Consider again what arguments are most likely to appeal to your audience, and be sure that you have an answer to *every* opposing argument, no matter how obvious (to you) that answer might be! We often become so convinced of the correctness of our view that we cannot imagine any sane person failing to share it once it is presented. Don't get caught in this trap.

REVISION　During revision, strive for a balance between logical and emotional arguments. Break up statistics to show the real people behind them; be sure to use statistics to show that the story you are telling about an individual applies broadly. Remember, statistics are dry and stories are not arguments.

Finally, review your entire speech or document to be sure you have used clear, precise, and vivid language. Remove all clichés (phrases or opinions that are overused and reveal a lack of original thought) at this point and replace them either with fresh images or direct and clear expressions.

What about visual aids? If you are able to use **visual aids**, it is best to think about them at this stage in your speech preparation. You should know from your speech-situation analysis whether you will have a computer and projector, a transparency projector, or if it is appropriate to use physical charts. During your research, you may well have come upon some striking images or graphs showing important statistics. Now is the time to consider whether such visual aids will enhance your message. Don't simply assume that they will.

All too often, speeches are hijacked by PowerPoint slides. Instead of working on evidence and argument or on rhetorical organization, novice speakers overly rely on PowerPoint slides because visual aids give them a crutch during a speech. However, the most effective visual aids are those that support a well-formed argument. If your argument is really well formed, the visual aid may not be necessary at all. Visuals aids should do one of these two things: (a) make complex information easier to grasp and (b) increase the impact of an argument.

So don't use a PowerPoint slide that gives the title of your speech and your name. Don't use slides of bullet points. Don't show YouTube clips. Don't show cartoons. On the other hand, if it really helps, show a graphic or an image that bolsters a point you are making. For example, show a large clear graph that reveals the rise in crime over the years in a client's neighborhood. Give the audience time to absorb it. Point out striking data and explain the significance of this information. Then turn the PowerPoint projector off and get back to your oral presentation.

Always be prepared for the very real possibility that the technology will not be working when you get up to speak. Don't waste any time trying to get it to work! Have handouts of your absolutely essential graphics—and make the number of handouts as small as possible. Ask for a volunteer from the audience to distribute the handouts so you can go on with the speech.

Step Four: Process of Practice and Fine-Tuning

You have arrived at step four; this is when you practice a lot, in front of a mirror and in front of real people who can give you feedback. Get a friend to take a video of you as you practice and then look at it. The video will show you how long you are speaking and whether you look like you are delivering an important message or just trying to say the words so you can escape the spotlight.

PRACTICE It takes a lot of practice for most people to learn to be expressive when they give an oral presentation, but even the best delivery makes no difference unless the presentation itself is well researched, well organized, and persuasive. Here's a true story—from numerous historical accounts, Abraham Lincoln was described as a terrible speaker. His voice was high and he spoke in a monotone. Still, he is remembered as a superior speaker because he wrote superb speeches.

So do your best to be expressive, but remember that what is essential is that your audience hears all your words. Therefore, speak slowly enough and loudly enough to ensure that your audience hears your presentation. Don't speak faster to cram everything in—ultimately, less is more in this case. Stick to the time limit even if it means deleting parts of your presentation. It would be wise to time yourself as you practice giving your oral presentation and have a strategy to end your presentation in the event the allotted time is limited.

FINE-TUNING   As you practice, continue to revise your presentation. Because you will think of ways to say things that sound better, you will think of new formulations of your arguments, you will think of all kinds of things that should go into the speech. This process is called fine-tuning—it reveals the importance of starting the practice stage well before the date for your presentation.

Step Five: Process of Delivering the Speech

The final step is the delivery of the talk. Many of you will ask if there is a way to overcome stage fright. Sadly, no. Each time I give a paper at a conference I have butterflies, but after the start of the talk the butterflies typically go away. Don't be fooled by street wisdom. Don't drink vodka. Don't think about the audience naked. Don't look over the heads of the audience instead of at their eyes. The best way to decrease your stage fright is to do your research, compose the speech carefully, and practice. If you are prepared and well-rehearsed, it is more likely that you will be less nervous before an audience.

If giving speeches is going to be part of your career (and it can be a big part of a human services career), try to take a speech course, join Toastmasters, and take every opportunity to give speeches. Eventually it will become easier as you do it more.

Advocacy in a Human Services Context

Let's sum up our persuasive practices and techniques and then see how they apply to typical situations in human services work that might call for advocacy. First, have a very clear picture of what you are advocating for; in other words, know exactly what you intend to propose. Research the situation thoroughly to avoid wasting your time or putting yourself and your agency in a false position.

Find out how to conduct the form of advocacy (e.g., agency, community, legislative) appropriate for what you are proposing. In some situations, beginning an advocacy campaign requires you to go through a standardized process that begins with filling out forms or writing a formal proposal. In addition, figure out what particular people or groups to approach to determine who can make the decision you seek.

Write out an advocacy plan that identifies these submissions, people, due dates, and so on. If there is no standard process, make a plan that makes sense for your project. Identify your allies to determine who will support you when you make your proposal. Contact them early, let them know what you are planning, and keep them in the loop.

Remember that persuasive communication can be achieved by using the five-part form of rhetorical organization: (a) finding the best arguments, (b) arrangement, (c) composition, (d) practice and fine-tuning, and (e) delivery. This will allow you lay out your proposal in the most compelling terms. Don't skip these persuasive communication steps—they will be your most important tool, even if you don't ever give a long speech or write a long proposal. Carry out your plan, and then constantly revisit the techniques for persuasion that we have been studying and constantly refine your messages to make them crisp, concise, and compelling.

Advocating for Client Services

If you are a case manager, one of your duties will be to make referrals. Whether or not you obtain the services of a specific program for an individual client or family depends on whether the client qualifies for services under the program guidelines. Take your time with the first step and clearly identify the client's need that must be met, then go to the second step and identify the programs that can meet the need. Collect the data from those programs about how to satisfy their requirements that are set out in the formal guidelines. Services can hinge on whether an agency accepts a client's insurance or whether a client meets income guidelines.

Program rules can be tricky and baffling not only to clients but to those who work in the program. What are the rules for getting an unemployment insurance extension? What documents do you need to obtain Medicaid, TANF (Temporary Assistance for Needy Families), or other services? What zip codes are covered by the emergency aid declaration?

When a referral fails, you may feel that it is appropriate to advocate for your clients in order to obtain needed services. The borderline cases are the toughest ones, of course—and these are the ones that will call on your advocacy skills. Take the third step and find people in the target agencies that seem helpful and sympathetic. Find out if there are others working on the same problem with whom you can make common cause. Identify community leaders or elected officials who might have some influence. You may find that you and your client are part of a larger issue that calls for rule changes or collective action.

Human Services Delivery Systems

Understanding and Mastery: Skills to effect and influence social policy.

Critical Thinking Question: Calculate what it would take to live in your community for one month for a single adult with two preschool children. Consider necessities such as rent, utilities, food, transportation, childcare, clothing, and entertainment. Next, note the income eligibility level for TANF in your state* and assume that our imaginary family makes exactly the maximum allowable income. Calculate how much money this family of one adult and two children would have after one month's expenditures. Does your state's TANF legislation make it possible for a family such as this to live comfortably? If not, what arguments might persuade them to change that legislation?

*Explore the <u>National Center for Children in Poverty</u> website to see what the income eligibility criteria are for a recipient to qualify for benefits in your state.

Advocating for a New Program

While working in human service agencies you may find that your program is not helping clients in the manner expected. To alter a program for the benefit of your clients, you might have to engage in a two-prong advocacy effort in the agency and in the community served by the agency. According to Ezell (2001), agency advocacy involves using tactics and activities to cause change in a program or organization. Community advocacy involves community education that focuses on changing community members' attitudes and beliefs so they will support particular policies and practices. Once again, you will have to make a case to the agency and community to explain your position about altering a program in an agency.

Advocating in the Legislative Arena

There will be times that the problems your clients are experiencing are caused by outdated, incomplete, or unjust laws and policies. In this instance, some of you will engage in legislative advocacy, which deals with persuading legislators to change or create laws that will benefit a legally deprived population (e.g., illegal immigrants). To change policies and laws, advocates must learn to effectively maneuver the legislative process (Patti & Dear, 1975) and employ strategic tactics to increase their chances that a bill would have a favorable outcome. In Chapter 9, "Lobbying in the Political Arena," you will examine how to lobby at the state level. Your ability to master the five-part form of rhetorical organization will again be used to create persuasive arguments designed to change legislators' positions on different legislation or policies affecting people in communities.

Communication Formats for Persuasion

A formal presentation such as the one we have just studied assumes that the advocate has time to prepare and time to deliver a thoughtful case. However, the same principles apply in other communication situations that human service professionals might find themselves in. There are several communication situations in which you might produce short pieces of writing to succinctly express your ideas. In an op-ed piece (an abbreviation for an opinion article that is opposite to the editorial page) for a local newspaper you might attempt to generate public support for your cause but you typically will be limited to approximately 350 words. In a letter to the editor for the same purpose, that limit might be as little as 125 words. For an "elevator speech"—for example, a chance meeting with the mayor at an event where you can grab the mayor's attention for a few seconds at best—you may be able to say no more than 30 words or so (maybe more if the mayor shows interest). On a flyer to hand out at a neighborhood rally, use one picture and 12 words. On a bumper sticker or button, there is typically space for only three or four words. Other communication situations in which you might express your ideas or position are in interviews on a radio or television talk show. In these situations, you might get 30 seconds for an introduction and about 5 minutes of questions and answers.

Communication Format	Words or Time Allowance
Newspaper op-ed	About 350 words
Letter to the editor	About 125 words
Elevator speech	About 30 words
Community flyer	About 12 words
Bumper sticker or button	About 3 words
Interview on radio or television	About 5 minutes

In short, you need to be prepared to speak and write persuasively in a variety of situations. The same techniques of persuasion work for just about every occasion, but the delivery must be adjusted to the circumstances. It pays to write and rehearse short versions of your argument suitable for opportunities to generate interest and support when time and printed space are at a premium. Your advocacy messages will be more effective when they have these qualities:

1. The proposition can be stated accurately in relatively few words.
2. Memorable key words identify the idea.

3. Striking images are associated with the idea.
4. Multiple examples or illustrations can be offered.
5. Benefits are easy to identify and articulate.
6. Objections have been anticipated and are readily refuted.
7. Advocacy statements are passionate.
8. Supporters are praised for their support.
9. Supporters know how to express their support.

All of these elements are or should be present in the long formal presentation we have examined. Now they should be extracted and refined, ready to be used when the moment is right.

A Case Study: Advocating for a Community Bus Line

Let's look at an example of how a human services practitioner might go through the process of advocating for a community improvement. The following case study is about how a human services practitioner prepares a proposal for her clients and their community.

Sondra, a human services case manager at a vocational services agency in a medium-sized city, has become concerned about the absence of a bus route on Green Boulevard, a big street in a poor neighborhood where many of her clients live and work. It is difficult for the residents to get to their jobs or to shop for food. There had been a bus on Green Boulevard for quite some time, but the Mass Transportation Agency (MTA) cancelled it. Sondra's agency is committed to advocacy and she takes the lead on trying to get that bus line restored for her clients and their communities. Let's follow Sondra through this process of advocacy.

First, she must find out who makes the decision about bus lines. Is it the MTA or the city council? What is the history of the Green Boulevard line? When and why was it cancelled? Who made that decision? Is Sondra correct in her assumption that the line would be used if it were restored? After some extensive research, the answers to her questions convince Sondra that restoring the bus route would improve the lives of many different communities along the Green Boulevard bus line and her clients. She learns that there is a committee of the city council that hears proposals about public transportation: She must send them an abstract (brief overview) of the proposal and later appear at a public hearing to explain and defend the proposal. How shall she go about preparing for this task?

Analyzing and Researching to Make an Argument

The first step calls for Sondra to do more research. She will attempt to answer questions like: Who are the members of the Mass Transportation Committee? What is their review process and what are the circumstances of their meetings? The information about who is on the committee is public information, so Sondra can learn a good deal about the individual members, for example, where they live and what constituencies (voters) in the city they serve. She can sit in on the hearings for other cases because they are public. All proposal abstracts are publicly registered, which makes them available to anyone interested in reading them. This allows Sondra to note which succeeded and which failed.

Sondra must also begin collecting information and other arguments that support her proposal. In addition to what she has already learned about the history of the Green Boulevard line, Sondra gets clients involved in collecting signatures on a petition to restore the line. She also gets agency workers to record brief interviews with clients and community residents who talk about their difficulties in getting around the city without bus transportation. Additional information can be collected from the city census report that quantifies how many people live in the area, how many people would be served by the bus line, and other data about community demographics.

Structuring the Presentation

The second step calls for Sondra to arrange her case in a way that will be likely to persuade the members of the Mass Transportation Committee. Sondra sets up a preliminary outline:

> **Introduction:** First, a story about a long-time resident who used the bus and is now suffering without it; next, a brief reference to the number of people who are in a similar situation; finally, a statement of the proposal to restore the line.
>
> **Narrative:** A history of the Green Boulevard bus line, its ridership over the years, the reasons for its cancellation, and the consequences of that cancellation.
>
> **Arguments:** Restoring the line would result in a significant improvement of the quality of life for the residents at little to no cost to the transportation authority, a claim backed up in a number of ways: an estimate of the number of new riders, the lack of job opportunities in the neighborhood, the distance of supermarkets from the neighborhood, a petition to restore the line signed by many residents, the responsibility of the city to serve its citizens, and the increase in the value of property on streets with public transportation.
>
> **Refutation:** Sondra anticipates several objections: that her estimate of new ridership is too high, that many residents now have cars, that they are increasingly elderly and don't travel as much, that many are unemployed and do not have jobs to go to, that the line had been cancelled because the cost was not sufficiently offset by ridership and that other neighborhoods needed the lines more. Sondra sees that these objections are focused on cost and utility, so her refutation of them is to demonstrate that the buses now being used are cheaper to operate, that the demographics of the neighborhood show a rise in the number of people in the "employable" age range (and she can speak to this issue from her experience at the vocational service agency), and that other bus lines with lower ridership remain in operation in other neighborhoods.
>
> **Conclusion:** Returning to the story of the resident in her introduction, Sondra will describe the improvement in community life if the bus line is restored and call on the committee to do the right thing for the citizens of their city.

Composing and Revising the Presentation

The third step is when Sondra goes back to her speech-situation analysis and audience analysis and revises the speech to be sure that it suits the occasion and really appeals to the audience. She wonders, for example, whether the whole presentation can be done in the time that the committee typically allows advocates to speak. There will be a question-and-answer period, she has learned, so she can perhaps take out some of the objections and responses she has prepared, assuming that the committee will ask about them. Watching some of the public sessions has shown Sondra the kinds of questions that are typically asked.

Sondra has also learned about some of the positions that members of the committee have taken on previous similar issues. She will be able to show, for example, that her proposal is *not* like one that was turned down recently on the objection of two committee members. Furthermore, the committee appears to like summaries of statistical findings, but does not always meet in a room that has projection equipment. She and her staff can make a big poster with essential information and she can prepare a written summary, but that seems to be the limit for visual aids.

Practice and Fine-Tuning

Step four involves Sondra practicing and fine-tuning, which takes place in her own agency's meeting room, and she asks some colleagues to help her by playing the role of committee members. After a few practice rounds, another colleague makes a video recording while Sondra gives her whole speech and then her co-workers grill her with questions. The speech is too long and Sondra fumbles over some of her answers. Interestingly, her co-workers come up with some arguments she hadn't thought of—and ask some questions she was unprepared for. The video is embarrassing but very helpful and over the next few days, Sondra tightens up the speech and finds ways to answer key questions more concisely.

Delivering the Speech

After everything is said and done the final step means it is show time. Sondra begins nervously making her case before the committee, but after a minute or so she forgets to be nervous and finds that her passion for the issue is her dominant emotion. She forgets to say something she planned to say—how could she miss it when it was right there in her notes? Nobody is perfect the first time out the gate. Over time Sondra will get better.

The practical skills of persuasion that we have worked on in this chapter will be applicable in a wide variety of advocacy situations. Community organizing (covered in Chapter 8) is simply another name for social advocacy, and lobbying (covered in Chapter 9) is also called legislative advocacy. Don't limit your advocacy to individual clients: Always consider whether the problems they face are shared by many and whether your efforts may serve a population in addition to a single person!

Summary

It was not until the mid-1890s that a group of activists made organized efforts for social reform in areas such as child welfare, equitable economic conditions for all, raising the standard of living, and using the nation's resources to solve urban social problems. With little government involvement to help alleviate the social problems, much of the job fell to private citizens and organizations. Over the next several decades, dedicated advocates for social welfare continued to seek improvements through legislation, government support, and social consciousness and by the end of the 20th century had achieved considerable success.

Currently, advocating is a professional responsibility of human services practitioners and other helping professionals. However, advocacy theories and models have yet to be developed as evidence-based approaches. As a result, advocating professionals appear to be left to employ nonscientific advocacy approaches when working in the field. Yet the ancient discipline of rhetoric has sound theories of persuasion that can be used by advocates. The established rhetorical process explains the importance of researching a position, arranging specific elements of an oral or written presentation for persuasive effect, composing an argument with rhetorical appeals, fine-tuning an argument through practice, and making the presentation as a polished performance. All of these practices are essential to successfully persuading others. Overall, the advocate's job is to get others to see things from his or her perspective in order to get the things needed to advance the social good.

Assess your analysis and evaluation of this chapter's content by completing the **Chapter Review.**

CHAPTER 8

Becoming a Community Organizer

· ·

The overall objective of community organizing is to mobilize people to engage in collective action to address a social problem. Many people before you have attempted community organizing; some have had varying degrees of success and others have not achieved what they intended. If you have questioned whether you have what it takes to be a community organizer, you need to know that it is possible to be an effective agent of change. However, you must believe in social change and possess a broad range of knowledge about social, economic, and political factors that influence the structure and function of communities. Furthermore, you must have courage, insight, cultural awareness, compassion, empathy, humility, a sense of humor, and a desire to work tirelessly on social issues. Community organizing is a form of advocacy, so you must also master the practical skills of persuasion covered in Chapter 7.

In this chapter, you will examine the meaning of community, social justice, and hegemony in society. In addition, you will learn about the community organizer's three primary roles as recruiter, facilitator, and educator. According to the *Ethical Standards of Human Service Professionals* you have an ethical obligation to be a community advocate:

> **Statement 13:** Human service professionals act as advocates in addressing unmet client and community needs. Human service professionals provide a mechanism for identifying unmet client needs, calling attention to these needs, and assisting in planning and mobilizing to advocate for those needs at the local community level.

> (*Ethical Standards for Human Service Professionals* (1996) Reprinted by permission of the National Organization for Human Services)

The Meaning of Community and Social Justice

Before we get to the nuts and bolts of community organizing, you must learn what makes a community. Is a community geographically determined? Is a community defined by a formal governing body that oversees day-to-day operations? You might conceptualize a community much like those portrayed on popular television programs. Or you might conceptualize a community as the geographic space where you have spent the majority of your life. No matter how community is defined, a community organizer needs to know that all communities have problems, needs, and opportunities. In addition, the way in which the community perceives itself can impact how a community organizer will strategize to make needed or desired changes.

Community Imagined and Real

Let's examine different concepts of **community**. One of the largest communities we all belong to is our nation. A nation is a community with enduring comradeship among citizens (Anderson, 2006). In a nation, citizens are aware that most other citizens will remain unknown to them. Despite the lack of direct connection and the wide range of difference among citizens, many vehemently claim their allegiance to the nation, and when the nation is threatened—as in the 9/11 attack on the New York World Trade Center—many citizens demonstrate a loyalty that may lead them to forfeit their lives to preserve the boundaries of their nation. There is great power in the belief in the nation-state, which should not be ignored.

Now let's consider how communities are defined within a nation. In the community-theory literature, there is an ongoing debate about how best to characterize the changing pattern of community life, which has made it difficult to develop a rigid definition for community (Warren, 1978). Despite the debates, people have developed definitions for community. Saul Alinsky, a famous American community organizer, defined community as people engaged in an organized communal life and living in an organized fashion (see Box 8.1). Another way to define community is in terms of relationships between individuals. As a result, community is defined as a site where citizens consent to enter a relationship with other citizens and make a commitment to care for each other (McKnight, 1995). Community can also be defined as a web of affect-laden relationships among a group of individuals. These relationships often crisscross and reinforce one another and require a measure of commitment to a set of shared values, norms, and meanings, as well as a shared history and identification with a particular culture (Etzioni, 1996). Others have defined community as a group of people with similar geographic proximity, ethnicity, sexual orientation, religious affiliation, or a common cause (Rubin & Rubin, 2008); communities are sites for consumer production and consumer consumption (Kretzman, 1995), or communities are a mixture of social units and systems, which serve as the major social functions having locality significance (Warren, 1978).

Our traditional way of thinking about community as a large or small cluster of people living in close proximity to stores and services does not adequately capture what constitutes community life in the modern world (Warren, 1978). There have been transformations in community living such as the increased number of people living in

Saul Alinsky was a community organizer and political writer. He is also considered the founder of the modern community organizing. During his four decades as an organizer in poor and working-class neighborhoods, he sought to improve the living conditions of workers and African Americans in urban areas throughout the United States. He authored several books, including *Rules for Radicals* and *Reveille for Radicals*.

metropolitan areas that contain hundreds of communities. The overlapping and inter-mingling of city, suburb, and rural communities has also changed the concept of com-munity. With increased autonomy and transiency of people, the development of close relationships among residents has been inhibited, and the concept of community remains elusive.

Outside the cities are suburbs that have overlapping boundaries with urban centers. Large networks of highly efficient roads and transportation systems have made it possi-ble for people to travel great distances to their jobs and for products or services. On the one hand, this type of mobility has created suburbs, but on the other it has undermined the stability of small community business centers and the infrastructure of many sub-urban communities. Businesses (from all sectors) located in communities are often run by state and national systems, which headquarter the decision makers outside the pur-view of the community (Warren, 1978). In other words, banks, drug stores, and mega shopping centers such as Target, Home Depot, and Wal-Mart may employ community residents but are not managed within the community.

The Meaning of Social Justice

As a community organizer, you will need to understand what makes a community and how social injustice affects some communities more than others. If you are endeavoring to bring social justice to a community, you must understand what social justice is and is not.

In the 1840s, the person credited with coining the phrase "social justice" was Luigi Taparelli d'Azeglio (Miller, 1999). Taparelli believed that social justice focused on a just approach to helping people in need by way of social associations (e.g., family, neighbor-hood, and religious community) that were outside of the government.

In the next century, social reformers would use the term *social justice* in their appeals to make those in power attend to the needs of the growing number of working poor, racial minorities, and other vulnerable populations who were nega-tively impacted by political and economic forces in society. Since the 1960s, there has been an interest in the philosophical concept of social justice in the United States. Some believe this interest in social justice was due to a growing significance of public controversies over civil rights, war, Black power, and women's rights, which all impacted political, social, and economic spheres throughout the United States (Miller, 1999).

SOCIAL JUSTICE ACCORDING TO RAWLS   John Rawls, a preeminent political philosopher of the 20th century, reignited the field of political philosophy around the topic of social justice. In 1971, Rawls published *A Theory of Justice,* in which he proposed: "Each person possesses an inviolability [sacredness] founded on justice that even the welfare of society as a whole cannot override. For this reason justice denies that the loss of freedom for some is made right by a greater good shared by others" (p. 3). Rawls's (1999) theory of justice centers on what he called "*justice as fairness*," which is based on two fundamental principles:

LIBERTY PRINCIPLE   Each person is to have an equal right to the most extensive total system of equal basic liberties compatible with a similar system of liberty for all.

DIFFERENCE PRINCIPLE   Social and economic inequalities are to be arranged so that they are both: (a) to the greatest benefit of the least advantaged, consistent with the just savings principle and (b) attached to offices and positions open to all under conditions of fair equality of opportunity (p. 302).

Let's now closely examine the two fundamental principles. The liberty principle focuses on equal basic liberties, which means every person should have equal rights to basic personal and political liberties including freedom of thought, the right to influence, the right to be involved in politics, and freedom of association (Cohen, 2004). The difference principle holds that social and economic inequalities are just only if they bring benefits to everyone, especially the neediest people in society. Furthermore, the distribution of income and wealth should not be based on accidental differences or what Rawls calls the "natural lottery." In other words, people's inborn traits such as intelligence, beauty, and strength come by way of a natural lottery. To lessen excessive economic inequality (typically created by the natural lottery), income would be limited; but in a just society, those who are capable of creating social innovations would maximize the economic expectations, including disadvantaged social groups, ultimately leading to a system of social cooperation that offers a fair life to all.

CREATING A JUST AND FAIR SOCIETY   Rawls (1999) asks us to imagine how we might create a truly just society. He proposes that a group wishing to do so should begin with something he calls the "original position," which has two features. First, the group commits to the attempt to create conditions that guarantee the greatest political and social justice for all. Second, the group agrees to operate under the "veil of ignorance," which means that each member of the group is ignorant of his or her own characteristics in the "natural lottery" of inborn traits (gender, race, intelligence, strength, beauty, and so on) and circumstances of birth. The veil of ignorance should help the framers remember that it is in their own best interest to maximize fairness for all, as they don't know where they themselves might wind up in society. Those in this original position are now to choose among the possible principles of social justice to select the principles that would ensure the greatest fairness. Rawls proposes that the two principles described earlier—the liberty principle and the difference principle—are the most likely to succeed in creating a just society.

CHALLENGES TO RAWLS'S THEORIES OF JUSTICE   The relevance of Rawls's work is extensively debated and written about in the literature. Political philosophers argue that standard

---

Human Systems

Understanding and Mastery: An understanding of capacities, limitations, and resiliency of human systems..

Critical Thinking Question: As a community organizer, a human services practitioner needs to understand how a human system—such as a community—is affected by social injustice. Play the Natural Lottery game with your classmates to explore what social justice means and what it takes to create a just society. The game will give you the opportunity to think critically about social justice and consider all the factors that make a just and fair society..

. . . .

concepts related to justice, such as natural rights, reaping the fruit of one's labor, collective wealth, and liberty are in opposition to Rawls's concept of justice. Other scholars argue that Rawls's theory of justice does not consider issues such as women and childcare (Bojer, 2002), equality in the context of globalization (Christensen, 2005), the complexity of eradicating poverty (Lotter, 2010), or same-sex marriage (Gray, 2004). On the other hand, it has been argued that Rawls's principles of social justice will work if three things are in place: (a) there must be a bounded society with a group membership; (b) there must be an institution to implement and modify the principles of social justice; and (c) there must be an entity—such as a government— that is capable of implementing and managing institutional changes to promote social justice (Miller, 1999).

Moreover, scholars who debate Rawls' theory of justice have offered other theories and concepts of social justice. Some propose social justice theories in terms of redistribution of resources, some propose social justice theories in terms of recognition (or identity) politics, and others propose to achieve social justice by employing both redistribution and recognition theories as a bivalent conception. Let's examine these three different theoretical perspectives.

REDISTRIBUTIVE THEORY OF JUSTICE   From a redistributive theoretical perspective, injustice is caused by political and economic factors such as labor exploitation, low paying jobs, and an inadequate standard of living for many workers. To achieve social justice in terms of political economics, there would have to be a just redistribution of resources and goods (Fraser, 1996). In other words, the remedy for injustice would be to have economic restructuring that would include redistributing income more equally, reorganizing the division of labor, and transforming political and economic structures.

RECOGNITION THEORY OF JUSTICE   From the recognition theoretical perspective, injustice is based on cultural domination, nonrecognition of other social cultures, and disrespect for cultural differences. To achieve social justice, there has to be an acknowledgement of ethnicity, race, gender (Bojer, 2002), and sexual minorities (Gray, 2004) to create a difference-friendly world (Fraser, 1996). The remedy for injustice requires cultural changes such as recognizing cultural distinctiveness, revaluing disrespected social identities, and transforming oppressive societal patterns. In this form of justice, marginalized groups would not be faced with the choice of assimilating into the dominant cultural norms to get respect and have the right to equal participation in society.

BIVALENT CONCEPTION OF JUSTICE   It has been argued that the redistributive and recognition theories of justice used by themselves fail to ensure that the greatest number of people in society would be justly treated and have the right to equal participation in society (Fraser, 1996). However, adopting both theories results in a bivalent conception—also known as paired conceptions—of justice, which ensures a norm of participatory equality in society despite factors such as class or a distinctive social identity.

Women in society experience gender-specific status injuries such as being denied the full rights and protections of citizenship, enduring sexual assault and domestic violence, lack of reproductive autonomy, demeaning stereotypical depictions in the mass media, sexual harassment on the job, unequal pay in employment, and marginalization in public decision-making bodies. How would you address all these problems? Let's examine how using a bivalent conception of justice helps more broadly address women's social problems in society. It is statistically evident that gender creates an economic inequality between men and women here in the United States (Hochschild & Machung, 2012) and in other countries. In addition, across many societies women are a devalued cultural group, which also makes gender a recognition problem as opposed to simply a redistribution problem. Therefore, efforts to remedy injustice due to one's gender may require challenging cultural attitudes, which involves the use of a recognition theory of justice. However, remedying women's economic problems would involve use of redistribution theories of justice. Not recognizing that classism, racism, and sexism require a bivalent conception of justice may impede the ability to fight the injustices within society. The bivalent approach to justice is far from simple, but it is promising:

> To be sure, not all oppressed collectivities are bivalent in the same way, nor to the same degree. Some axes of oppression, such as class, tilt more heavily toward the distribution end of the spectrum; others, such as sexuality, incline more to the recognition end; while still others, such as gender and "race," cluster closer to the center. (Fraser, 1996, p. 22)

The Generalist as a Community Organizer

Social and community psychology scholars have found it hard to define social justice and to implement social justice approaches that actually improve the condition of oppressed groups in society (Drew, Bishop, & Syme, 2002). Nevertheless, there is much discussion and fascination about social justice in many different academic disciplines. In the human services discipline, there is little discourse or scholarship about social justice concepts or approaches (Kincaid, 2009). However, if you hope to be a community organizer it will benefit you to understand the complexities of social justice theories and the limitations of implementing social justice approaches. There are also many other things community organizers must know to do their job.

Here is a story of a community organizer. In 1985, a young man named Barack Obama started his human service career in Chicago after graduating from Harvard Law School. He became a community organizer at the Altgeld Gardens, a public housing project on the Southside of Chicago. Obama did volunteer training and developed different poverty programs. Years later, Obama ran for the highest political office in the United States. During his 2008 presidential campaign, a woman from Altgeld Gardens complained to news reporters that Obama hadn't really done much work in the community. She went on to say that Obama had not taken a leadership role in the community nor was he visible during their successful community change process.

In fact, Obama had begun training community members in the political process, organizing groups, and facilitating contacts with government leaders. He also arranged for mass media exposure but all the while remained out of the limelight. So the woman was correct: He had not taken a leadership role. But he was not supposed to do that. The lesson to be learned from this story about President Obama's job as a community organizer is that the role of the organizer is behind the scenes, while the community members take center stage. Simply put, the community organizer guides a community and then quietly slips away when his or her services are no longer needed.

You should be mindful of the fact that human services professionals and their organizations have sometimes been accused of destroying the sense of community and of reducing the overall strength and capacity of the community to do the thing they do best, which is caring for each other (McKnight, 1995). You must be open to the fact that when community members are seeking collective power to change their lives, they need an organizer who will be passionate about helping them move toward their collective empowerment. The organizer will also respect the fact that community members are experts about their community and have the right to self-determination.

What It Takes to Be a Community Organizer

According to Alinsky (1971), one key quality needed to be a **community organizer** is strong interpersonal skills to genuinely communicate to the membership and leadership of a community organization. He believed it is also essential for a community organizer to be sincere, caring, respectful, and committed. Moreover, a community organizer must have courage, insight, cultural awareness, compassion, empathy, humility, a sense of humor, and a desire to work tirelessly on social issues. An organizer must have a vision of change and believe that change can occur.

What does a community organizer actually do? Lee Staples (2004), an activist scholar, states the majority of a community organizer's time is spent with people in their homes around the kitchen table, on the front stoops of their homes, or speaking with people on the phone. The organizer also spends a tremendous amount of time in an endless array of recruitment meetings, evaluating organizational operations, fundraising, negotiating, strategic planning, and doing action research. The organizer's time is also absorbed by doing community education, leadership training, and lobbying.

What type of education should a community organizer have? A community organizer's education should cover topics such as power dynamics, mobilization, effective communicating, operational problems, field tactics, and development of community leaders, but several volumes would be needed to adequately examine the complexities of community organizing. Let's examine where the community organizer works and the basic roles the community organizer plays.

Learning About the Community Organization

Community organizations typically are nonprofit businesses that have a 501(c)(3) or (c)(4) tax-exempt designation (see Chapter 4). These entities have the trappings of most businesses, such as a formal name, a building, or rented offices. They also have formal business structures that often lean more toward a democratic culture with very little bureaucracy. Hence, administration, managers, line workers, and volunteers work in a culture that promotes (or should promote) participation, transparency, and debate. In addition, community members may be sponsored into paid positions in these nonprofit organizations.

An established nonprofit community organization has longevity and could be involved in solving multiple interrelated chronic community problems (e.g., substandard education, poverty, or lack of housing and viable jobs) at the local, state, or national levels. These organizations help to stimulate targeted communities to address the community problems (Gittell & Vidal, 1998). These entities strongly communicate to those in power that they are focused on results and will maintain their efforts until progress is made (Rubin & Rubin, 2008).

The special feature of these nonprofit organizations is that they are in close contact with their constituents, so they can quickly respond to immediate threats and issues. These organizations also have the means to share expert knowledge, offer financial support, and teach technical skills to community members. Economic and social development organizations are examples of organizations that bring communities together as an organized body so that they have the power to sustain a collective action to solve their common issues. In Table 8.1 is a list of different types of nonprofit organizations that function in American communities. This table is not a comprehensive list, but it is representative of organizations that work for specific people on issues or progressive social change.

Nonprofit community organizations employ more direct service workers than community organizers (Rubin & Rubin, 2008). However, the presence of a professional community organizer (hired by an agency) can have far-reaching effects in a

Table 8.1	Nonprofit Community Organizations	
Organization Type	Purpose	Examples
Identity Organizations	General purpose is the development of collective pride of a specific group formed by a common identity (Native American, LGBT) and to collectively work on shared problems.	Janitors for Justice National Organization for Women (NOW) International Gay and Lesbian Human Rights Commission (IGLHRC)
Social Action Organizations Radical Social Action Radical Community Organization	General purpose is to compel those in power to respond to community needs	ACT UP pressured government and health systems to be more responsive to PWAs
Issue-based Coalitions	General purpose is to have a group of organizations temporarily come together to accomplish a common objective.	GOTV (Get Out the Vote) Group of organizations came together to register the poor, the homeless, and minority to vote.
Ad Hoc Neighborhood Organizations Community Power Organizations Consensus-Building Community Organizations	General purpose is to have a group of organizations temporarily come together to accomplish a common objective.	Neighborhood Watch LA Bus Riders Union

Organization Type	Purpose	Examples
National Advocacy Coalitions	Come together to accomplish shared goals.	Gray Panthers National Council of La Raza Center for Community Change
Social and Economic Development Organizations	General purpose is to restore neighborhoods, service the poor, and work to create a more equitable and justice society.	ACORN Gamaliel *Boston Dudley Street Neighborhood Initiative started the growth of businesses and the training of new entrepreneurs. Southern Poverty Law Center fights to protect minorities from racist actions
Church-based Organizations Faith-based Organizations	Work for redevelopment to create new supermarket, affordable housing, and employment training center; support ongoing workers' employment problems such as low wages.	PICO *PIA (Peninsula Interfaith Action) CLUE (Clergy and Laity United for Economic Justice)

community. Professional community organizers typically come from outside the community and work with, and not on, the community. A compilation of the qualification, skills, and responsibilities from different ads for a community organizer is given in the following box. This will give you a sense of what many organizations are looking for in a professional community organizer.

LEARN ABOUT THE ORGANIZATIONAL CULTURE As you begin your work with an agency, your first job is to learn about the organizational mission and the

---

**A Generic Ad for a Community Organizer

Job description: Seeking a community organizer to work with a diverse community. This is an opportunity to create and initiate innovative programs. You must be focused on developing a relationship with community stakeholders and leaders, be committed to social equity and justice, and work to alleviate community problems.

Qualifications

- Associate or bachelor's degree from an accredited college or university
- Knowledge about the political and policy process.
- Experience with analysis and development of human service policy.

Skills

- Strong interpersonal and relational skills
- Strong written and verbal communication skills.
- Cultural competency to work with people from diverse backgrounds.

- Capacity to recruit residents and move them into action in a public or political arena.
- Training and facilitating skills to develop community leaders.
- Demonstrated ability to organize and mobilize a community.
- Demonstrated capacity to lead others in community outreach, surveying, and canvassing.
- Capable of running community meetings,
- Can mobilize a campaign, shape the message, and assess responses.
- Capable of managing multiple priorities and use a team approach.
- Strong community outreach, organization and engagement skills.
- Supervisory abilities to work with staff and volunteers.
- Capable of doing a community needs assessment.

Essential Responsibilities

- Engaging in advocacy efforts with identified communities.
- Initiating and developing relationships with key stakeholders in the community.
- Developing community membership, track member contacts with membership database.
- Assisting with meeting preparations, scheduling, coordinating activities and events.
- **Participating** in coalition member workshops, trainings, and meetings.
- Maintaining community relationships between actions and meetings.
- Working with the campaign leadership to build the cross-neighborhood committee.
- Increasing awareness of specific community problems.
- Participating in strategic organizational planning and development.
- Supervising staff of six or more employees.

specific set of issues the organization is working on with the community. Initially, this information can be obtained by examining organization material or talking with people in your organization. You should also do a systematic and thorough analysis of the organization and the community in which you work. Don't forget, you are a social scientist, which means that before you draw any conclusions it is essential to have the facts. Your work in the field should not be a "fly-by-the-seat of your pants" effort. Rather, it should be done with scientific precision to ensure facts are facts—rather than assumptions. Start with an **organizational scan**. In the organizational scan, you will examine and record the history of the organization and discover how the organization became involved with the community around a specific set of issues. Your research should reveal the organizational players, perspectives, and existing or previous efforts to assist the community in addressing their collective problems. Treat this investigation as a formal academic research project: Develop a hypothesis, keep detailed records, do systematic analysis of your data, revise your hypothesis as necessary, and draw your conclusions.

Learning About the Community Culture

Your second job is to become educated about the community culture; this can be accomplished by doing a community needs assessment. A needs assessment is a process that provides estimates about perceived needs (Royse et al., 2009). It is typically used by agencies to determine the service needs of a community and to determine how to efficiently make use of resources to provide those services. A community needs assessment should focus not only on deficiencies but also on community power dynamics. Therefore, the needs assessment should have two sets of questions:

Perceived needs of the community:

- What characteristics of the service populations (e.g., vulnerable children) can be determined from public records?
- What needs can be identified by direct contact with service users?
- What perceptions do community service providers have about the ways that community problems are being handled?
- What services are available in the community?
- Are there gaps or redundancies in current service delivery?
- What perceptions do members of the community have about services provided and services needed?

Power dynamics in the community:

- What problems seem to be getting the most attention?
- What is the history of the community's problems?
- What resources are being used to solve community problems?
- Who has power in the community's government, organizations, agencies, and institutions?
- Who are the allies and who are the enemies in the community?
- Which politicians are involved and in what ways?
- What are the agendas of the players and stakeholders?
- What other agencies or organizations are involved in the community problems?

If you can answer questions such as these (the list here is by no means exhaustive), you will have a good sense of what is needed in the community and whether you can work with the community and generate change.

POWER GAMES IN A CULTURAL CONTEXT According to Saul Alinsky (1971), the education of an organizer requires an analysis of power patterns. An earlier theorist, Antonio Gramsci (1892–1937), developed the concept of *hegemony* to explain the fundamental—and often invisible—patterns of political power. Gramsci argued that all parts of our social reality are dominated by and supportive of the most powerful social groups within society. Gramsci called this powerful and pervasive influence that a dominant culture has on society "**hegemony**." There are three main applications of hegemonic power: (1) the social, cultural, ideological, or economic influence exerted by a dominant group; (2) the predominant influence of one state over others; and (3) the processes by which a dominant culture maintains its leading position. Gramsci focused on the first and the third. His analysis showed that the successful use of hegemonic power made unequal social arrangements seem natural and unequal distributions of power seem necessary and inevitable. Thus, simply becoming aware of the idea of hegemony is an important starting point because it means questioning these assumptions of naturalness and inevitability.

Understanding hegemonic forces within society will make you aware of the challenges you will face when engaging in social change activities as a community organizer. Hegemonic forces, for example, engulf modern communication and data systems that function within domains such as national politics, global business, and intelligence (Gosovic, 2001). Therefore, much of the information that comes through mass media is designed to give the appearance that the world as it is has order and is functioning normally. If things are as they must be, then change is threatening.

Poverty is a particularly intractable problem, even in the wealthy United States. Many of us (if we are honest) don't know what causes poverty in America. Mass media creates simplistic information bits for general consumption that greatly influence the public's perceptions of the poor, so that poverty may seem inevitable and unchangeable. Very little critical analysis is offered about poverty in the information that comes through mass media systems. Many consumers digest these simplistic information bits but remain relatively uninformed. More detailed analyses are available, to be sure—but they are generally not widely disseminated. So if you are a community organizer trying to educate people about complex social issues such as the causes of poverty, you can't depend on mass media to inform people about poverty. In fact, you will have to work against the prevailing dominant culture to offer a different view about poverty and its solutions.

Hegemonic forces may be observed in action in surprising forms. For example, NPR (National Public Radio) and PBS (Public Broadcast Services) have both been threatened with budget cuts when their reporting strayed too far from the party line of conservative foundations and government. Defunding threats came from Republican administrations under Richard Nixon, Ronald Regan, and George W. Bush when NPR and PBS programming focused on social and political issues that placed the government in an unfavorable light.

Moreover, global intellectual hegemony (perpetuated by the control of mass media) tends to homogenize public opinion, which leaves millions of people around the world interpreting and explaining social processes through the dominant conceptual framework. In turn, people limit or forego critical debates about social issues, efforts to maintain social and political pluralism, and attempts to challenge authority—even when not doing these things will be detrimental to their own lives.

Is it hopeless to try to alter the existing hegemonic dynamic within society? Not at all! We are examining (what seems like) the invisible forces of power so you will be aware of this dynamic and can plan accordingly, but this means you must take the time to understand hegemony and acquire some skills to address it, especially if you intend to engage in community organizing.

What must you learn about the hegemonic dynamic within society? Gramsci argued that for ordinary people to change their social conditions they had to master the dominant culture prior to attempting to transform society. Mastering the dominant culture, for instance, would involve learning facts such as how intellectual hegemony discredits, undermines, neutralizes, and targets anything that is significantly different or challenges the current social orthodoxy or calls into question the current social structure (Gosovic, 2001).

At present, the American government is probably one of the best examples of a functioning democratic public body. Under American democracy, people have rights that protect their freedom of speech, freedom to assemble, and freedom to seek redress from the government. These rights have enabled citizens to engage in struggles over social equity and equality within our society. Historical struggles for rights and freedoms in the United States are exemplified by those who fought for the abolition of slavery, women's right to vote, and desegregation of public schools. Currently, there are social struggles such as greater gender equality in the workplace, an increase of the minimum wage, and finding a legal path to U.S. citizenship for illegal immigrants, just to name a few. These basic rights are crucial to the ability to challenge hegemony and reach for positive social change.

In the United States, when people's movements have pushed the government for greater equity and justice, there has been a predictable push back from government. All you need to do is look at what has happened to activist groups such as Green Peace and Occupy America to observe how government attempts to retain power. Frances Fox Piven (2008), an activist scholar and political scientist, believes the government has a limited repertoire of strategies to retain its power. The first strategy typically begins with the public officials attempting to co-opt the activist group's leadership by requesting that they join government ad hoc committees, commissions, or take a professional position within the government. If the leadership of the activist group refuses to be enticed by official titles or obtaining power within the government, the next strategy is used.

The second strategy involves public officials offering conciliatory remedies such as grants or changing oppressive legislation targeted by activist groups (Piven, 2008). When conciliatory remedies are taken by activist groups, they view them as gains for the movement. However, once social order is restored, historically the government has retracted their financial support, restored oppressive measures, and taken back other gains made by the protest movement. A historical example of government using this second strategy occurred after the Civil War when social order had been restored, freed slaves were assisted by the government to resettle and begin a free life. However, in short order, government funding was withdrawn, and new laws (Jim Crow laws) stripped these new citizens of their right to own land, vote, or use public facilities.

The last strategy used by the government to retain its power occurs when the previous two strategies fail to disrupt activist groups (Piven, 2008). At this point, public officials may resort to coercive interventions: fining, imprisoning, or using police or military forces to disband groups. For example, after months of Occupy America activists living in urban public spaces and peacefully demonstrating against corporations and the wealthy elite, encampments around the country were asked by public officials to disband. When the activists would not leave the public space, many were threatened with fines and imprisonment and in some cities the police forcefully removed activists.

As a community organizer, if you are intent on changing the social structure, you must master the dominant culture (i.e., learn all aspects of the dominant culture). You also must create social networks, learn new social concepts, and begin spreading new ideas, to help others create a new cognitive framework or a new way of thinking as they begin to challenge the status quo. It may seem daunting to contemplate making changes in communities as you read and think about theories that envision building a drastically different social system. However, it is very important that you understand the influence that hegemonic dynamics have on society, government, organizations, and most importantly on you.

The Roles of the Professional Community Organizer

If you are hired to be a community organizer for an agency there are three critical roles: recruiter, facilitator, and educator (see Table 8.2). While working as an organizer in the community you must adopt the mindset that you are working to help others live their lives, so your personal desires and ambitions must be held in abeyance.

The Recruiting Role

Recruiting is one of the roles of the community organizer. To recruit people for social action, the community organizer will use a tactic called *canvassing*. Canvassing is the age-old method of knocking on doors in the community and engaging people face to face to explain the issues and explain why community members should sign on to help (Staples, 2004). The organizer's prior research about the community problems is distilled down to a short persuasive "elevator speech," which is designed to get people involved (see Chapter 7). During the canvassing process, the organizer might even have the opportunity to do short semi-structured interviews, which allows for the collection of in-depth data for later use. Collecting data means keeping systematic records, which allows for an analysis of what is and is not occurring in the field.

Information Management

Understanding and Mastery: Performing elementary community needs assessment.

Critical Thinking Question: Community organizers must know how to do an analysis of community needs, including an assessment of community power dynamics. Using the questions provided in this chapter as a starting point, perform a basic needs assessment for a community that you are familiar with and have access to. Try to answer as many questions in both areas—needs and power dynamics—as possible. How does the needs assessment help you to think about planning for providing services to a community? What power arrangements in the community seem to have a hegemonic character?

Table 8.2	Roles and Tactics of the Community Organizer
Roles Played by Organizer	**Tactics Used by Community Organizer**
Recruiter Role	1. Canvasses to mobilize a people. 2. Motivates people to work collectively work on a problem. 3. Interviews people to gather community data on issues. 4. Uses social media to inform, mobilize, and follow-up with community members. 5. Engages in house meetings to raise consciousness and mobilize community members into action.
Facilitator Role	1. Oversees daily operations of the community organization. 2. Builds a broad base participation of volunteers. 3. Coaches volunteers about the community organizational operations. 4. Identifies potential community leadership. 5. Helps with leadership development.
Educator Role	1. Teaches people about community problems. 2. Initiates leadership training. 3. Teaches community members to run their organization. 4. Teaches community members to influence political, economic, and social spheres.

Another recruiting tactic to consider is the **house meeting**. The house meeting is a laid-back gathering where community volunteers invite their friends and the community organizer, which gives them an opportunity to discuss problems in a safe venue. Food or dessert should be provided at the meeting because it typically draws people in and keeps them around. The objective for the house meeting is to raise consciousness of people about community problems and to mobilize people into action. Remember, the role of the organizer as the recruiter is to act as a catalyst and guide the community members. Despite how well prepared you may be, recruiting people is hard work and it is even harder to get people to join and participate in a sustained collective action, even if it is beneficial to them. Expect modest recruiting results and remain mindful that recruiting is an ongoing process. After recruiting community members, the community organizer can use social media such as Facebook and Twitter to keep people and stay connected. Social networks can be a rich resource for retaining people, but the community organizer must learn about the dynamics of these networks before using it.

The Facilitator Role

A professional community organizer often functions as a **facilitator** who will help build and run a community group. (Remember the community group is separate from the formal organization that the professional organizer works for.) Hence, the organizer helps the community members build a democratic organizational structure and process, which allows for greater member commitment, member participation, member growth in numbers, and power (Staples, 2004).

To have a democratic and progressive community organization, leaders must be chosen from the community. The organizer must refrain from taking the position of power and ensure that power remains in the hands of the people who must lead their community or group (Alinsky, 1971). The organizer should help the community group identify potential leaders. An effective leadership should emerge from the community. Leaders are typically among the recruited community members and have the necessary strengths, assets, and resources to fulfill the leadership function (Staples, 2004). The professional organizer must help with leadership development but must be aware that identification of leaders occurs when they come to the attention of a group because they are self-selected, elected, or are specifically recruited (Homan, 2004).

The community organizer is usually responsible for initially overseeing the daily operations of the organization. Volunteers work for the community organization when time permits, which may leave a lot of operational work undone. It is important that an organizer coach community leaders to be inclusive of all volunteers in the organization because it makes available an array of opinions, experiences, and expertise. By employing individual strengths and skills of volunteers, they feel better utilized and challenged and that in turn grows and strengthens the organization. Ultimately, community volunteers and leaders must acquire a full range of skills and the psychological confidence to run their organization and to engage in social action to achieve their goal.

The community organizer must also build a broad base of participation among the volunteers to ensure that daily operations are completed because this is their organization and the ultimate goal is for the community to have complete oversight. The community organizer encourages volunteers to engage in organizational functions such as running meetings, doing strategic planning, filling new positions, and marketing, which leads to building a powerful organization. High volunteer participation ensures that the community members do not become overly reliant on the professional community organizer, because the decision-making power should reside with the members of the community organization. Moreover, a professional organizer is responsible for sharing information with community leaders and members in the context of a safe working environment. It is also essential that organizers remain mindful of not creating a hierarchical relationship between themselves and community members.

The Community Educator Role

The third role of the community organizer is being a **community educator**. To be a good educator requires the organizer to have a broad educational foundation that includes knowledge of social change, social justice, political science, public policy, community psychology, and economics (just to name a few topics). The organizer must also be informed about social problems that stem from poverty, such as the lack of health care, unemployment, under-performing schools, and the lack of affordable housing, because community work often deals with one or more of these problems.

When teaching in the community, the organizer must be able to explain how the different external factors cause social problems. Teaching people how external factors cause social problems will help them formulate better arguments for social change; without this type of information people tend to believe that personal problems are of their own making and not related to broad structural failings. Also local community issues are influenced by political, economic, and social spheres beyond the borders of any specific community. An organizer should be teaching community members how to influence all three spheres, which may involve creating winnable campaigns, initiating nonviolent protests, generating publicity for their cause, and exercising electoral and consumer power to achieve social change.

The Purpose of Grassroots Organizing

The terms *grassroots organizing* and *community organizing* are often used interchangeably, but they are different. Grassroots organizations typically spring up around a single issue and mobilize members for a specific problem, whereas community organizations as we just learned, sets out to address a variety of issues that affect a community. In grassroots organizing, according to Staples (2004):

> Community members make their own decisions about social change—what needs to be added, altered, or eliminated to make their lives better. The community provides its own leadership for the change effort. [And] community members take collective action that employs "people power" to achieve shared goals, resolve common problems, and gain a greater measure of control over the circumstances of their lives. (p. 2)

Grassroots organizing is not based in a formal agency, and there is rarely a paid position for a grassroots organizer. Nevertheless, you should know about grassroots organizing and how it differs from agency-based community organizing.

The Structure of Grassroots Organizations

Grassroots organizations often form to bridge service gaps left by government when it fails to be responsive to basic human needs of communities or groups. These organizations are like ad-hoc committees, which means that they are short lived. There are approximately 7.5 million grassroots organizations in America, outnumbering nonprofit entities, but both have similar social change missions within communities (Sobeck, Agius & Mayers, 2007).

Grassroots organizations typically have a fluid and informal leadership; the membership fluctuates depending on how pressing the issue is; and the organization is formed to make specific demands, and is not intended to be a permanent organization (Delgado, 1997). Furthermore, grassroots organizations are loosely structured, which allows for easy membership and participation from a broad section of society. The assembly of community members can occur in geographical communities, virtual communities, or among groups of people with similar identities.

GRASSROOTS LEADERSHIP   Citizen participation in grassroots organizations enhances community development and civic engagement and serves to educate people about politics, leadership, and empowerment (Sharpe, 2005). There are typically four levels of participation in a grassroots organization (Homan, 2004):

1. Leadership—the core group participants
2. Workers—ongoing active participants
3. Assisters—occasionally active participants
4. Inactive members—general supporters

Grassroots leadership must create structures so that all have a sense of the collective goals. Thus, leadership responsibilities must be shared among volunteers to ensure there is a democratic process and to ensure there will be trained future leaders. Leadership must create an environment of inclusivity to ensure an array of opinions, experiences, and expertise that broadens viable approaches to social issues.

Most people who participate in grassroots movements are volunteers and have other obligations and have limited time. Volunteers initially experience exhilaration when they become aware of their ability to be involved in social change. To maintain volunteers' initial enthusiasm, they must be engaged in meaningful work that employs their individual strengths and skills. However, over time there will be a decline in participation due to personal exhaustion, personal economic costs, or because the movement achieved its goal by winning the grievances (Piven, 2008).

Grassroots Organizing as a Political Tool

Grassroots organizing can be used as a political tool to advance social or economic agendas of communities. This type of organizing is more often used by marginalized groups and serves as a public outlet for their dissenting expressions. Typically, grassroots organizers use social action strategies to achieve their goals. Social action is an adversarial or confrontational strategy. The primary goals of social action are (a) building a large power base of constituents, (b) problem resolution, and (c) decreasing the overall power disparities between the movement and the official decision makers. In other words, social action brings a group of people (a power base) together to pressure, embarrass, and compel those in power to respond to community needs.

A perfect example of a social action is represented by the Arab Spring—also known as the Arab Awakening—that occurred in 2010 in Tunisia and quickly spread across the region. The Arab Spring occurred after Mohamed Bouazizi, a young vegetable vendor in Tunisia, protested against abusive government officials by setting himself on fire in the town square. Bouazizi's extreme action occurred because of repeated episodes of harassment and continual confiscation of his wares, which impeded him from making a living.

Ultimately, Bouazizi's extreme act served as the catalyst for a series of grassroots movements across the Arab world. Within weeks of Bouazizi's death, civil protests were occurring against oppressive governments in Tunisia, Egypt, and Libya, which later resulted in the dismantling of these governments. Major civil protests were also inspired in Algeria, Bahrain, Iraq, Jordan, Kuwait, Morocco, Oman, Saudi Arabia, Sudan, Syria, and Yemen.

How were people in all these different countries so quickly informed and organized? The answer is Facebook and Twitter. These electronic platforms were instrumental in the quick dissemination of uncensored information and replaced dependence on the state-censored Arab national media (Owais, 2011).

In Tunisia alone, there are nearly 2 million Facebook and Twitter users. With social networking, grassroots organizers could rapidly coordinate, synchronize, and gather support. The social network allowed people to communicate and also allowed for real-time updates of events occurring at ground zero. In the case of the civil protests in Egypt, the technological know-how of activists outpaced and circumvented their government's attempts to limit or block the information available to and from citizens (Dunn, 2011) and to the outside world. In fact, the Egyptian government's attempts to stop communications that were fueling the uprising ultimately proved ineffective in preventing the spread of information and further galvanized citizens against them. Ultimately, the government regime fell.

Grassroots organizing accomplished during the Arab Spring is an example of using electronic platforms as a political tool for social change. Throughout the Middle East, twenty-something Arab citizens had become tech savvy like their peers around the globe, but their elder statesmen were behind the technological curve. State officials in many Middle East countries were unable to keep up with the tech savvy activists.

In the West, communication technology has been in the hands of different groups to advance their agendas. Electronic grassroots strategies are also used by "Astroturf" companies. Astroturf refers to artificial grassroots organizing, which uses manipulative methodology to create the appearance of an actual community mobilization (McNutt & Boland, 2007). The unique feature of artificial grassroots organizing is that it appears to be supported by individuals in a local community when in fact it is not. Astroturf grassroots organizing was originally created to manipulate the political process at all levels of government, while masking the true identities of corporate organizations that desired political outcomes that would benefit them. Now electronic grassroots organizing has become a staple of social activist groups. For example, activists use websites such as www.protest.net to notify members of a pending demonstration, initiate an automated letter writing campaign, or send a variety of announcements on issues such as pending legislation.

Summary

The concept of community has no rigid definition. The community called *nation* is expansive while the community of like-minded peers could be small. Traditional communities have been transformed by numerous social factors such as technology and transportation. Despite how a community is conceptualized, it will take a lot of knowledge and skill to advance social change within it.

Social justice is more than a concept; it is also something that many have sought to implement within society. From the theoretical side, scholars have attempted to explain the essential components needed to create a just society. However, limitations of the theories of justice demonstrate that to achieve a socially just society there are numerous factors to consider such as race, gender, sexual orientation, and socioeconomics.

Beyond theory, there is the work of professional community organizers that requires them to have courage, insight, cultural awareness, compassion, empathy, humility, a sense of humor, and a desire to work tirelessly on social issues. Human service practitioners who are hired by an agency to be a community organizer will learn that much is required of them.

Community organizers will need to understand both the organizational and community cultures in which they work. They will have to learn to do an analysis of power patterns in social systems they hope to change. At the same time, a community organizer will take on three critical roles as recruiter, facilitator, and educator while working with a community group to address specific community problems.

Assess your analysis and evaluation of this chapter's content by completing the Chapter Review.

Lobbying in the Political Arena

···

In many countries, citizens have the right to advocate for legislation by directly addressing members of the government. This form of advocacy, called lobbying, enables citizens and groups to bring a wide variety of concerns—political, social, and economic—to the attention of government and to attempt to persuade legislators to take action on them. Lobbying is thus a significant form of citizen participation in government and a major force for social change. Human services professionals, who so often encounter social problems and whose ethical standards oblige them to pursue social change, must be prepared to engage in lobbying as one of the chief forms of advocacy.

In the United States, the right to lobby the government is offered to all citizens under the Constitution. Because lobbying is undertaken precisely to affect legislation, it is critically important to understand the legislative process, beginning with the Constitution itself. Under the *Ethical Standards,* as a human services practitioner you are obligated to lobby for legislative change:

> **Statement 10:** Human service professionals are aware of local, state, and federal laws. They advocate for change in regulations and statutes when such legislation conflicts with ethical guidelines and/ or client rights. Where laws are harmful to individuals, groups, or communities, human service professionals consider the conflict between values of obeying the law and the values of serving people and may decide to initiate social action.
>
> (*Ethical Standards for Human Service Professionals* (1996). Reprinted by permission of the National Organization for Human Services)

In this chapter, we will review the U.S. Constitution to ensure that you are knowledgeable about laws that protect you and others who engage in social action. In the United States, there are thousands of organized groups that lobby the government to ensure that legislation favors them, sometimes at the expense of other groups. This chapter will also address the issue of the scope and power special interest groups have over our legislators.

We will then examine policies and laws that define a lobbyist, lobbying practices, and limitations of lobbying in government venues. Lobbying at the state level is particularly important for human service organizations. Topics related to lobbying at the state level include building a coalition in and outside of the workplace, developing strategies to become acquainted with the political arena, making a bill into law, and learning about legislators' activities in the State House. Finally, you will examine how to initiate a lobbying campaign, so you can advocate for the needs of communities in which you may work.

By no means is this chapter an exhaustive review of lobbying. What you do get in this chapter is a substantial amount of information to form a solid foundation on which you can build.

A Brief History of the Bill of Rights

Many of you have taken a high school civics course and have learned about the U.S. Constitution and the Bill of Rights, including the right to bring concerns to the attention of the government. When I began teaching undergraduate human services students about lobbying, I was surprised to discover that most of my students were unaware of this right. Moreover, my students did not know who their state or federal representatives were. The importance of these rights and the necessity of understanding the legislative process make this section a very useful review—even if you remember your civics lessons well. A comprehensive discussion of the U.S. Constitution is beyond the scope of this book, but I would strongly encourage you to read this document because it is what the democratic process within our country is based on.

The U.S. **Constitution** was initially adopted by members of the Constitutional Convention in Philadelphia on September 17, 1787. This legal document outlines the organizational structure and function of the U.S. government's three federal branches: (a) the executive branch, (b) the judicial branch, and (c) the legislative branch, Congress, which comprises the Senate and the House of Representatives. The Constitution is considered the supreme law of the land and outlines the federal government's legal relationship to each state, each citizen, and other individuals in the United States. This legal document outlines how the government functions within the framework of a participatory democracy. (Go to the Internet and retrieve a copy of the U.S. Constitution and then take a moment to closely examine it.)

At a later date, the first United States Congress ratified 10 separate amendments known as the **Bill of Rights**. The Bill of Rights was added to the original Constitution in 1791 because there were no provisions in the original document to protect the fundamental principles of liberty and freedom. Furthermore, the Bill of Rights ensured limitations on the power of the federal government and increased protections of the people's rights to liberty, specific freedoms, and the right to own property. Box 9.1 lists the 10 amendments in the Bill of Rights. Can you determine which amendment states you can lobby the government?

Box 9.1 **The United States Bill of Rights**

Amendments to the U.S. Constitution

The Conventions of a number of the States having, at the time of adopting the Constitution, expressed a desire, in order to prevent misconstruction or abuse of its powers, that further declaratory and restrictive clauses should be added, and as extending the ground of public confidence in the Government will best insure the beneficent ends of its institution;

Resolved, by the Senate and House of Representatives of the United States of America, in Congress assembled, two-thirds of both Houses concurring, that the following articles be proposed to the Legislatures of the several States, as amendments to the Constitution of the United States; all or any of which articles, when ratified by three-fourths of the said Legislatures, to be valid to all intents and purposes as part of the said Constitution, namely:

Bill of Rights

Amendment I

Congress shall make no law respecting an establishment of religion, or prohibiting the free exercise thereof; or abridging the freedom of speech, or of the press; or the right of the people peaceably to assemble, and to petition the government for a redress of grievances.

Amendment II

A well-regulated militia, being necessary to the security of a free state, the right of the people to keep and bear arms, shall not be infringed.

Amendment III

No soldier shall, in time of peace be quartered in any house, without the consent of the owner, nor in time of war, but in a manner to be prescribed by law.

Amendment IV

The right of the people to be secure in their persons, houses, papers, and effects, against unreasonable searches and seizures, shall not be violated, and no warrants shall issue, but upon probable cause, supported by oath or affirmation, and particularly describing the place to be searched, and the persons or things to be seized.

Amendment V

No person shall be held to answer for a capital, or otherwise infamous crime, unless on a presentment or indictment of a grand jury, except in cases arising in the land or naval forces, or in the militia, when in actual service in time of war or public danger; nor shall any person be subject for the same offense to be twice put in jeopardy of life or limb; nor shall be compelled in any criminal case to be a witness against himself, nor be deprived of life, liberty, or property, without due process of law; nor shall private property be taken for public use, without just compensation.

Amendment VI

In all criminal prosecutions, the accused shall enjoy the right to a speedy and public trial, by an impartial jury of the state and district wherein the crime shall have been committed, which district shall have been previously ascertained by law, and to be informed of the nature and cause of the accusation; to be confronted with the witnesses against him; to have compulsory process for obtaining witnesses in his favor, and to have the assistance of counsel for his defense.

Amendment VII

In suits at common law, where the value in controversy shall exceed twenty dollars, the right of trial by jury shall be preserved, and no fact tried by a jury, shall be otherwise reexamined in any court of the United States, than according to the rules of the common law.

Amendment VIII

Excessive bail shall not be required, nor excessive fines imposed, nor cruel and unusual punishments inflicted.

Amendment IX

The enumeration in the Constitution, of certain rights, shall not be construed to deny or disparage others retained by the people.

Amendment X

The powers not delegated to the United States by the Constitution, nor prohibited by it to the states, are reserved to the states respectively, or to the people.

If you guessed the First Amendment, you are correct! The First Amendment reads: "Congress shall make no law respecting an establishment of religion, or prohibiting the free exercise thereof; or abridging the freedom of speech, or of the press; or the right of the people peaceably to assemble, and to petition the Government for a redress of grievances." What phrase in the First Amendment actually speaks specifically to lobbying? Carefully examine the very end of the First Amendment—the phrase "to petition the Government for a redress of grievances" speaks to your right to lobby the government.

The U.S. Supreme Court maintains that the First Amendment should be broadly interpreted to include public petitions of grievances. But is the right to petition the government a permanent right? What could be done to take away the right or limit it? Why would government want to take that right away from people? Even though the Constitution provides us the right to petition the government for a redress of grievances, there have been attempts by the federal government to take away that right. For instance, in 1835, abolitionists petitioned the government to end slavery of African Americans, but the House of Representatives drafted and adopted the Gag Rule (Miller, 1996). The Gag Rule allowed Congressional representatives to automatically table antislavery petitions, memorials, or resolutions brought by abolitionists of the American Anti-Slavery Society. This rule suspended the House of Representatives protocol for reading the petition and assigning it to the appropriate committee for consideration. By refusing to take action on citizens' petitions, the Representatives of Congress were in direct violation of the First Amendment and were able to momentarily leave the institution of slavery intact. It took approximately a year to repeal the Gag Rule. Nearly a decade later in 1844, the Thirteenth Amendment was ratified, banning slavery in the United States and its territories.

There are other instances in American history where the government has limited the right to petition for a redress of grievances for what appears to be relatively good reasons. Since the 1850s, for instance, lobbying had been growing in direct proportion to the growth of industry in the United States. Lobbyists increasingly flooded Washington, DC, for the purpose of influencing legislators on behalf of industrialists who wanted to protect their profits and fortunes. To stem the influence of lobbyists, the government eventually created the Merchant Marine Act of 1936 to control the growing influence of lobbyists in all types of businesses. Under the act, employees in firms governed by the U.S. shipping laws had to file with the Commerce Department prior to engaging in lobbying to influence legislation or administrative decisions (Birnbaum, 1992). Two years later, the Foreign Agents Registration Act of 1938 was enacted due to the threat of Nazism. Under this act, anyone representing either a foreign government or a foreign individual was required to register with the Justice Department.

In 1946, the Regulation of Lobbying Act came into law and required all lobbyists to register with Congress and to give an accounting of their lobbying income and its sources. In addition, under the Lobbying Act of 1946, a lobbyist was defined as a person or organization whose primary job was to influence legislation by direct or indirect lobbying and who received payment for lobbying (Birnbaum, 1992). In *United States vs. Harriss*, the Supreme Court upheld the constitutionality of the Regulation of Lobbying Act of 1946 but narrowed the scope and application of the act with respect to the amount of time that a person could engage in lobbying and who could be lobbied. Furthermore, individuals who specifically solicited and collected money for lobbying public officials were required by the government to register, which included organizations that collected fees for lobbying public officials. Despite the narrow interpretation of the Lobbying Act of 1946, over the next decade there was an increase in the formation of lobbying groups and an increase in lobbyists who directed their attention to the power center of the federal government (Cigler & Loomis, 2007). Inadvertently, the "Third House" of the legislature had been born!

The Third House: Organized Interest Groups

Lobbyists have been dubbed the "Third House" of the legislature because of the great influence that lobbyists and special interests have upon policy and the legislative process. Is there a problem with having the third house in government? Mass media has negatively represented lobbyists as engaging in backroom deals and lavishly spending to entertain government officials. The arrest of Jack Abramoff, the nation's top lobbyist, for example, didn't help the image of lobbyist or that of special interest groups. According to mass media coverage, Abramoff and his associate Michael Scanlon allegedly overbilled their Native American clients for lobbying and unduly influenced government officials by bribing them with gifts and money. In 2006, both Abramoff and Scanlon were found guilty of defrauding their Native American clients of approximately $85 million in lobbying fees. Many of the officials who had taken bribes were forced to resign their government positions.

You should not be swayed by negative portrayals of a handful of unethical lobbyists. Lobbying is also a critical tactic for positive social change. More importantly, you should not be intimidated by the lobbying process; instead you should learn the rules and play the game. However, to play the lobbying game you need the knowledge and skills to boldly go where few human services practitioners have gone before!

Special Interest Groups

What do special interest groups lobby for? Table 9.1 lists registered special interest groups—also known as lobbies—which fall into three major categories:

1. Private interest lobbies
2. Noneconomic lobbies
3. Demographic lobbies

PRIVATE INTEREST LOBBIES Trade associations are industry-specific organizations that set industry standards and offer information and services to group members. However, they also engage in lobbying so they can influence laws and policies that affect their organizations. Examples of trade associations that you might be familiar with are the American Iron and Steel Institute, American Bankers Association, National Coal Association, Soy Protein Council, and the Sugar Association. Each trade association serves industry-specific needs versus umbrella organizations that fall in the category of noneconomic lobbies. Industry lobbies are typically single minded in the promotion of their interests to gain economic advantage through manipulation of public policy and to ensure that the free market benefits themselves (Navarro, 1984).

Noneconomic lobbies are not monolithic, which means they comprise different types of groups and organizations such as public interest groups, single issue groups, religion groups, ethnic groups, and educational groups. The reason to have a lobby with different groups and organizations is because there is strength in numbers. In some instances, similar types of groups belong to a noneconomic lobby and

Table 9.1	Registered Special Interest Groups.	
Private Interest Lobbies	**Noneconomic Lobbies**	**Demographic Lobbies**
Business Federated Organizations	**Public Interest**	**Age-Related Issue Groups**
Business Roundtable	Common Cause	AARP
National Association of Manufacturers	American Civil Liberties Union	American Federation for Children
Trade Associations	Americans for Peace Now	Children's Aids Society
American Bankers Association	**Single Issue Groups**	**Gender Issue Groups**
American Soy Protein Association	National Rifle Association	National Black Women's Health Project
American Sugar Alliance	Right to Life	League of Women Voters
Labor Groups	In Defense of Animals	National Women's Law Center
Federated Organizations	**Ideological Issue Groups**	**Sexual Orientation Issue Groups**
AFL-CIO	Americans for Democratic Action	Gay Men's Health Crisis
Independent Unions	Socialist Movement for Integration	National Gay & Lesbian Task Force
Longshoremen's Association	Log Cabin Republicans	**Socioeconomic Issue Groups**
National Union of Healthcare Workers	**Religious Groups**	Law Center on Homelessness &
Farm Groups	American Jewish Congress	Poverty
Federated Organizations	American Muslim Council	Metropolitan Council on Jewish Poverty
American Farm Bureau	Christian Coalition	Child Welfare League of America
Farmers for Clean Air & Water	National Council of Jewish Women	
Corporate Farm Groups	**Racial/Ethnic Groups**	
Monsanto Company	NAACP	
Smithfield Foods	Hispanic Communications Network	
Commodity-Specific Groups	Native American Resource Partners	
American Meat Institute	**Universities Groups**	
United Egg Producers	Harvard University	
National Chicken Council	New England College	
Dairy Farmers of America	Rutgers University	
Professional Groups	Catholic University of America	
American Medical Association	**Research Organizations**	
American Bar Association	American Foundation for AIDS	
National Education Association	Research	
Government Groups	Hastings Center	
Council of State Governors	RAND Corporation	
US Conference of Mayors	National Center for Public Policy	
Council of State Governments	Research	
Commonwealth of Puerto Rico		
Foreign Interest Groups		
Air France-KLM		
China Currency Coalition		
Japan Automobile Manufacturers		
Association		
US Poland Business Council		

have competing interests. Having competing interest can cause conflicts among group members, especially when their lobby focuses on changing public policy in a way that won't equally benefit all members. For example, both the Americans for Democratic Action and the Log Cabin Republicans are ideological issue groups. However, when it comes to taxes, their respective lobbies might be working for a different type of outcome when attempting to influence public policy.

DEMOGRAPHIC LOBBIES　　Demographic lobbies are structured around a set of human characteristics such as race, ethnicity, religion, political affiliation, gender, age, or sexual orientation. A demographic lobby that you might be familiar with is the American Association of Retired Persons (AARP). AARP lobbies the government on behalf of members who are 55 and older about issues such as Medicare. AARP is an example of a demographic lobby that has successfully developed a powerful presence in Washington and throughout the country and has been effective in lobbying for their constituents. Overall, demographic lobbies typically work to mobilize a constituency that desires a greater voice in the political decision making that may affect their lives and status in society.

Despite all the good that lobbies do, we should be concerned about the perceived power and influence lobbies have over our government. Box 9.2 lists the largest and most influential lobbies.

All the lobbies listed above are currently registered with the government. Typically, registered lobbies are monitored by organizations such as Open Secrets. Open Secrets is

---

Box 9.2　　　　**The Largest and Most Influential Lobbies**

American Association of Retired Persons
National Federation of Independent Business
American Israel Public Affairs Committee
National Rifle Association of America
AFL-CIO
Association of Trial Lawyers of America
Christian Coalition
National Right to Life
American Medical Association
US Chamber of Commerce
Credit Union National Association
Independent Insurance Agents of America
National Association of Manufacturers
American Farm Bureau Federation
National Restaurant Association
National Association of Home Builders
National Association of Realtors
National Association of Broadcasters
Motion Picture Association of America
American Bankers Association
National Education Association
Health Insurance Association of America
American Council of Life Insurance
Veterans of Foreign Wars

a nonprofit organization that maintains a free online lobbying database where anyone can access and find information such as:

1. A specific client/group.
2. A specific lobbying firm.
3. An individual lobbyist.
4. A specific industry.
5. A specific issue a lobby is addressing.
6. Government agencies that were lobbied.
7. Specific bills that were lobbied.
8. Total spending of a company for lobbying.

The wealthiest corporations and special interest groups usually pepper legislators and public officials with large amounts of money in hope of influencing the political process. If you're interested in knowing how much money is being spent to lobby and by whom, Open Secrets tabulates lobbying expenditures of organizations (for some examples, see Table 9.2).

Lobbies cannot spend or use money to influence legislators as they please because there are legal controls placed upon them, which presumably ensures they don't have undue influence on policymaking throughout the country. Yet in the United States, the decentralization of political power creates a system where public policy decision making occurs in three separate venues, at the federal level, state level, and local levels of government. Having three different venues allows lobbies to have multiple points of access to government with virtually no coordinated monitoring among the different levels of government. Some believe that lobbies threaten the functioning of American government (Navarro, 1984) while others believe lobbies might not have has much power as we might think (Baumgartner, Berry, Hojnacki, Kimball, & Leech, 2009). Whatever the case, lobbying is a reality in all government arenas and you need to know the players and how to play the game.

Political Action Committees

How are **political action committees (PACs)** different from special interest groups? PACs are organizations that are solely involved in influencing legislation, ballot initiatives, and political campaigns for or against a candidate.

Table 9.2	Top 10 Most Powerful Lobbies in 2011
Organization	**Lobbying Expenditure**
ActBlue	$51,124,846
AT&T	$46,292,670
Federation of State, County & Municipal Employees	$43,477,361
National Association of Realtors	$38,721,441
Goldman Sachs	$33,387,520
American Association for Justice	$33,143,279
Intl Brotherhood of Electrical Workers	$33,056,216
National Education Association	$32,024,610
Laborers Union	$30,292,050
Teamsters Union	$29,319,982

There is no single definition for a PAC across all 50 states, but under federal law an organization that raises more than $1,000 is legally considered a PAC. There are three types of PACS recognized by the federal government: (a) connected PACs, (b) non-connected PACs, and (c) super PACS.

CONNECTED POLITICAL ACTION COMMITTEES The connected PACs are created by groups from businesses, corporations, unions, and health organizations. This type of PAC can collect donations from a restricted class of people that includes managers, members, and shareholders.

NON-CONNECTED POLITICAL ACTION COMMITTEES Non-connected PACs are created by politicians and single-issue groups. Donations for a non-connected PAC can come from connected PACs, individuals, and organizations.

SUPER POLITICAL ACTION COMMITTEES The last category of PACs is the super PAC. This type of PAC can legally raise unlimited amounts of money from individuals, corporations, and unions. Furthermore, a super PAC can independently engage in unlimited political spending on behalf of a candidate's political campaign. However, a super PAC cannot make a direct donation to a candidate's campaign or a political party, and this entity is not permitted to directly coordinate with a political party or a political candidate.

There are approximately 4,000 PACs in the United States. In Table 9.3 is a list of prominent PACs representing groups that are unabashed about spending money to influence the outcomes of political campaigns, legislation, and state ballot initiatives. There are laws in place to ensure transparency of all financial contributions made to PACs. For instance, the Federal Election Campaign Act of 1971/Amendment 1974 is supposed to curb the improper influence of PACs that funnel soft money—unreported contributions to candidates—to national political parties (Cigler & Loomis, 2007). In 2009, campaign finance laws were challenged with regard to restrictions on political advertising. By 2010, two federal court rulings made super PACs possible: The first ruling came after the Supreme Court heard the case *Citizens United vs. Federal Election Commission* and the Court ruled that the government could not prohibit corporations

Table 9.3	Political Action Committees in 2011
PAC Names	**Total Amount Spent**
National Association of Realtors	$3,791,296
Honeywell International	$3,654,700
National Beer Wholesalers Association	$3,300,000
AT&T Incorporated	$3,262,375
Intl Brotherhood of Electrical Workers	$2,993,373
American Bankers Association	$2,870,154
American Association for Justice	$2,820,500
Operating Engineers Union	$2,789,220
National Auto Dealers Association	$2,483,400

or unions from contributing money to be used for political purposes. The second ruling came from the federal Court of Appeals for the DC Circuit that heard the case of *Speechnow.Org vs. Federal Election Commission* and ruled that PACs that made no donations to other PACs, political candidates, or political parties could accept unlimited donations from corporations (both for profit and nonprofit), unions, and individuals to be used for political purposes.

It is important for you to understand how PACS can influence politicians and public policy because it can affect your agency, it can affect your job, and it can affect your clients. Many of my students told me they had no interest in politics because it seemed so divisive, petty, and unappealing. Understanding the political landscape, however, is not an option if you intend to advocate for disenfranchised groups and communities.

Lobbying has an impact of the political process in the United States, and it is a good thing we have websites such as www.lobyists.info and www.opensecrets.org that inform us about lobbyists' and PACs' activities. In addition, an annual book publication titled the *Washington Representatives* is another resource that reports the activities of PACs and other lobby groups. Ask your college or public librarian to order a copy so it will be available to anyone who is interested in monitoring the lobbying activities of different groups.

The Lobbyists in the Halls of Government

The term "lobbyist" was first used in England, and it referred to journalists who were waiting to interview newsmakers in the lobby of the House of Commons (Birnbaum, 1992). Similarly, in the United States the term "lobby-agent" was considered to be a person who was a seeker of information in the lobbies or halls of government. Eventually, the term *lobby-agent* was abbreviated to lobbyist.

If you engage in human services lobbying, you would most likely work at influencing changes in policies and legislation to improve the condition of marginalized groups. In addition, you would bring a variety of social problems and concerns to the attention of government officials. The last time I checked, our legislators were busy passing legislation that affects our lives and the human service delivery systems we are working or will work in. It may take a national organization to create a lobbying force at the federal level, but any group or organization that can be affected by state government should have a lobbyist in their State House.

Five Shades of a Lobbyist

There are five different types of lobbyists involved in the political arena (Rosenthal, 1993). First, there is the category of *governmental lobbyists* who are hired by local and county governments such as boards of education, public associations, and public agencies to represent their concerns and interest to public officials. Second, there are *association lobbyists* who work for a specific trade association, professional group, or labor group. These full-time in-house lobbyists are responsible for communicating to legislators and dealing with legislation on behalf of the specific group they work for. Association lobbyists may also have other duties that are unrelated to lobbying, so their work efforts are divided.

The third lobbyist category is *corporate lobbyists,* who typically are employed by only a single corporation, for example, Verizon Communications, AT&T, or Exxon Mobil. Corporate lobbyists are highly paid and are the largest lobbying group in Washington, DC. Corporations typically have their lobbyists working in multiple state governments, which ensures policies don't harm or impede corporate interests at all levels of government. The fourth category of lobbyist is the *contract lobbyists* who work as independent contractors. This type of lobbyist is referred to as a "hired gun" and usually works for multiple clients at the same time. The employment opportunities for a contract lobbyist can include working as an independent practitioner, working with a lobbying firm, or working with a law firm. Interestingly, some law firms offer multiple services and engage in lobbying, business consulting, and handling legal matters.

The last category of lobbyists includes *cause lobbyists*, who serve community-based agencies or an organized community group. Typically, a cause lobbyist commonly represents and works with nonprofits or single-issue groups. This lobbyist also is ideologically motivated to bring a human cause to the attention of legislators at different levels of government. It is possible that you might take on the role of a cause lobbyist and you need to be prepared for that eventuality.

> Watch the movie *Thank You for Smoking*. After watching the movie, explain what type of lobbyist Aaron Eckhart portrays and what methods he employs to persuade people.

Laws Governing Lobbyists

In general, a lobbyist is anyone who engages in direct contact with public officials or legislators, to influence legislation or policy of a government body (Cigler & Loomis, 2007). Here is the legal definition of lobbyist according to the Lobbying and Disclosure Act of 1995 Public Law 104-65-DEC. 19, 1995 109 STAT. 695 Section 3:

> (10) The term "lobbyist" means any individual who is employed or retained by a client for financial or other compensation for services that include more than one lobbying contact, other than an individual whose lobbying activities constitute less than 20 percent of the time engaged in the services provided by such individual to that client over a six month period.

In addition, the Lobbying and Disclosure Act contains 24 sections that outline who, what, and when lobbyists can and cannot lobby. Another piece of legislation that you should be acquainted with is the Honest Leadership and Open Government Act of 2007 (P.L. 110-81), which was enacted after the Abramoff lobbying scandal that was mentioned earlier. President George W. Bush signed the Honest Leadership and Open Government Act (HLOGA) into law to ensure there would be greater transparency in the legislative process. Under this law, there is to be more frequent disclosure of lobbying contacts and activities between lobbyists and public officials. In Box 9.3 is Title II of the Honest Leadership and Open Government Act, which outlines what is now required of registered lobbyists. In 2009, President Barack Obama signed executive orders that addressed the scope of lobbying. Additional restrictions were enacted to stem the influence of lobbyists and lobby groups.

The Honest Leadership and Open Government Act of 2007 requires that lobbyists register with the federal Clerk of the House of Representatives and the secretary of the Senate. Failure to register as a lobbyist is punishable by a civil fine of up to $50,000.

Box 9.3

Honest Leadership and Open Government Act of 2007 (P.L. 110—81): Title II—Full Public Disclosure of Lobbying

Sec. 201. Quarterly filing of lobbying disclosure reports.

Sec. 203. Semiannual reports on certain contributions.

Sec. 204. Disclosure of bundled contributions.

Sec. 205. Electronic filing of lobbying disclosure reports.

Sec. 206. Prohibition on provision of gifts or travel by registered lobbyists to Members of Congress and to congressional employees.

Sec. 207. Disclosure of lobbying activities by certain coalitions and associations.

Sec. 208. Disclosure by registered lobbyists of past executive branch and congressional employment.

Sec. 209. Public availability of lobbying disclosure information; maintenance of information.

Sec. 211. Increased civil and criminal penalties for failure to comply with lobbying disclosure requirements.

Sec. 212. Electronic filing and public database for lobbyists for foreign governments.

Every state in the union also requires lobbyists to register. Table 9.4 identifies three state offices in which a person would register to be a lobbyist. The first step to registering is to read the Lobbyist Registration Office's website information very carefully. If you have any questions or need clarification about the information call their office.

Explore **Alliance for Justice.** Search for your state's lobbying registration office.

Are You Ready to Lobby?

Many human service organizations have never lobbied their state or federal legislators. Often, this occurs because human service administrations believe lobbying takes lots of money and time. However, having little money or time shouldn't stop an organization from lobbying. With the right information and the right strategies, almost anyone can engage in some form of lobbying.

Table 9.4	Examples of State Lobbyist Registration Offices		
State	**Office**	**Website**	**Phone**
New Jersey	New Jersey Election Law Enforcement Commission PO Box 185 Trenton, NJ 08605-0185	http://www.elec.state.nj.us/	609-292-8700
New York	New York Temporary State Commission on Lobbying Two Empire State Plaza, 18th Floor Albany, NY 12223-1254	http://www.nylobby.state.ny.us	518-474-7126
Pennsylvania	Pennsylvania Department of State, Division of Campaign Finance and Lobbying Disclosure 210 North Office Building Harrisburg, PA 17120	http://www.ethics.state.pa.us/ethics/site/default.asp	717-787-5280

Many people think of their government as an untouchable entity they have no power over. They create imagined barriers between themselves and their government officials. One of the greatest barriers is the lack of information about government. Take a moment and answer the following questions: Do you know what state district you live in? Who are your local state legislators and where are their offices located? How would you bring an issue to the attention of your state legislators? Have you been inside your State House for any public meetings that focus on a piece of legislation? This information is clearly critical for lobbying.

The benefits of lobbying for your agency and your client constituency can be considerable, and at least some lobbying can been done on a shoestring budget. We will now examine the methods, both direct and indirect, for engaging in successful lobbying.

Direct Lobbying

Let's imagine that you were chosen to lobby at the state level for a client such as a community action group. You would engage in direct lobbying of legislators on behalf of your client, who is concerned about a pending bill that might negatively affect the community. **Direct lobbying** involves having personal communications with legislators and their staff in order to persuade them about, for example, an alternative policy position. There are three forms of direct lobbying—a face-to-face meeting with a legislator or government official, giving testimony at a hearing, and onsite observation.

FACE-TO-FACE MEETING   The first and most potentially effective form of direct lobbying is a face-to-face meeting between the lobbyist and the public official. While it may seem daunting to make an appointment with a legislator to have a one-on-one discussion about an alternative policy position, don't be afraid to try it. Legislators typically want to meet their constituents to learn about the issues that affect them. Don't be afraid—but be very prepared! Review Chapter 7, where you learned about putting a persuasive argument together; you should do this review before taking a meeting.

When the moment comes for your meeting with a legislator, dress in business attire and be courteous. In a face-to-face meeting you need to introduce yourself, and then quickly and succinctly pitch a persuasive argument that should include the bill you're talking about, what the bill does, the costs of implementing the bill, and how many constituents are for the bill or against the bill. This succinct persuasive argument is referred to as your "elevator speech" (see Chapter 7). What's the rush? Legislators have very tight schedules and that means you will have a limited amount of time in their office—if you're lucky, the scheduled meeting will last five minutes. Despite the brief amount of time you may have, you must be prepared to make a clear argument about your concerns.

In the fast-paced legislative arena, you also want to create a one-page fact sheet on the bill, based on solid research. Doing good research and counter-research demonstrates that you are informed about the bill (from the pro and con sides). In other words, the fact sheet should contain accurate information from both sides of the argument. During your face-to-face meeting, the prepared fact sheet can also be used to quote from (especially if you get nervous) to ensure you present all points. Then at the end of the meeting, a copy of the fact sheet can be handed directly to the legislator and his or her staffers. Legislators and their staff appreciate the efforts to inform them about a specific bill that might not have caught their attention. Be especially polite to the staffers, because they are the gatekeepers to the legislators and they can give you an insider's view of the workings of the State House.

GIVING TESTIMONY   Another form of direct lobbying is giving testimony at legislative committee meetings that occur in the State House. Testimony is designed to persuade legislators to a group's position about pending legislation. Testimony can be given by the lobbyists, legislators who support your case, or members of the group who will be affected by the bill. For instance, in Massachusetts, cochlear implants for hearing impaired children are not covered by most health insurance plans. As a result, a parents group began a campaign to get their children's cochlear implants covered by medical insurance. In this instance, the job of the lobbyist involved preparing the parents to give testimony before a state legislative committee. Preparing people to give testimony takes a lot of planning. However, when the committee met on this issue, the parents were brilliantly prepared, along with their hearing impaired children. Both the parents and children gave testimony before the legislators about the need to compel insurance companies to cover the cost of the cochlear implant procedure. Overall, they were extremely effective (especially the children) in persuading legislators to change the law so insurance companies would cover the cost of the cochlear implant.

What makes testimony effective? A mixture of different types of testimony creates a more persuasive argument, so it is important to have different people testify. For instance, a portion of the testimony should include a technical explanation of what the bill does, which the lobbyist could present. There should also be personal stories from individuals affected by the bill, explaining how the bill might solve a problem. Finally, legislators supporting the bill could also testify on your behalf (Meredith, 2000). Having a legislator on your side, in many instances, brings credibility to your cause.

ONSITE VISITS   The last type of direct lobbying deals with onsite visits. Legislators conduct the majority of their business publicly but are infrequently observed by their constituents (voting citizens). Observation of the government doing the business of the people is a legal right. However, if it is your intent to influence legislators, observation has to be taken to another level. For instance, you can make an onsite observation of a legislator during the voting process in the State House and bring along a hundred constituents who you rallied together for that occasion (you can bet you'll get the legislator's attention).

Another way to do an onsite visit is to have a large group of constituents walking through the State House, which demonstrates to legislators and other public officials that constituents have specific concerns. There is power in numbers and power in watching legislators who will act in a manner that will keep them in office.

Indirect Lobbying

Let's now examine **indirect lobbying**, which is an approach used by a lobbyist to bring an issue to the attention of legislators and public officials without having face-to-face encounters. In this instance, the lobbyist creates a coordinated plan designed to flood one or more legislators with phone calls, letters, tweets, text messages, or emails.

LETTER WRITING CAMPAIGN   One of the most powerful indirect lobbying approaches is a letter writing campaign that involves getting your mobilized base members to send a form letter or personal letter to their legislator. Typically, organizations send email alerts or send form letters for their members to sign and resend electronically to their legislator. Written communications such as letters, tweets, text messages, or emails cost virtually nothing. However, all electronic communications to public officials become public information. In other words, communication between legislators and the public are not confidential; therefore, your mother, friends, neighbors, boss, and the world can access your communications if they go through the right channels.

Another tactic for a letter writing campaign involves pressure mailing. This type of mailing is used to coax or pressure legislators to meet the demands of a mobilized group. Any communication made to a public official should focus on the issue and also indicate that if something is not done constituents would not support or vote for that person in a future public election. Communications to a public official should contain no direct or veiled threats because if it does you will find yourself in a world of trouble. In a human services course I taught, my students were required to write their federal legislators about a pending bill. To my surprise, after writing letters to different federal legislators, one of my students had an unexpected visit from several FBI agents. Agents came to the student's home because the letter to the public official contained language that appeared (to the FBI) to be threatening. The students in this class learned an important lesson: When writing a letter to a legislator you must be polite, accurate, and nonthreatening. All written communications that are sent to legislators are categorized and responded to by legislative staff. Threatening letters and other communications are sometimes forwarded to the FBI for review.

Public Relations and Mass Media

The final indirect lobbying approach we will examine involves the use of public relations (PR) and mass media. Persuasion of public officials can occur when groups use press conferences, op-eds in newspapers, magazines, and interest group journals to make their argument. Public relations and mass media strategies are used to create a favorable press or can be used to create unfavorable press in newspapers, blogs, message boards, and electronic social networks. Feature-length movies have been created to get groups' political positions across, for example, about the meat and food industry in *Food, Inc.* by Robert Kenner, or about the state of healthcare in America in *Sicko* by Michael Moore.

In most of the lobbying strategies we have examined, it is beneficial to engage a group of people in the lobbying effort. An effective lobbying effort must be able to draw upon the contributions of many individuals or groups. One email is not a campaign; one visitor is not a constituency. How can coalitions be built to make lobbying a group advocacy project?

How to Build the Coalition

The federal government has been retreating from financial commitments to states in different social spheres since the Nixon era (Rosenthal, 1993). During this era, in the early 1970s, state governments were left to deal with regulating things such as consumer affairs, workplaces, environmental pollution, and decreased funding to social services. At the same time, lobbying groups were on the rise and becoming very active in many of the same social issues. For instance, social cause lobbies throughout the country targeted their State Houses to ensure nonpublic issues (e.g., funding for day-care) and public issues (e.g., abortion rights for the poor) were not forgotten by their state legislators.

Federal and state budget cuts are still the reality in today's market, and human service organizations are often the first to be cut, leaving these entities to do more with fewer resources. Decreased funding is a major reason to understand the process of lobbying and to be prepared to engage in lobbying to ensure your organization or agency survives economic downturns. The adage that the "squeaky wheel gets the oil first" holds true in the political world; so those who work in nonprofit human service organizations must make legislators pay attention to the fact that work for the public good can't be done if government financial support is withdrawn. To get the attention of legislators, you need to build a coalition. There is power in numbers. Quite simply, organized groups have more power to influence policy compared to an individual (Haynes & Mickelson, 2000).

UNDERSTANDING THE NATURE OF GROUPS   Before you attempt to build a coalition for a lobbying campaign, you need to learn why groups form, how groups function, and what makes groups important to social change. A widely known hypothesis about group lifecycles holds that every group takes on a life of its own and progresses through a group development that occurs in five stages: (1) forming, (2) storming, (3) norming, (4) performing, and (5) adjourning (Tuckman & Jensen, 1977). In the first stage of this group lifecycle model, members of the group decide on their leader, structure, and purpose. In the second stage, the group will face their differences of opinions, while also struggling over who will become the leader of the group. In the third stage, the group members have developed relationships within the group, and there is a relative cohesiveness building. In the fourth stage, the group is focused on getting the task done, and in the final stage the group becomes aware that they can disband because the task is completed.

If you understand group stage development, you can anticipate changes that will occur in the group dynamics that can impede or activate the group toward its common goal. It is important that you understand group development because it will make it easier for you to work with and in a group. You'll have a sense of how group formation affects leadership selection, how groups approach decision making, and how groups work toward a common goal.

CREATING THE COALITION   First, you need to know the difference between creating a coalition that is democratic versus creating a coalition run with a core group of informed organizers. In the long run, knowing how the group will operate will save you a lot of heartache. Moreover, when you begin coalition building the people who might join the coalition will have a clear sense of how the organization operates. However, a decision must be made about whether the group will be or will not be democratically run.

Ideally, a democratic coalition seems like a good idea, but it will probably hinder the effectiveness and efficiency of the group advancing a lobbying campaign. Why? In a democratic group, all group members have equal influence in the decision-making process with their votes. So in terms of a lobbying campaign, the majority determines how the group will be run and what public policy will be focused on. Overall, a democratic coalition will slow the lobbying efforts because everyone has a say in how the group approaches each group task and goal. On the other hand, if the coalition is run by a core group of informed organizers, they will be more efficient and effective at working on the ground and getting a bill passed through the legislature. In this type of group, the leadership subgroup effectively calls all the shots, and the members of the base are guided in their work toward achieving a common goal. If you are working for an organization and are acting as a professional lobbyist or community organizer, there are a few things you must consider before you begin building a coalition that will involve your organization.

COALITION BUILDING 101   Before building a coalition in the workplace, you must get your leadership and administration onboard, especially if your organization functions under a bureaucratic model. In other words, first deal with the person in charge before attempting to organize a coalition for a lobbying campaign, because organizing in the workplace will affect the organizational system (Ezell, 2001).

When you talk to the administration, you must present a sound argument about how building a coalition to engage in a lobbying campaign will benefit the organization. This is an opportunity for you to practice developing that persuasive "elevator speech" we talked about in an earlier chapter. Don't forget that the administration and other leadership are the bosses, and it is wise to keep them informed about your activities because they could reflect upon the organization as a whole.

Who should be a part of the member base of the coalition? Once you have approval (and more importantly, buy-in) from the administration, it's time to begin coalition building. The administrators in your organization should be in the member base and if they have bought into the cause, they will use their power to promote the coalition. Furthermore, they have the power to allocate resources to the cause such as offering free conference space, office materials, postage, and other essentials needed to run a lobbying campaign. Remind your administration that people are volunteering their time, and it is very important to have the tools that make it easier to efficiently and effectively gather and transmit information that supports the lobbying campaign. Other people who should be recruited into the coalition are middle managers, supervisors, staff, and affiliated organizations.

Clients should also be recruited for the coalition, but due to client confidentiality it would be prudent to have them work through their own grassroots organization. This means that you will have to educate clients about the lobbying campaign and train them to start a grassroots effort to get new members from the community. A grassroots movement controlled by clients is empowering to this collective. Furthermore, clients who are part of a grassroots movement then have the choice to reveal or not to reveal their affiliation with your organization from which they may be receiving services. As a human services practitioner, you are expected to preserve client confidentiality and only the client can give his or her written permission to break confidentiality.

This rule was brought home to me years ago when I was working with HIV/AIDS clients. Before making a move to do community campaigns, I first asked my clients whether they wanted to be involved in the campaign or if I could use their names to get to community gatekeepers to join the campaign. I thought that asking was a mere formality, because, after all, this campaign would benefit them greatly. However, I was doing this work during the early years of the AIDS epidemic, and most of my clients were frightened to be associated with any public campaigns. It was not at all the case that they were willing to put themselves on the line and face possible scorn and ostracism. I soon learned never to assume that a client would be willing to publicly admit to needing direct services of any type. So if you intend to involve clients in a lobbying campaign, you must remain aware of client confidentiality and be sensitive to their desires. If you want to get community members into the coalition, you can also do it without involving clients. Other members can be employed to do canvassing in the community.

Once people have joined the coalition, you will need to have a group of volunteers who can help run the lobbying campaign with you. This group of volunteers will first be tasked with helping to gather, organize, manage, and protect information about coalition members. Each person who joins the coalition needs to give contact information that includes name, street address, email address, Twitter account, and phone numbers and the way he or she prefer to be contacted. Once a person is a member of the base, he or she should be given written information about the cause just in case they meet others who are interested in joining the coalition.

With new technology such as electronic tablets, it is easy to organize or access information. You should systematically catalog all member information and legislator personal information, record legislative visits arranged by date with pictures, link to public documents, and so on. Plus you can easily share files through a cloud platform that can be used to store everyone's information in one secure centralized place. If you have electronic capability for face-to-face contact (using videoconferencing), you can communicate directly with members, legislators, or anyone else you need to be in contact with. Most tablets and many computers have encryption hardware that protects stored data, mail messages, and attachments.

As you are building a coalition, it important to stay in touch with the member base by sending out updates. With social networks and email, you can also mobilize your member base by sending electronic alerts to assemble for a certain reason. Having assembled a coalition, it's now time to begin the lobbying campaign.

> ### Administration
>
> *Understanding and Mastery: Constituency building and other advocacy techniques such as lobbying, grassroots organizing, and community development and organizing.*
>
> **Critical Thinking Question:** Lobbying is not an individual activity, so forming a coalition group for the purpose of undertaking a lobbying campaign is a critical step. Form groups of four or five participants to act as a leadership group and identify an issue that interests you or seems important for your community. (1) Identify legislative remedies that might be helpful in addressing your issue. (2) Identify groups, agencies, or individuals who should be part of your coalition. What would induce them to join your lobbying effort? (3) Identify the initial research tasks that must be completed before starting the lobbying effort itself. Many such tasks are named in the chapter: Are there others that your issue calls for as well? How might your hoped-for coalition partners be meaningfully engaged in these pre-lobbying tasks?

A Lobbying Campaign in the State House

For our example, we will imagine a lobbying campaign focused on supporting a bill to maintain state funding for nonprofit human service organizations helping troubled teens. In this scenario, you are the lobbyist with a core group of informed organizers who are working on the ground to get the bill passed through the legislature. You are having your first meeting with the total member base to discuss the lobbying campaign. As you know from group theory, every group goes through a series of developmental stages. Leaders will emerge from the base, some members will choose to be workers, and other members will take less active roles. Tempting as it may be to plunge into the issues themselves or to start strategizing about the campaign, remember that the formation of the group is a critical stage in the project. Allow time for group process.

If a lobbying campaign is to be successful, you must identify the group's strengths and weaknesses, and carefully let the group evolve by guiding leadership development, clarifying roles among the membership, and helping the group maneuver beyond conflicts and dissensions. Then you will guide the group into the planning phase. Planning means preparing a flexible strategy that outlines the who, what, where, how, and when of the campaign. This part of the process is critical: Allow time for discussing these critical details. The lobbying campaign should be given a name that captures the essence of what the group is trying to achieve, for example, *Teen Care Supported by Human Services, Advocates for Teen Support,* or *Policy for Children in Troubled Waters.*

Once the group has formed, leaders have emerged, a plan is created, and the group has picked a name, it is time for the core group of informed organizers to educate members about the issues and explain the strategies that will be used in the lobbying campaign. Once members are clear about the campaign issues, the group must decide on its primary message. Judith Meredith (2000), a lobbyist for the poor, offers a simple list of fill-in statements that will assist with the development of the campaign message (Figure 9.1).

After the campaign message is developed, a group of volunteers from the base will be needed to help with the task of doing in-depth research and fact finding to advance the campaign. Information is power and the more information you have at your disposal the better you can argue your point, but getting reliable and accurate information takes time and energy. You can start with collecting current research that supports the cause, such as information about human service programs that successfully support troubled teens in their own communities.

If there is little published research or information on your issue, it will be incumbent upon you and the volunteers to do your own research. Research could be done on topics such as the effectiveness and efficiency of current services for teens or an analysis of policy affecting teens. A research project can be either qualitative or quantitative, but it must be done in a scientifically rigorous manner. Qualitative and quantitative research take time and are labor intensive but sometimes yield critical information that can support the position of your cause. When possible, appropriately match the talents of base members to the task, which will make members feel that they are being utilized for their expertise. In short, research assignments should go to volunteers who have the knowledge and skills to do the project.

Researching may take great expertise, but fact finding can be done by almost anyone. Fact finding can yield vital information in a much shorter period of time in comparison to a research project. Fact finding can also be done via computer search engines such as Google, Yahoo, Ask, and Bing, which make accessible a broad range of databases that contain public records (e.g., demographics and legislators' voting records) and other printed sources (e.g., newspapers, scholarly articles, and books).

FIND YOUR STATE LEGISLATORS   One major objective of campaign lobbying in a political arena is to make contact with different legislators. How do you find your state legislators? You find them by looking them up on a state government webpage. I found my state legislators at the following web address: www.MAlegislature.gov/People/House.

FIGURE 9.1

Sample of Lobbying Campaign Statement List

1. _____ is in crisis because _____.
2. You should care because _____.
3. We think we can begin to fix it by _____.
4. You can help by _____.

This Massachusetts legislature webpage lists the names of legislative leadership, senate members, and members of the House of Representatives. In addition, the webpage has each legislator's picture, email, and phone number, plus information about the number of elected public officials. I discovered that Massachusetts has 40 state senators and 160 members in the State House of Representatives.

It is important that you learn and remember your public officials because they are the people who might help or who might work against the cause. Commit to memory information such as the legislators' names, policy positions, level of political influence, and their battles inside and outside of the legislative arena. Having this information stored in your brain (and electronic tablet or smart phone) allows you to act in the moment with legislators who might come into your immediate sphere. Other useful information about legislators includes their voting patterns, affiliations with special interests, and involvement with different causes. Knowing what causes legislators have supported in the past will give you a sense of who to approach to help push your cause.

Your lobbying campaign is focused on ensuring that new legislation is passed that supports the increased funding of your agency and similar agencies offering services to troubled teens. To make this happen, you would be looking for legislators to join or support your lobbying campaign if they have been credited with pushing similar legislation to increase funding for other human service programs. If possible, it would be beneficial to have a legislator who appears regularly in the news media because he or she can garner greater attention for your cause and the more you get your name in the news the more influential the cause becomes.

Coalition base members who serve as the fact finders for the lobbying campaign can get answers to questions such as, What previous policies related to the cause have passed and why? Which if any did not pass? What other similar policies have passed? Will legislators likely support or not support the cause? What opposition might come from outside of the legislature or from within the legislature? What groups might oppose the cause? What does the current governor's administration think of the bill the cause is promoting? Does the cause's bill create jobs? Are there legislators with expertise or interest in the bill the cause is promoting? Once you have information about the pros and cons of the legislation you're attempting to get passed, it should be shared with legislators who will likely support it. Don't forget to review Chapter 7 to help put a persuasive argument together.

KNOW YOUR WAY AROUND THE STATE HOUSE The gatekeepers of our legislators are their staff members—referred to as staffers—so it is important that you learn their names and backgrounds. In a legislative office, staffers have different jobs: Some are tasked with the analysis of pending legislation that a legislator will use to make a decision and other staffers serve as personal aides or manage requests from constituents (Meredith, 2000). Staffers do the bidding of their boss (the legislator), but if you have summarized information about your cause and the legislation that you (and your group) support, staffers may help get your information passed forward to all the right places. Staffers and legislators both serve the public and want to retain their jobs, so they are there to listen to their constituents. They don't want to lose donations or votes. If they respond or help your cause, it's important that you thank legislators and their staffers with personal notes and emails.

There are numerous strategies of how and when to call upon your legislator, but before you attempt to do direct lobbying make sure you have done your homework. For example, you want new legislation passed to support teen programs in your community.

You must have comprehensive factual information about the bill you intend to lobby. Then you must have an organized and persuasive argument that you can use to get others to understand both the benefits and problems related to the bill.

What's it like talking to legislators? Many of you will get nervous the first time you engage in a conversation focused on your cause; to be honest I still get a little nervous. Many of you will make mistakes (everyone makes mistakes) but what counts is how you move beyond your mistakes. Some of you will hate lobbying and some of you will love it! But when you get the knack of pitching your persuasive argument about a cause to people (no matter who they are), the excitement will take over and supplant your nervousness. Getting acclimated to the frantic pace of the political arena will also take some effort. Your first visit to a State House may seem surreal, which is not an uncommon feeling.

I remember my first visit to Capitol Hill in Washington, DC. I felt like Mr. Smith in the 1939 political drama film *Mr. Smith Goes to Washington*. Standing in the halls of Congress, I saw legislators of all stripes doing the business of the people. When Senator Ted Kennedy walked by I initially was utterly amazed, but then I realized, no matter how famous our legislators may or may not be, they have been put into office by their constituents to ensure there is greater equity and justice in our communities and society.

Part of lobbying legislators entails understanding the political arenas in which they work. I encourage you to explore the State House in your state or, if possible, the U.S. Capitol before initiating a lobbying campaign. Visit these venues and find all the places that are open to the public; find the public bathrooms; find the cafeteria and see if legislators eat there; and find your representative's office and go in and introduce yourself. In addition, find different public sessions to sit in on. This will give you an opportunity to see people giving testimony or an opportunity to observe legislators debating about different issues on the floor. In Chapter 7, you learned the importance of understanding your audience. So when you attend a public session, this would be the time to do an audience analysis to determine how best to prepare yourself or coalition members to make testimonies in similar public sessions.

UNDERSTANDING THE JOB OF LEGISLATORS   As you become acquainted with the sounds, smells, sights, and feel of a political venue, you will be less apprehensive about working in them. In addition, the time spent in the State House and in public hearings allows you a bird's eye view of how legislators, in the House and Senate, debate the merits of the bills that come to their respective floors. Legislators debate during the second reading of a bill, at which time there are extended debates and proposed amendments. Typically, this is when you will observe groups engaging in direct lobbying of legislators. If the bill is controversial, you might hear testimony delivered by constituents, supportive legislators, or sympathetic experts who have insight and knowledge about the bill. If you think at this point the policymaking process is a done deal, you are mistaken.

If your lobbying campaign is focused on getting a bill passed through the state legislature, every member of the coalition needs to understand how a bill becomes a law. Figure 9.2 shows a flow chart of the process by which a bill becomes law. But there is much more to know about the different committees' rules, procedures, and loopholes for accepting, tabling, or killing a bill, all of which is beyond the scope of this book . You can buy a rule book in the State Clerk's office to learn about all the procedural rules that can and do occur on the floor, including how to kill a bill. What is most important is you review how a bill ultimately becomes law.

Understanding and Mastery: Skills to develop goals, and design and implement a plan of action.

Critical Thinking Question: Go back to the previous critical thinking question, get your group together again, and start to collect the information you identified as necessary for your lobbying effort, assigning research tasks to each member of the group. The plan for your lobbying campaign will be based on the information you discover, so be strategic in your research. You will certainly need (1) names of three legislators or influential community figures who should be visited personally; (2) the committees in government that affect or oversee issues such as yours; (3) current or recent legislation affecting your issue; and (4) one page of talking points or key arguments for your issue. What else do you need to find out right away? How will you use the information you are discovering? How long do you think you will need to sustain the lobbying effort to achieve your goal? What lobbying activities will you undertake during that time?

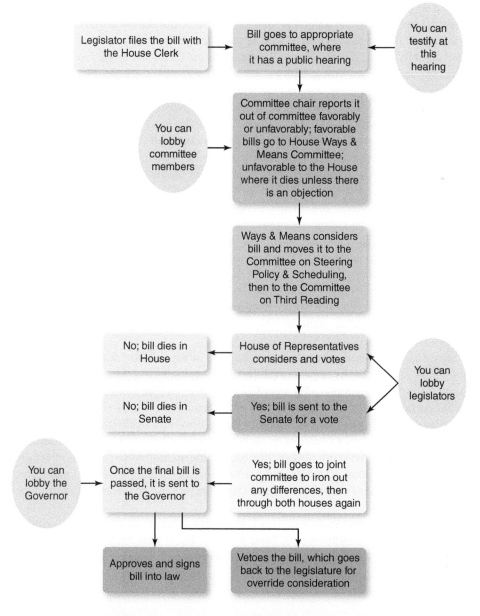

FIGURE 9.2

Flow Chart of How a Bill Becomes Law

FULL STEAM AHEAD   After getting a sense of what happens in the State House, you will be prepared to get your lobbying campaign underway. Contact the State House to obtain a calendar of bills and the dates when they will be publicly discussed. Having this calendar will ensure you have the most accurate dates and times for the coalition to gather at the State House. Electronic alerts can be sent to the coalition in a timely fashion containing information about the status of the bill and when and where to meet. When the coalition is mobilized, the member base should be armed with an updated fact sheet about the bill. A member should be able to read the fact sheet aloud in less than 15 seconds, which is equivalent to a news media sound bite you typically hear on TV or radio. During the lobbying campaign, members need to be reminded to stay on message (by reading the fact sheet) when asked questions about the cause, no matter who is asking the questions. Members should also be given cause buttons or t-shirts, which is an effective way to visually advertise the cause to the general public. Most importantly, remind coalition members to be polite to all legislators and that no members are to engage in a public argument with anyone. Similarly, if the coalition is called to attend a public meeting of the House Ways and Means (W&M) Committee in the State House, the same tactics should be used to make legislators aware that the coalition is watching.

What is the W&M Committee? The W&M committee holds the purse strings of the state government, which make it an extremely powerful force within the State House. The committee's overall function is to analyze bills that need funding and then report out on bills they feel should be funded by the state. Why should this be of concern to you? If the funding of your organization is dependent on the bill that is under consideration in the State House, it might be wise to lobby legislators who sit on the W&M committee.

Lobbying the W&M committee means you and members from the base will have to research, do fact finding, and devise an appropriate campaign message. When waging a lobbying campaign on a matter that concerns state funding (as in the case of maintaining teen programming), the issues will be restoring full funding, avoiding underfunding, and avoiding funding cuts. The coalition will need to be informed about the state budget process and so will the organizations and legislators backing your bill. In addition, you will need to understand how the line items in the budget are relevant to your program (Meredith, 2000).

State and federal budgets are line item budgets in which individual financial statement items are grouped by department, the budget contains a comparison of financial data, and the past budget period is recorded. Such budgets take a historical approach in which expenditure requests are based on past expenditures and current revenue data. In addition, the line-item budget includes the figures for a future period. Line-item budgeting is widely used because of its simplicity and flexibility. The shortcoming of a line-item budget is that it offers very little useful information to anyone who needs to determine the functions, activities, and performance of each department. In addition, no justification or explanations are offered about the proposed expenditures within the budget.

In the Massachusetts State line-item budget, the account number and description are consistent with expenditure data. Table 9.5 is the Fiscal Year 2012 Budget Summary of the state budget. The Summary is an outline of different line items, and the proposed amount of tax revenue to be expended on different things in the state.

Table 9.5	Massachusetts Government Fiscal Year 2012 Budget Summary ($000)		
Government Area	FY2012 Conference	FY2012 Vetoes*	FY2012 GAA
Judiciary	709,223	0	709,223
Independents	3,473,181	0	3,473,181
Administration and Finance	2,548,402	0	2,548,402
Energy & Environmental Affairs	187,008	0	187,008
Health and Human Services	16,203,399	0	16,203,399
Transportation	187,934	0	187,934
Housing & Economic Development	354,578	0	354,578
Labor & Workforce Development	33,522	0	33,522
Education	5,926,679	0	5,926,679
Public Safety	913,091	0	913,091
Legislature	60,908	0	60,908
TOTAL	**30,597,924**	**0**	**30,597,924**

Independents 11%
Administration and Finance 8%
Health and Human Services 54%
Education 19%

Table 9.6 is an All Account Listing that gives an accounting of each state department and what was spent, including a column for an explanation of vetoes. All state budget information is on your state's webpage and can be viewed by the public. In addition, in the state budget reports you get a full view of what programs, services, and infrastructure the government is putting taxpayers' dollars into. To do a comprehensive analysis of the state budget, it would be advisable to get someone in the community who knows how to scrutinize these reports, so you have a real sense of what you're looking at.

Learn How Your Government Works

What other things will you need to know to advance a lobbying campaign? To effectively lobby in the political arena, you need to know how your government functions at all levels. Many think that they know how government functions. Yet it was reported that U.S. students who took the National Assessment of Educational Progress exam had little knowledge about how the federal government functions. In response to this educational crisis, Sandra Day O'Connor (a former U.S. Supreme Court justice) established a nonprofit organization that offers a free web-based education project named iCivics.

The iCivics website has free games, lesson plans, and interactive modules about the functioning of the federal government. You can use this website to further educate yourself and use it as a teaching tool to educate coalition members, staff, and community members who are involved in a lobbying campaign. Be mindful of the fact that it will take time to learn about the complex industry of government. Despite the complexities of government, you need to know how government works if you hope to influence or alter it on behalf of your clients. Remember, lobbying government helps to sustain our democracy.

Table 9.6	Massachusetts Government All Account Listing Data Current as of 7/11/2011			
Account	Description	FY2011 Spending	FY2012 GAA	Veto Explanation
0320-0003	Supreme Judicial Court	7,588,951	7,437,172	
0320-0010	Clerk's Office of the Supreme Judicial Court for the County of Suffolk	1,147,536	1,131,858	
0321-0001	Commission on Judicial Conduct	512,657	575,359	
0321-0100	Board of Bar Examiners	1,061,436	1,057,789	
0321-1500	Committee for Public Counsel Services	32,255,081	45,304,806	
0321-1510	Private Counsel Compensation	158,706,173	93,255,462	
0321-1518	Indigent Counsel Fees Retained Revenue	750,000	8,900,000	
0321-1520	Indigent Persons Fees and Court Costs	13,464,300	9,010,351	
0321-1600	Massachusetts Legal Assistance Corporation	9,500,000	9,500,000	
0321-2000	Mental Health Legal Advisors Committee	707,599	781,177	
0321-2100	Prisoners' Legal Services	902,016	902,016	
0321-2205	Suffolk County Social Law Library	1,000,000	1,000,000	
0321-2215	Suffolk Social Law Library Chargeback	506,704	0	
0322-0100	Appeals Court	10,642,967	10,501,429	
0330-0101	Trial Court Justices' Salaries	48,424,649	47,307,647	
0330-0300	Office of the Chief Justice for Administration and Management	197,946,450	185,437,997	
0330-0312	Trial Court Civil Motor Vehicle Infractions	300,000	0	
0330-3333	Trial Court Retained Revenue	537,306	0	

Explore iCivics to learn about how the U.S. government works.

Summary

The First Amendment of the U.S. Bill of Rights protects your right to lobby the government. The First Amendment protects the rights of special interest groups and political action committees to lobby the government. Special interest lobbies influence public policy to ensure that the legislation works in their favor and in some cases to gain economic advantage. Political action committees are formed to influence legislation, ballot initiatives, and political campaigns. Because of the power these groups have on government, they are referred to as the Third House of the legislature.

A person whose sole job is to influence changes in policies and legislation would be considered a lobbyist. There are five types of lobbyists: governmental lobbyists, association lobbyists, corporate lobbyists, contract lobbyists, and cause lobbyists. All lobbyists have to register with the state or federal government. Laws regulate the behavior of lobbyists who work to influence public officials, legislators, and government bodies.

Direct lobbying means personal contact with legislators. Indirect lobbying refers to email campaigns or group demonstrations. A lobbying campaign involves coalition building, focusing on the cause, mobilizing the member base, and understanding how government operates. Lobbying requires knowledge of how government operates: what legislators do, how bills become law, and how the government spends tax dollars.

Assess your analysis and evaluation of this chapter's content by completing the Chapter Review.

References and Further Readings for Introduction

Chenault, J. (1974). Career education and human services: Monograph on career education. Retrieved from http://eric.ed.gov/ERICWebPortal/custom/portlets/recordDetails/detailmini.jsp?_fpb=true&_ERICExtSearch_SearchValue_0=ED109507"

Chenault, J., & Burnford, F. (1978). *Human services professional education: Future directions.* New York: McGraw-Hill Book Company.

Clubok, M. (1997). Baccalaureate-level human services and social work: Similarities and differences. *Human Service Education, 17(1)*, 7–17.

Ginsberg, M.I., Shiffman, B.M., & Rogers, M. (1969). Nonprofessionals in social work. In C. Grosser, W.E. Henry, & J.G. Kelly, *Nonprofessionals in the human services* (pp. 193–202). San Francisco: Jossey-Bass.

Grant, G., & Riesman, D. (1978). *The perpetual dream.* Chicago: The University of Chicago Press.

Kadish, J. (1969). Programs in the federal government. In C. Grosser, W.E. Henry, & J.G. Kelly, *Nonprofessionals in the human services* (pp. 228–242). San Francisco: Jossey-Bass.

Kincaid, S. (2009). Defining human services: A discourse analysis. *Human Service Education, 29(1)*, 14–23.

McPheeters, H.L., & King, J.B. (1971). *Plans for teaching mental health workers: Community college curriculum objectives.* Washington, DC: National Institute of Mental Health. Retrieved from ERIC database (ED079210).

Nixon, R.A. (1969). Congressional actions. In C. Grosser, W.E. Henry, & J.G. Kelly, *Nonprofessionals in the human services* (pp. 203–227). San Francisco: Jossey-Bass.

Osher, D., & Goldenberg, I. (1987). The school of human services: A case study in social intervention and the creation of alternative settings. In E.M. Bennet, *Social intervention: Theory and practice* (pp. 57–91). New York: The Edwin Mellen Press.

Pearl, A., & Riessman, F. (1965). *New careers for the poor: The nonprofessional in human service.* New York: Vintage Book.

Roszak, T. (1995). *The making of a counter culture: Reflections on the technocratic Society and its youthful opposition.* New York: Doubleday.

Sweitzer, H.F. (2003). Multiple forms of scholarship and their implications for human service educators. *Human Service Education, 11(1)*, 3–15.

Thompson, N. (2003). *Theory and practice in human services.* New York: Open University Press.

True, J.E., & Young, C.E. (1974). Associate degree programs for human service workers. *Personnel and Guidance Journal, 53(4)*, 304–307.

Wheeler, B.R., & Gibbons, W.E. (1992). Social work in academia: Learning from the past and acting on the present. *Journal of Social Work Education, 28(3)*, 300–311.

Woodside, M., & McClam, T. (2006). *An introduction to human services.* Belmont: Brooks/Cole.

Young, C.E., True, J.E., & Packard, M.E. (1974). A national survey of associate degree mental health programs. *Community Mental Health Journal, 10(4)*, 446–476.

References and Further Readings for Chapter 1

Ackerson, B.J., & Karoll, B.R. (2005). Evaluation of an assertive community treatment harm reduction program: Implementation issues. *Best Practices in Mental Health, 1(2)*, 34–49.

Arean, P.A., Ayalon, L., Chengshi, J., McCulloch, C.E., Linkins, K., Chen, H., Estes, C. (2008). Integrated specialty mental health care among older minorities improves access but not outcomes. *International Journal of Geriatric Psychiatry, 23*, 1086–1092.

Bigelow, D.A., & Young, D. (1991). Effectiveness of a case management program. *Community Mental Health Journal, 27(2)*, 1–8.

Bond, G.R., Drake, R.E., Mueser, K.T., & Latimer, E. (2001). Assertive community treatment for people with severe mental illness: Critical ingredients and impact on patients. *Diseases Management Health Outcomes, 9(3)*, 141–159.

Bjorkman, T., Hansson, L., & Sandlund, M. (2002). Outcome of case management based on the strengths model compared to standard care. *Social Psychiatry & Psychiatric Epidemiology, 37*, 147–152.

Bronfenbrenner, U. (1979). *The ecology of human development*. Cambridge: Harvard University Press.

Bronfenbrenner, U., ed. (2005). *Making human beings human: Bioecological perspective on human development*. Thousand Oaks: Sage Publications.

Brun, C., & Rapp, R.C. (2001). Strengths-based case management: Individuals' perspectives on strengths and the case manager relationship. *Social Work, 46(3)*, 278–287.

Burns, T. (2010). The rise and fall of assertive community treatment? *International Review of Psychiatry, 22(2)*, 130–137.

Burns, T., & Perkins, R. (2000). The future of case management. *International Review of Psychiatry, 12*, 212–218.

Cairns, R., & Cairns, B. (2005). Social ecology over time and space. In U.Bronfenbrenner (ed.), *Making human beings human: Bioecological perspectives on human development*. (pp. 16–26). Thousand Oaks: Sage Publications.

Chenault, J. (1975). *Human services education and practice: An organic model*. New York: Human Science Press.

Coldwell, C.M., & Bender, W.S. (2007). The effectiveness of assertive community treatment for homeless populations with sever mental illness: A meta-analysis. *American Journal of Psychiatry, 164(3)*, 393–399.

Dvoskin, J.A., & Steadman, H.J. (1994). Using intensive case management to reduce violence by mentally ill persons in the community. *Hospital and Community Psychiatry, 45(7)*, 679–684.

Finkelman, A.W. (2011). *Case management for nurses*. Boston: Pearson Education.

Greene, R.R., & Kropf, N.P. (1995). A family case management approach for level I needs. In A.C. Kilpatrick & T.P. Holland (eds.), *Working with families: An integrative model by level of functioning* (4th Edition) (pp. 94–113). Boston: Allyn & Bacon.

Hasenfeld, Y. (1992). The nature of human service organizations. In Y.Hasenfeld (ed.), *Human services as complex organizations* (pp. 3–23). Newbury Park: Sage Publications.

Hoffman, D., & Rosenheck, R. (2001). Homeless mothers with sever mental illnesses and their children: Predicators of family reunification. *Psychiatric Rehabilitation Journal, 25(2)*, 163–169.

Holt, B.J. (2000). *The practice of generalist case management*. Boston: Allyn and Bacon.

Intagliata, J. (1982). Improving the quality of community care of the chronically mentally disabled: The role of case management. *Schizophrenia Bulletin, 8*, 655–674.

Knight, L.W. (2005). *Citizen: Jane Addams and the struggle for democracy*. Chicago: The University of Chicago Press.

Law, S. (2007). The role of a clinical director in developing an innovative assertive community treatment team targeting ethno-racial minority patients. *Psychiatry quarterly, 78*, 183–193.

Marshall, M., & Francis, C. (2000). Assertive community treatment—Is it the future of community care in the UK? *International Review of Psychiatry, 12*, 191–196.

McGrew, J.H., & Wilson, R.G. (1996). Client perspectives on helpful ingredients of assertive community treatment. *Psychiatric Rehabilitation Journal, 19(3)*, 13–22.

Mills, C.S., & Usher, D. (1996). A kinship care case management approach. *Child Welfare, LXXV (5)*, 600–618.

Milkis, S.M. (2005). Lyndon Johnson, the great society and the "twilight" of the modern presidency. In S.M. Milkis & J.M. Mileur, *The great society and the high tide of liberalism* (pp. 1–49). Boston: University of Massachusetts Press.

Moseley, C. (2004). Support brokerage issues in self-directed services. *NASDDDS Technical Report*, pp. 1–13.

Mowbray, C., Plum, T., & Materson, T. (1997). Harbinger II: Deployment and evolution of assertive community treatment in Michigan. *Administration & Policy in Mental Health, 25*, 125–139.

Murphy, R., Tobias, C., Rajabium, S., & Abuchar, V. (2003). HIV case management: A review of the literature. *AIDS Education & Prevention, 15*, 93–108.

Preston, N.J. (2000). Predicting community survival in early psychosis and schizophrenia populations after receiving intensive case management. *Australian and New Zealand Journal of Psychiatry, 34*, 122–128.

Prince, P.N., Demidenko, N., & Gerber, G.J. (2000). Client and staff members perceptions of assertive community treatment: The nominal group technique. *Psychiatric Rehabilitation Journal, 23(3)*, 284–289.

Roberts-DeGennaro, M. (1993). Generalist model of case management. *Journal of Case Management, 2(3)*, 106–111.

Rothman, J. (1991). A model of case management: Toward empirically base practice. *Social Work, 36(6)*, 520–528.

Rothman, J., & Sager, J.S. (1998). *Case management: Integrating individual and community practice.* Boston: Allyn and Bacon.

Schaedle, R. (1999). *Critical ingredients of intensive case management: Judgments of researchers/administrators, program managers and case managers.* Dissertation.com. Retrieved from http://www.bookpump.com/dps/pdf-b/1120508b.pdf

Schaedle, R., McGrew, J.H., Bond, G.R., & Epstein, I. (2002). A comparison of experts' perspectives on assertive community treatment and intensive case management. *Psychiatric Services, 53(2)*, 207–210.

Schein, E.H. (1997). *Organizational culture and leadership.* San Francisco: Jossey-Bass.

Spence-Diehl, E. (2004). Intensive case management for victims of stalking: A pilot test evaluation. *Brief Treatment and Crisis Intervention, 4(4)*, 323–341.

Stein, L.I., & Test, M.A. (1980). Alternative to mental hospital treatment: Conceptual model treatment program and clinical evaluation. *Archives of General Psychiatry, 37(4)*, 392–397.

Sytema, S., Wunderink, L., Bloemers, W., Roorda, L., & Wiersma, D. (2007). Assertive community treatment in the Netherlands: A randomized controlled trial. *Acta Psychiatrica Scandinavia, 116*, 105–112.

Udechuku, A., Olver, J., Hallam, K., Blyth, F., Leslie, M., Nasso, M., & Burrows, G. (2005). Assertive community treatment of the mentally ill: Service model and effectiveness. *Australasian Psychiatry, 13(2)*, 129–134.

Vanderplasschen, W., Wolf, J., Rapp, R.C., & Broekaert, E. (2007). Effectiveness of different models of case management for substance-abusing populations. *Journal of Psychoactive Drugs, 39(1)*, 81–95.

Woodside, M., & McClam, T. (2003). *Generalist case management.* Pacific Grove: Brooks/Cole.

Young, H.M. (2003). Challenges and solutions for care of frail older adults. *Online Journal of Issues in Nursing, 8(2)*, 109–126.

References and Further Readings for Chapter 2

Alinsky, S. (1971). *Rules for radicals: A practical primer for realistic radicals.* New York: Vintage Books.

Anthony, P., & Crawford, P. (2000). Service user involvement in care planning: The mental health nurse's perspective. *Journal of Psychiatric and Mental Health Nursing, 7,* 425–434.

Austin, D.M. (2002). *Human services management.* New York: Columbia University Press.

Cannon, M. D., & Edmondson, A.C. (2001). Confronting failure: Antecedents and consequences of shared beliefs about failure in organizational work groups. *Journal of Organizational Behavior, 22(2),* 161–177.

Dickson, D.T. (1995). *Law in the health and human services.* New York: Free Press.

Fischer, J. (1978). *Effective casework practice: An eclectic approach.* New York: McGraw-Hill.

Gans, S.P., & Horton, G.T. (1975). *Integration of human services.* New York: Praeger Publishers.

Houston, S. (2003). A method from the 'Lifeworld': Some possibilities for person centered planning for children in care. *Children & Society, 17(1),* 57–70.

Jenson, J.M., & Fraser, M.W. (2006). *Social policy for children and families: A risk and resilience perspective.* Thousand Oaks: Sage Publications.

Rothman, J. (1991). A model of case management: Toward empirically base practice. *Social Work, 36(6),* 520–528.

Rothman, J., & Sager, J.S. (1998). *Case management: Integrating individual and community practice.* Boston: Allyn and Bacon.

Sauber, S. R. (1983). *The human services delivery system.* New York: Columbia University Press.

Schneider, B., & Amerman, F. (1997). Clinical protocols: Guiding case management assessment and care planning. *Generations, 21(1),* 68–73.

Thomson, C., & Walker, F. (2010). How to involve children in care planning. *Community Care 1807,* 34–44.

References and Further Readings for Chapter 3

Barbara, H., & Sheeley, V.L. (1987). Privileged communication in selected helping professions: A comparison among states. *Journal of Counseling and Development, 65,* 479–483.

Dickson, D.T. (1995). *Law in the health and human services.* New York: The Free Press.

Glosoff, H.L., & Pate, R.H. (2002). Privacy and confidentiality in school counseling. *Professional School Counseling, 6(1),* 1–13.

Herlihy, B., & Sheeley, V.L. (1988). Counselor liability and the duty to warn. *Counselor Education and Supervision, 27(3),* 203–215.

Krinidis, S., & Pitas, I. (2010). Statistical analysis of human facial expressions. *Journal of Information Hiding and Multimedia Signal Processing, 1(3),* 241–260.

Leigh, J.W. (1998). *Communicating for cultural competence.* Boston: Allyn & Bacon

Mandell, B.R., & Schram, B. (2011). *An introduction to human services: Policy and practice.* Boston: Allyn and Bacon.

Murphy, B.C., & Dillon, C. (1998). *Interviewing in action: Process and practice.* Pacific Grove: Brooks/Cole Publishing Company.

Rubin, H.J., & Rubin, I.S. (2005). *Qualitative interviewing: The art of hearing data.* Thousand Oaks: Sage Publications.

Russell, J.A. (1994). Is there universal recognition of emotion from facial expression? A review of the cross-cultural studies. *Psychological Bulletin, 115(1),* 102–141.

Seidman, I. (2006). *Interviewing as qualitative research.* New York: Teachers College Press.

Ulin, P.R., Robinson, E.T., & Tolley, E.E. (2005). *Qualitative methods in public health: A field guide for applied research.* San Francisco: Jossey-Bass.

Wigmore, D. (1961) cited page 127 in Donald T. Dickson (1995). *Law in the health and human services.* New York: The Free Press.

References and Further Readings for Chapter 4

Anheier, H.K. (2005). *Nonprofit organizations: Theory, management, policy*. New York: Routledge Press.

Austin, D.M. (1988). *The political economy of human service programs*. Greenwich: Jai Press Inc.

Cheng, T. (2002). Welfare recipients: How do they become independent? *Social Work Research, 26(3)*, 159–170.

Commission on Private Philanthropy and Public Needs (1975). *Giving in America: Toward a Stronger Voluntary Sector*. Retrieved from https://archives.iupui.edu/handle/2450/889

De Tocqueville, A. (2006). *Democracy in America* (G. Lawrence, Trans.). New York: Harper Perennial Modern Classic (Original work published 1832).

Drucker, P.F. (2003). *The essential Drucker*. New York: Harper Collins Publishers.

Fremont-Smith, M.R. (2004). *Governing nonprofit organizations: Federal and state law and regulation*. Cambridge: Harvard Press.

Friedman, L.J., & McGarvie (2003). *Charity, philanthropy, and civility in American history*. Cambridge: Cambridge University Press.

Frumkin, P. (2002). *On being nonprofit: A conceptual and policy primer*. Cambridge: Harvard Press.

Grigsby, J.E. (1998). Welfare reform means business as usual. *Journal of the American Planning Association, 64(1)*, 19–22.

Hall, P.D. (2005). Historical perspectives on nonprofit organizations in the United States. In R. D. Herman (ed.), *The Jossey-Bass handbook on nonprofit leadership & management*. (pp. 3–38). San Francisco: Jossey-Bass.

Hasenfeld, Y. (1992). *Human services as complex organizations*. Newbury Park: Sage Publications.

Hawkins, R. (2005). From self-sufficiency to personal and family sustainability: A new paradigm for social policy. *Journal of Sociology and Social Welfare, 32(4)*, 77–92.

O'Neill, M. (2002). *Nonprofit nation: A new look at the third America*. San Francisco: Jossey-Bass.

Piven, F.F., & Cloward, R.A. (1993). *Regulating the poor: The functions of public welfare*. New York: Vintage Books.

Salamon, L. (2002). *The state of nonprofit America*. Washington, DC: Brookings Institution Press.

Salamon, L.M., & Anheier, H.K. (1997). *Defining the nonprofit sector: A cross-national sector*. New York: Manchester University Press.

Schmid, H. (2004). The role of nonprofit human service organizations in providing social services. In H. Schmid (ed.) *Organizational and structural dilemmas in nonprofit human service organizations* (pp. 1–21). Binghamton: The Haworth Social Work Practice.

Silk, T. (2005). The legal framework of the nonprofit sector in the United States. In R.D. Herman, *The Jossey-Bass handbook on nonprofit leadership & management* (pp. 63–80). San Francisco: Jossey-Bass.

Woodside. M., & McClam, T. (2011). *An introduction to human services*. Belmont: Thomson Brooks/Cole.

Zins, C. (2001). Defining human services. *Journal of Sociology and Social Welfare, 28(1)*, 3–21.

References and Further Readings for Chapter 5

Argyris, C. (1991). Teaching smart people how to learn. *Harvard Business Review, 69(3),* 99–109.

Ashforth, B.E., & Fried, Y. (1988). The mindlessness of organization behaviors. *Human Relations, 41(4),* 305–329.

Austin, D.M. (1988). *The political economy of human service programs.* Greenwich: JAI Press.

Austin, D.M. (2002). *Human services management.* New York: Columbia University Press.

Bedwell, R.T. (1993). How to adopt total quality management: Laying a sound foundation. *Nonprofit World, 11(4),* 28–33.

Beer, M., Eisenstat, R.A., & Spector, B. (1990). Why change programs don't produce change. *Harvard Business Review, 68(6),* 158–167.

Boezman, E.J., & Ellemers, N. (2008). Volunteer recruitment: The role of organizational support and anticipated respect in non-volunteers' attraction to charitable volunteer organizations. *Journal of Applied Psychology, 93(5),* 1013–1026.

Bolman, L.G., & Deal, T.E. (2003). *Reframing organizations: Artistry, choice, and leadership.* San Francisco: Jossey-Bass.

Brault, M.W. (July, 2012). *American with Disabilities: 2010 Household Economic Studies. Current Population Report.* Retrieved from http://www.census.gov/prod/2012pubs/p70-131.pdf

Brody, R. (2005). *Effectively managing human services organizations.* Thousand Oaks: Sage Publications.

Brownmiller, S. (1999). *In our time: Memoir of a revolution.* New York: A Delt Book.

Brundney, J.L. (2010). Designing and managing volunteer programs. In D.O. Renz, *The Jossey-Bass handbook of nonprofit leadership and management* (pp. 753–793). San Francisco: Jossey-Bass.

Bureau of Labor Statistics, Volunteers by annual hours of volunteer activities and selected characteristics (2012). Retrieved from http://www.bls.gov/news.release/volun.t02.htm

Cannon, M.D., & Edmondson, A.C. (2001). Confronting failure: Antecedents and consequences of shared beliefs about failure in organizational work groups. *Journal of Organizational Behavior, 22(2),* 161–177.

Carlsen, K.G. (1991). Worn paths, unbroken trails: Volunteer coordinators at the turning point. *Nonprofit World, 9(1),* 29–33.

Chait, R.P., Holland, T.P., & Taylor, B.E. (1996). *Improving the performance of governing boards.* Phoenix: Oryx Press.

Coutu, D.L. (2002). The anxiety of learning. *Harvard Business Review, 80(3),* 100–106.

Deming, W.E. (2008, July 25). Retrieved from www.M07_GOOD6981_11_SE_C07.QXD

Drucker, P.F. (1954). *The Practice of Management.* New York: Harper Collins Publishers.

Drucker, P.F. (2005). *Managing the nonprofit organization principles and practices.* New York: Harper Collins Publishers.

Forsyth, J. (1999). Volunteer management strategies: Balancing risk and reward. *Nonprofit World, 17(3),* 40–43.

Frumkin, P. (2002). *On being nonprofit: A conceptual and policy primer.* Cambridge: Harvard Press.

Galindo-Kuhn, R., & Guzley, R.M. (2001). The volunteer satisfaction index: Construct definition, measurement, development, and validation. Journal of Social Service Research, 28, 45–68.

Hager, M.A., & Brudney, J.L. (2011). Problems recruiting volunteers nature versus nurture. *Nonprofit Management & Leadership, 22(2),* 137–156.

Halpern, D., & Osofsky, S. (1990). A dissenting view of MBO. *Public Personnel Management, 19(3),* 321–330.

Hardina, D., & Montana, S. (2011). Empowering staff and clients: Comparing preferences for management models by the professional degrees held by organization administrators. *Social Work, 56(3),* 247–257.

Hasenfeld, Y. (1992). The nature of human service organizations. In Y. Hasenfeld, *Human services as complex organizations.* (pp. 3–23). Newbury Park: Sage Publications.

Harvey, C.P., & Allard, M.J. (2012). *Understanding and managing diversity: Readings, cases, and exercises.* Boston: Pearson Education.

Heimovis, R., Herman, R., & Coughlin, C. (1993). Executive leadership and dependence in nonprofit organizations: A frame analysis. *Public Administration Review, 53(5),* 419–427.

Herman, R.D., & Heimovics, R. (1991). *Executive leadership in nonprofit organizations: New strategies for shaping executive-board dynamics.* San Francisco: Jossey-Bass.

Hochschild, A., & Machung, A. (2012). *The second shift: Working families and the revolution at home.* New York: Penguin Group.

Hong, Y.J. (2011). Developing a new human services management model through workplace spirituality in social work. *Journal of Workplace Behavioral Health, 26,* 144–163.

Jackson, P.M. (2006). *Sarbanes-Oxley for nonprofit boards*. Hoboken: John Wiley & Sons, Inc.

Joslyn, H. (2009). A man's world. *E-Journal of the Chronicle of Philanthropy*. Retrieved from http://philanthropy .com/article/A-Mans-World/57099/

Katz, J. (1989). *White awareness: Handbook for anti-racism training*. Norman: University of Oklahoma Press.

Kegan, R., & Lahey, L.L. (2001). The real reason people won't change. *Harvard Business Review, 79(10)*, 85–92.

Kennedy, M.T., & Fiss, P.C. (2009). Institutionalization framing, and diffusion: The logic of TQM adoption and implementation decision among US hospitals. *Academy of Management Journal, 52(5)*, 897–918.

Kettner, P.M. (2002). *Achieving excellence in the management of human service organizations*. Boston: Allyn and Bacon.

Koontz, H. (1977). Making MBO effective. *California Management Review, 20(1)*, 1–6.

Leonard, R., Onyx, J., & Hayward-Brown, H. (2004). Volunteer and coordinator perspectives on managing women volunteers. *Nonprofit Management & Leadership, 15(2)*, 205–219.

Macduff, N. (2005). Principles of training for volunteers and employees. In R. Herman, *The Jossey-Bass handbook of nonprofit leadership and management* (pp. 703–730). San Francisco: Jossey-Bass.

Mackelprang, R., & Salsgiver, R. (1999). *Disability: A diversity model approach in human service practice*. Pacific Grove: Brooks Cole.

Martin, L.L. (1993). *Total quality management in human service organizations*. Thousand Oaks: Sage Publications.

McConkey, D.D. (1973). Applying management by objectives to non-profit organizations. *Advance Management Journal, 38(1)*, 10–20.

McCurley, S. (2005). Keeping the community involved: Recruiting and retaining volunteers. In R.D. Herman, *The Jossey-Bass handbook of nonprofit leadership and management* (pp. 587–622). San Francisco: Jossey-Bass.

Nagada, B., & Gutierrez, L. (2000). A praxis and research agenda for multicultural human services organizations. *International Journal of Social Welfare, 9*, 43–52.

Nashman, H.W., Morrison, E., & Duggal, R. (2008). Baby boomers as volunteers: Are nonprofit organizations prepared? *Human Service Education, 27(1)*, 5–16.

Netting, F.E., Nelson, H.W., Borders, K., & Huber, R. (2004). Volunteer and paid staff relationships: Implications for social work administration. In H. Schmid (ed.) *Organizational and structural dilemmas in nonprofit human service organizations* (pp. 69–90). Binghamton: The Haworth Social Work Practice.

Nolan, T., & Johnson, K. (2011). *The essential handbook for human service leaders*. Indianapolis: Dog Ear Publishing.

O'Neill, M. (2002). *Nonprofit nation: A new look at the third America*. San Francisco: Jossey-Bass.

Pardeck, J.T. (205). An analysis of the Americans with Disabilities Act (ADA) in the twenty-first century. In J.W. Murphy & J.T. Pardeck (eds.) *Disability issues for social workers and human services professional in the twenty-first century* (pp. 121–151), Binghamton: The Haworth Social Work Practice.

Pecora, P.J., & Austin, M.J. (1987). *Managing human services personnel*. Newbury Park: Sage Publications.

Peters, J.B., & Masako, J. (2000). A house divided how nonprofits experience union drives. *Nonprofit Management & Leadership, 10(3)*, 305–317.

Quinn, R. (1988). The competing values model: Redefining organizational effectiveness and change. In *Beyond rational management: Mastering the paradoxes and competing demands of high performance*. San Francisco: Jossey-Bass.

Renz, D.O. (2010). Leadership, governance, and the work of the board. In D.O. Renz and Associates, *The Jossey-Bass handbook on nonprofit leadership & management*. (pp. 125–156). San Francisco: Jossey-Bass.

Robbins, S.P., & Coulter, M. (2009). *Management*. Upper Saddle River: Pearson.

Robinson, F.M., West, D., & Woodworth, D. (1995). *Coping + plus: Dimensions of disability*. Westport: Praeger Publishers.

Rodgers, R., & Hunter, J.E. (1992). A foundation of good management practice in government: Management by objectives. *Public Administration Review, 52(1)*, 27–37.

Sand, M.A. (2005). *How to manage an effective nonprofit organization*. Franklin Lakes: Career Press.

Sandberg, S. (2013). *Lean in: Women, work, and the will to lead*. New York: Random House.

Schwab, K. (2011). Volunteers: Recruit, place, and retain the best. *Nonprofit World, 29(6)*, 16–17.

Silk, T. (2005). The legal framework of the nonprofit sector in the United States. In R.D. Herman, *The Jossey-Bass handbook on nonprofit leadership & management*. (pp. 68–80). San Francisco: Jossey-Bass.

Stewart, M. (2006, June). The management myth. *The Atlantic Monthly*, pp. 80–87.

Stone, D.A. (1984). *The disabled state*. Philadelphia: Temple University Press.

Swiss, J.E. (1992). Adapting total quality management (TQM) to government. *Public Administration Review, 52(4)*, 356–362.

Tauber, M. (1983). MBO a practical approach to increasing productivity. *Nonprofit World Report, 1(2)*, 26–37.

Taylor, F.W. (1911/2001). The principles of scientific management. In J.M. Shafritz, & J.S. Ott, *Classics of organization theory* (pp. 61–72). Belmont: Wadsworth Group.

Wigens, L. (1997). The conflict between 'new nursing' and 'scientific management' as perceived by surgical nurses. *Journal of Advanced Nursing, 1997(25)*, 1116–1122.

Wolf, T. (1999). *Managing a nonprofit organization in the twenty-first century*. New York: Simon & Schuster.

References and Further Readings for Chapter 6

Alexander, G.D., & Carlson, K.J. (2005). *Essential principles for fundraising success*. San Francisco: Jossey-Bass.

Allen, J. (2000). *Event planning*. Ontario: Wiley Publishers.

Anheier, H.K. (2005). *Nonprofit organizations: Theory, management, policy*. New York: Routledge Press.

Austin, D. (2002). *Human services management: Organizational leadership in social work practice*. New York: Columbia Press.

Barnes, N.G., & Mattson, E. (2009). Retrieved May 2013 from http://www.umassd.edu/media/umassdartmout/cmr/studiesandresearch/socialmediacharity.pdf

Bekkers, R., & Crutzen, O. (2007). Just keep it simple: A field experiment on fundraising letters. *International Journal of Nonprofit Sector Marketing, 12*, 371–378.

Bell, B. (2009). The psychology of giving. *Nonprofit World, 27(1)*, 9–10.

Bloom, L., & Kilgore, D. (2003). The volunteer citizen after welfare reform in the United States: An ethnographic study of volunteerism in action. *International Journal of Voluntary and Nonprofit Organizations 14(4)*, 431–454.

Boezman, E.J., & Ellemers, N. (2008). Volunteer recruitment: The role of organizational support and anticipated respect in non-volunteers' attraction to charitable volunteer organizations. *Journal of Applied Psychology, 93(5)*, 1013–1026.

Brody, R. (2005). *Effectively managing human services organizations*. Thousand Oaks: Sage Publications.

Bureau of Labor Statistics, Volunteers by annual hours of volunteer activities and selected characteristics (2012). Retrieved from http://www.bls.gov/news.release/volun.t02.htm

Burnett, K. (2002). *Relationship fundraising: A donor-based approach to the business of raising money*. San Francisco: Jossey-Bass.

Falasca, M., Zobel, C., & Ragsdale, C. (2011). Helping a small development organization manage volunteers more efficiently. *Interfaces, 41(3)*, 254–262.

Finch, A. (2009). The latest trends and how to master them. *Nonprofit World, 27(5)*, 18–20.

Giving USA (2012). *The annual report on philanthropy for the year 2011*. Chicago: Giving USA Foundation.

Hager, M.A., & Brudney, J.L. (2011). Problems recruiting volunteers nature versus nurture. *Nonprofit Management & Leadership, 22(2)*, 137–156.

Hager, M.A., Rooney, P., & Pollak, T. (2002). How fundraising is carried out in US nonprofit organizations. *International Journal of Nonprofit Sector Marketing, 7(4)*, 311–326.

Harris, T. (2011). How to engage the next generation of donors now. *Nonprofit World, 29(1)*, 6–8.

Hitchcock, S. (2004). *Open immediately! Straight talk on direct mail fundraising*. Medfield: Emerson & Church Publishers.

Hogan, C. (2012). The roller coaster ride driving your fundraising efforts in the new era. *Searcher, 20(1)*, 20–25.

Jacobs, F.A., & Marudas, N.P. (2006). Excessive, optimal, and insufficient fundraising among the Nonprofit Times 100. *International Journal of Nonprofit Sector Marketing, 11*, 105–114.

Keegan, P.B. (1990). *How to build a community partnership: Fundraising for non-profits*. New York: Harper Collins.

Klein, K. (2000). *Fundraising for social change*. San Francisco: Jossey-Bass.

Klein, K. (2004). *Fundraising in times of crisis*. San Francisco: Jossey-Bass.

Knaup, S. (2012). Turning the direct ask into gold. *Nonprofit World, 30(1)*, 6–8.

Lysakowski, L. (2003). What's in it for me? *New Directions for Philanthropic Fundraising, 2003(39)*, 53–64.

Lysakowski, L. (2005). *Nonprofit essentials: Recruiting and training fundraising volunteers*. Hoboken: John Wiley & Sons Inc.

Macduff, N. (2005). Principles of training for volunteers and employees. In R. Herman, *The Jossey-Bass handbook of nonprofit leadership and management* (pp. 703–730). San Francisco: Jossey-Bass.

Miller, B. (2009). Community fundraising 2.0—The future of fundraising in a networked society? *International Journal of Voluntary Sector Marketing, 14*, 365–370.

Miller, D. (2011). Nonprofit organizations and the emerging potential of social media and internet resources. *SPNHA Review, 6(1)*, 34–52.

O'Neill, M. (2002). *Nonprofit nation: A new look at the third America*. San Francisco: Jossey-Bass.

Ozdemir, Z.D., Altinkemer, K., De, P., & Ozcelik, Y. (2010). Donor-to-nonprofit online marketplace: An economic analysis of the effects on fundraising. *Journal of Management Information Systems, 27(2)*, 213–242.

Pecora, P.J., & Austin, M.J. (1987). *Managing human services personnel*. Newbury Park: Sage Publications.

Rice, R.B., & Keller, K. (2011). Strategic Fundraising Programs. *The Fourth Annual Financial Literacy Leadership Conference*, (pp. 1–45). Retrieved from http://www.mosaikstrategies.com/uploaded_files/SFEPD%20PPT%20%2010-4-11-FINAL.pdf

Salamon, L. (2002). *The state of nonprofit America*. Washington, D.C.: Brooking Institution Press.

Sargeant, A. (2001). Relationship fundraising how to keep donors loyal. *Nonprofit Management & Leadership, 12(2)*, 177–192.

Sargeant, A., & Shang, J. (2010). *Fundraising principles and practice*. San Francisco: Jossey-Bass.

Sargeant, A., West, D., & Jay, E. (2007). The relational determinants of nonprofit web site fundraising effectiveness: An exploratory study. *Nonprofit Management and Leadership, 18(2)*, 141–156.

Schwab, K. (2011). Volunteers: Recruit, place, and retain the best. *Nonprofit World, 29(6)*, 16–17.

Seltzer, M. (2001). *Securing your organization's future*. New York: The Foundation Center.

Stephens, C.R. (2004). Building the fundraising team. *New Directions for Philanthropic Fundraising, 2004(43)*, 83–94.

Warwick, M. (2000). *The five strategies for fundraising success: A mission-based guide to achieving your goals*. San Francisco: Jossey-Bass.

Waters, R.D., Burnett, E.L., & Lucas, J. (2009). Engaging stakeholders through social networking: How nonprofit organizations are using Facebook. *Public Relations Review, 35(2009)*, 102–106.

Wolf, T. (1999). *Managing a nonprofit organization in the twenty-first century*. New York: Simon & Schuster.

Wymer, W., & Sargeant, A. (2010). Managing fundraising volunteers. In A. Sargeant & J. Shang, *Fundraising principles and practice* (pp. 489–518). San Francisco: Jossey-Bass.

References and Further Readings for Chapter 7

Abood, S. (2007, June 9). Influencing health care in the legislative arena. *Online Journal of Issues in Nursing, 12(1)*, 3–19.

Alexander, M. (2012). *The new Jim Crow: Mass incarceration in the age of colorblindness*. New York: The New Press.

Astramovich, R.L., & Harris, K.R. (2007). Promoting self-advocacy among minority students in school counseling. *Journal of Counseling & Development, 85(3)*, 269–276.

Badger, A.J. (1989). *The new deal: The Depression years, 1933–1940*. Chicago: Ivan R. Dee Publishers.

Berg, R.M. (1977). An advocate model for intervention with homosexuals. *Social Work, 6*, 280–283.

Bizzell, P., & Herzberg, B. (2001). *The rhetorical tradition: Reading from classical times to present*. Boston: Bedford/St. Martin's.

Bu, X., & Jezewski, M. (2006). Developing a mid-range theory of patient advocacy through concept analysis. *Journal of Advance Nursing, 57(1)*, 101–110.

Byme, M. (2006). Patients in poverty. *American Organization of Registered Nurses Journal, 85(5)*, 832–839.

Dalrymple, J. (2004). Construction of child and youth advocacy: Emerging issues in advocacy practice. *Children & Society, 19*, 3–15.

Dear, R.B. & Patti, R. (1981). Legislative advocacy: Seven effective tactics. *Social Work, 26*, 289–296.

Ezell, M. (2001). *Advocacy in the human services*. Belmont: Wadsworth/Thomson Learning.

Gehart, D.R., & Lucas, B.M. (2007). Client advocacy in marriage and family therapy: A qualitative case study. *Journal of Family Psychotherapy, 18(1)*, 39–56.

Hanks, R.G. (2005). Sphere of nursing advocacy model. *Nursing Forum, 40(3)*, 75–78.

Haynes, K.S., & Mickelson, J.S. (2000). Social work and the Reagan Era: Challenges to the profession. *Journal of Social Work, 19(1)*, 169–183.

Herbert, M.D., & Mould, J.W. (1992). The advocacy role in public child welfare. *Child Welfare, 71(2)*, 114–130.

Hilfiker, D. (2003). *Urban injustice: How ghettos happen*. New York: Seven Stories Press.

Jalongo, M. (2006). The story of Mary Ellen Wilson: Tracing the origins of child protection in America. *Early Childhood Education Journal, 34(1)*, 1–4.

Landriscina, M. (2006). A calmly disruptive insider: The case of an institutionalized advocacy organization at work. *Qualitative Sociology, 29(4)*, 447–466.

Lindsey, D. (2004). *The welfare of children*. New York: Oxford University Press.

Marten, J. (2005). *Childhood and child welfare in the progressive era*. Boston, MA: Bedford/St. Martin's.

McDonald, M.J. (1995). The citizens' committee for children of New York and the evolution of child advocacy (1945–1972). *Child Welfare, 74(1)*, 283–304.

McGowan, B.G. (1983). Historical evolution of child welfare services. In Brenda G. McGowan, & William Meezan (Eds.), *Child welfare: Current dilemma future directions* (pp. 45–90). Itasca: F.E. Peacock Publishers.

McMahon, T.J. (1993). On the concept of child advocacy: A review of theory and methodology. *School Psychology Review, 22(4)*, 744–756.

McNutt, J. (2006). Building evidence-based advocacy in cyberspace: A social work imperative for the new millennium. *Journal of Evidence Based Social Work, 3(3/4)*, 91–102.

Mindell, R., Haymes, M.V., & Francisco, D. (2003). A culturally responsive practice model for urban Indian child welfare services. *Child Welfare, 82(2)*, 201–217.

O'Hair, D., Stewart, R., & Rubenstein, H. (2010). *A speaker's guidebook text and reference with the essential guide to rhetoric*. Boston: Bedford/St. Martin's.

Osborne, J.L., Collison, B.B., House, R.M., Gray, L.A., & Firth, J. (1998). Developing a social advocacy model for counselor education. *Counselor Education & Supervision, 37(3)*, 190–203.

Patti, R., & Dear, R.B. (1975). Legislative advocacy: One path to social change. *Social Work (20)*, 108–114.

Piven, F.F., & Cloward, R.A. (1993). *Regulating the poor: The function of public welfare*. New York: Vintage Books.

Polansky, N.A. (1986). There is nothing so practical as a good theory. *Child Welfare, 65(1)*, 3–15.

Rosenberg, A. (2005). Philosophy of science: A contemporary introduction. New York: Routledge.

Satterly, B.A., & Dyson, D.A. (2005). Educating all children equitably: A strength-based approach to advocacy for sexual minority youth in schools. *Contemporary Sexuality, 39*(3), 1–7.

Steves, L., & Blevins, T. (2005). From tragedy to triumph: A segue to community building for children and families. *Child Welfare, 84(2)*, 311–322.

Trattner, W.I. (1999). *From poor law to welfare state: A history of social welfare in America*. New York: The Free Press.

Ulin, P.R., Robinson, E.T., & Tolley, E.E. (2005). *Qualitative methods in public health: A field guide for applied research*. San Francisco: Jossey-Bass.

Wark, L. (2008). The advocacy project. *Human Service Education, 27(1)*, 69–82.

Whiteman, V.L. (2001). *Social security: What every human services professional should know*. Needham: Allyn and Bacon.

Woodside, M.R., & McClam, T. (2008). *An introduction to human services*. Belmont, CA: Thomson Brooks/Cole.

References and Further Readings for Chapter 8

Alinsky, S.D. (1989). *Reveille for radicals.* New York: Vintage Books.

Alinsky, S.D. (1971). *Rules for radicals: A pragmatic primer for realistic radicals.* New York: Vintage Books.

Anderson, B. (2006). *Imagined communities.* New York: Verso Publications.

Bens, I. (2006). *Facilitating to lead!: Leadership strategies for a networked world.* San Francisco: Jossey-Bass.

Bojer, H. (2002). Women and the Rawlsian social contract. *Social Justice Research, 15(4),* 393–407.

Chism, M. (2011). *Stop workplace drama.* Hoboken: John Wiley & Sons.

Christensen, B. (2005). Equality and justice: Remarks on necessary relationship. *Hypatia, 20(2),* 155–163.

Cohen, J. (2004). The importance of philosophy: Reflection on John Rawls. *South African Journal of Philosophy, 23(2),* 113–119.

Delgado, G. (1997). *Beyond the politics of place.* Oakland, CA: Applied Research Center.

Drew, N.M., Bishop, B.J., & Syme, G. (2002). Justice and local community change: Towards a substantive theory of justice. *Journal of Community Psychology, 30(6),* 623–634.

Dunn, A. (2011). Unplugging a nation: State media strategy during Egypt's January 25 uprising. *The Fletcher Forum of World Affairs Journal, 35(2),* 15–23.

Dyer, W.G., Dyer, J.H., & Dyer, W.G. (2013). *Team building: Proven strategies for improving team performance.* San Francisco: Jossey-Bass.

Etzioni, A. (1996). *The new golden rule: Community and morality in a democratic society.* New York: Basic Books.

Fraser, N. (1996). Social justice in the age of identity politics: Redistribution, recognition, and participation. *The Tanner Lectures on Human Values* (pp. 1–68). Palo Alto, California: Stanford University.

Ghasi, S. (2005). *Extreme facilitation: Guiding groups through controversy and complexity.* San Francisco: John Wiley & Sons.

Gittell, R., & Vidal, A. (1998). *Community organizing: Building social capital as a development strategy.* Thousand Oaks: Sage Publications.

Gosovic, B. (2001). Global intellectual hegemony and the international development agenda. *Cooperation South, 2,* 132–146.

Gramsci, A. (1977). *Selections from political writings 1910–1920.* New York: International Publishers.

Gray, J.S. (2004). Rawls's principle of justice as fairness and its application to the issue of same-sex marriage. *South African Journal of Philosophy, 23(2),* 158–172.

Guo, S. (2006). Adult education for social change: The role of a grassroots organization in Canada. *Convergence, 39(4),* 107–122.

Gutierrez, L., Alvarez, A.R., Nemon, H., & Lewis, E.A. (1996). Multicultural community organizing: A strategy for change.*Social Work, 41(5),* 501–508.

Hatashita, H., Hirao, K., Brykczynski, K., & Anderson, E. (2006). Grassroots efforts of Japanese women to promote services for abused women. *Nursing and Health Sciences, 8,* 169–174.

Hochschild, A., & Machung, A, (2012). *The second shift: Working families and the revolution at home.* New York: Penguin Books.

Homan, M.S. (2004). *Promoting community change: Making it happen in the real world.* Belmont: Brooks/Cole.

Ilkkaracan, P., & Amado, L. (2005). Human rights education as a tool of grassroots organizing and social transformation: A case study from Turkey. *International Education, 16(2),* 115–128.

Jackson, B. (2005). The conceptual history of social justice. *Political Studies Review, 3,* 356–373.

Jeris, L., Gajanayake, J., Ismail, J., Ebert, S., Peris, A., Wanasundara, L., et al. (2006). Grassroots empowerment of women: Portraits of four villages in Sri Lanka. *Convergence, 39(1),* 61–75.

Kettner, P., Daley, J.M., & Nichols, A.W. (1985). *Initiating change in organizations and communities: A macro practice model.* Belmont: Brooks/Cole.

Kincaid, S.O. (2009). Defining human services: A discourse analysis. *Human service education, 29(1),* 14–23.

Kretzman, J. (1995). Community organizing in the eighties: Toward a post-Alinsky agenda. In J. McKnight, *The careless society community and its counterfeits* (pp. 153–160). New York: Basic Books.

Lencioni, P. (2005). *Overcoming the five dysfunctions of a team: A field guide for leaders, managers, and facilitators.* San Francisco: Jossey-Bass.

Lotter, H. (2010). Refashioning Rawls as a true champion of the poor. *Polittkon,37(1),* 149–171.

Marbley, A., Bonner, F., Wimberly, C., Stevens, H., & Tatem, B. (2006). Harambee: Working together to engender change in communities of color. *The Educational Forum, 70,* 320–336.

Mayo, P. (2008). Antonio Gramsci and his relevance for the education of adults. *Educational Philosophy and Theory, 40(3),* 418–435. doi:10.1111/j.1469-5812.2007.00357.x.

McNutt, J., & Boland, K. (2007). Astroturf technology and the future of community mobilization: Implications for nonprofit theory. *Journal of Sociology and Social Welfare, 34(3),* 165–178.

McKnight, J. (1995). *The careless society community and its counterfeits.* New York: Basic Books.

Miller, D. (1999). *Principles of social justice.* Cambridge: Harvard University Press.

O'Donnell, K. (2003, January). Mayan women's struggle for a life with justice and dignity in Chiapas, Mexico. Paper presented at the meeting of the American Sociological Association Annual Meeting. Atlanta, GA.

Otis, M. (2004). One community's path to greater social justice: Building on earlier successes. *Journal of Gay & Lesbian Social Services, 16(3/4),* 17–33.

Owais, R. (2011). Arab media during the Arab spring in Egypt and Tunisia: Time for change. *Middle East Media Educator, 1(1),* 9–13.

Piven, F.F. (2008). *Challenging authority: How ordinary people change America.* New York: Rowan & Littlefield Publishers.

Piven, F.F., & Cloward, R.A. (1977). *Poor people's movements.* New York: Random House.

Pojman, L.P. (1993). *Life and death: A reader in moral problems.* Boston: Jones and Bartlett Publishers.

Rawls, J. (1999). *A theory of justice.* Cambridge: Harvard University Press.

Rosenthal, A. (1993). *The third house.* Washington, DC: Congressional Quarterly.

Royse, D., Staton-Tindall, M., Badger, K., & Webster, J. M (2009). *Needs assessment.* New York: Oxford University Press.

Rubin, H.J., & Rubin, I.S. (2008). *Community organizing and development.* Boston: Pearson Publications.

Schiola, S.A. (2011). *Making group work easy: The art of successful facilitation.* Lanham: Rowman & Littlefield Education.

Sharpe, E. (2005). Resources at the grassroots of recreation: Organizational capacity and quality of experience in a community sport organization. *Leisure Sciences, 28,* 385–401.

Sobeck, J., Agius, E., & Mayers, V. (2007). Supporting and sustaining grassroots youth organizations. *Voluntas,18,* 17–33.

Staples, L. (2004). *Roots to power: A manual for grassroots organizing.* Westport: Praeger Publishers.

Toman, C. (2006). The link between women's studies programs and grassroots organizations in Lebanon, the Balkans, and the Palestinian territories: A comparative study. *Arab Studies Quarterly,* 1, 55–67.

Tyner, J. (2006). Defend the ghetto: Space and the urban politics of the Black Panther Party. *Annals of Association of American Geographers, 96(1),* 105–118.

Veen, R.V. (2003). Community development as citizen education. *International Journal of Lifelong Education, 22(6),* 580–596.

Wainwright, J. (2010). On Gramsci's 'conception of the world.' *Transactions of the Institute of British Geographers, 35,* 507–521.

Warren, R.L. (1978). *The community in America.* Lanham:University Press of America.

Young, S.P. (2008). Reflections on Rawls. *The Review of Politics, 70,* 260–271.

References and Further Readings for Chapter 9

Baumgartner, F.R., Berry, J.M., Hojnacki, M., Kimball, D.C., & Leech, B.L. (2009). *Lobbying and policy change: Who wins, who loses, and why*. Chicago: University of Chicago Press.

Birnbaum, J.H. (1992). *The lobbyists: How influence peddlers get their way in Washington*. New York: Times Books.

Cigler, A.J., & Loomis, B.A. (2007). In *Interest Group Politics*. Washington, D.C.: CQ Press.

Deephouse, D.L. (1996). Does isomorphism legitimate? *Academy of Management Journal, 39*, pp. 1024–1039.

Ezell, M. (2001). *Advocacy in the human services*. Belmont: Wadsworth.

Greenwald, C. (1977). *Group power*. New York, New York: Praeger.

Haynes, K., & Mickelson, J. (2000). Social work and the Reagan era: Challenges to the profession. *Journal of Social Work, 19(1)*, 169–183.

Meredith, J.C. (2000). *Lobbying on a shoestring*. Boston, MA: MCLE.

Miller, W.L. (1996). *Arguing about slavery: The great battle in the United States Congress*. New York: Knopf.

Navarro, P. (1984). *How special interests and ideologues are stealing America*. New York: John Wiley & Sons.

Rosenthal, A. (1993). *The third house*. Washington, D.C.: Congressional Quarterly.

Sinema, K. (2009). *Unite and conquer: How to build coalitions that win and last*. San Francisco: Berrett-Koehler Publishers.

Teasdale, K. (1998). *Advocacy in health care*. Oxford: Blackwell Science.

Tuckman, B.W., & Jensen, M. (1977). Stages of small-group development revisited. *Group and Organization Studies, 2*, pp. 419–427.

Yalom, I.D. (1995). *Theory and practice of group psychotherapy*. New York, NY: Basic Books.

Index

· ·